CISTERCIAN FATHERS SERIES: NUMBER FIFTY-ONE

Bernard of Clairvaux: Sermons for Advent and the Christmas Season

Translated by
Irene Edmonds
Wendy Mary Beckett
Conrad Greenia OCSO

Edited by
John Leinenweber

Introduction by
Wim Verbaal

CISTERCIAN PUBLICATIONS
Kalamazoo, Michigan

Based on the critical Latin edition of Jean Leclercq and H. M. Rochais,
Sancti Bernardi Opera, vol. 4:161–334
Rome: Editiones Cistercienses, 1966.

*The work of Cistercian Publications is made possible in part
by support from Western Michigan University
to The Institute of Cistercian Studies.*

Library of Congress: Cataloging-in-Publication Data

Bernard, of Clairvaux, Saint, 1090 or 91–1153.
  [Sermons. English. Selections]
  Sermons for Advent and the Christmas season / Bernard of Clairvaux ;
translated by Irene Edmonds, Wendy Mary Beckett, Conrad Greenia ; edited
by John Leinenweber ; introduction by Wim Verbaal.
    p. cm. — (Cistercian fathers series ; no. 51)
    ISBN 978-0-87907-151-6 (hardcover) — ISBN 978-0-87907-451-7 (pbk.)
    1. Advent sermons. 2. Christmas sermons. 3. Sermons, Latin—Transla-
tions into English. I. Edmonds, Irene M. II. Beckett, Wendy. III. Greenia,
Conrad. IV. Leinenweber, John. V. Title. VI. Series.

BV4254.5.B4813 2007
252'.02—dc22

2007012357

Printed in the United States of America.

Table of Contents

Introduction   vii

Editorial Note   lxi

Table of Abbreviations   lxiii

THE SERMONS

On the Lord's Advent
    Sermon One: On the Six Aspects of Advent   3
    Sermon Two: On the Reading from Isaiah:
        The Lord said to Ahaz . . .   13
    Sermon Three: On the Seven Pillars   19
    Sermon Four: On the Twofold Coming and
        the Wings Covered with Silver   27
    Sermon Five: On the Intermediate Coming
        and the Threefold Renewal   33
    Sermon Six: On the Threefold Coming
        and the Resurrection of the Flesh   36
    Sermon Seven: On the Threefold Benefit   41

On the Eve of the Lord's Birth
    Sermon One: On the Proclamation of the Lord's Birth:
        Jesus Christ, the Son of God, is born in Bethlehem of Judea   43
    Sermon Two: On the Chant: *O Judah and Jerusalem*   50
    Sermon Three: On the Chant: *Today you shall know*
        that the Lord will come   59
    Sermon Four: On the Medicine of the Spouse's Left Hand
        and the Delights of His Right Hand   70
    Sermon Five: On the Chant: *Make yourselves holy today and be*
        prepared; tomorrow you shall see within you the majesty of God   80
    Sermon Six: On the Proclamation of His Birth   87

On the Lord's Birthday

Sermon One: On the Five Springs   99

Sermon Two: On the Three Comminglings of Divine Power   107

Sermon Three: On Christ's Birth and Passion,
On Mary's Virginity and Fruitfulness   113

Sermon Four: On the Lowliness and Humility of Christ's Birth   120

Sermon Five: On the Father of Mercies, Who Has Mercy
on Our Many Miseries   124

On the Feasts of Saint Stephen, Saint John, and the Holy Innocents 129

On the Lord's Circumcision

Sermon One: On the Lord's Circumcision, the Reason for
Circumcision, and the Name 'Jesus'   133

Sermon Two: On the Medicine of Circumcision and Its Value   138

Sermon Three: On Spiritual Circumcision   144

On the Lord's Epiphany

Sermon One: On the Three Appearances   154

Sermon Two: On the First Appearance   164

Sermon Three: On the Three Appearances, but Chiefly on
the First   169

On the Octave of Epiphany: On the Second Appearance   176

On the First Sunday after the Octave of Epiphany

Sermon One: On the Gospel Reading, Which Includes
the Miracle Performed at the Wedding; and, Before
That, On What the Lord Said: *You must be like those
waiting for their Lord when he returns from the wedding*   180

Sermon Two: On Changing Water into Wine   185

On the Feast of the Conversion of Saint Paul:
How We Ought to Be Converted to His Example   194

The Sermon Collection: Its Creation and Edition

Wim Verbaal

WRITING AND EDITING IN EARLY CISTERCIAN TRADITION

ALL TOO OFTEN one tends to forget that Bernard's activity as a writer was far from evident to his contemporaries. Early cistercian tradition does not seem to have been very indulgent toward literarily-gifted members. Stephan Harding wrote the first works of the Order, certainly, but, although they show him to be a remarkably gifted writer, they can hardly be considered as standing on their own. They are completely oriented to the goal of constructing and organizing an enduring community.[1]

---

[1] Stephan's writings consist of the *Monitum*, around 1109 [edited by Jean-Baptiste Auberger in *L'unanimité cistercienne primitive: mythe ou réalité?* Cîteaux: Studia et Documenta III (CîteauxVZW :Achel, 1986) 327]; a (circular) letter on the hymns to be used in the cistercian liturgy (1108–1113) [edited by Chrysogonus Waddell, *The Twelfth-Century Cistercian Hymnal* (Gethsemani Abbey-Kalamazoo, 1984) T. II 12]; the nucleus of the *Exordium Parvum* (around 1113) [edited by Chrysogonus Waddell, *Narrative and Legislative Texts from Early Cîteaux*. Studia et Documenta IX (Cîteaux – Commentarii cistercienses, 1999) 232–259]; the *Charta Charitatis Prior* (1114 and 1119) [edited by Waddell, 1999, 274–282]; a letter to the monks of Sherborne (between 1122 and 1133) [edited by Hugh Talbot, 'An Unpublished Letter of St. Stephen', *Collectanea Ordinis Cisterciensium Reformatorum* 3 (1936) 66–69]. In addition, two letters in Bernard's epistolary corpus are signed by him: letters 45 to Louis VI; and 49 to Pope Honorius II, both from 1129, and both edited by Jean Leclercq and Henri-Marie Rochais, *Sancti Bernardi Opera* [SBOp] 7:133 and 140–141 (Editiones Cistercienses: Rome 1974). Most of these texts are collected

Bernard is the first Cistercian to make a deliberate choice to write and to publish his writings and not to limit himself to the internal, institutional regulations of the young Order. What is more, his writings have an undeniably personal air and were allowed to circulate under his own name.[2] This again conflicts with the anonymity of the earliest cistercian documents. Both the *Charta Charitatis* and the *Exordium Parvum* may have been the work of Stephan Harding,[3] but they were not distributed, or even known, under his name.

In fact, it is not at all obvious that a congregation tending to the higher degrees of spiritual salvation by a strictly observed ascetism would allow its leading members to strive for literary reknown in 'the world'. None of the pioneers of the cistercian movement left any personal writings. From Robert de Molesme, the actual founder, no written documents are known, perhaps with the exception of two, again, institutional records.[4] The same is true for Alberic, the first abbot of Cîteaux, although the *Exordium Parvum* characterizes him expressly as 'a learned man, that is to say, well versed in things divine and human, a lover of the Rule and of the brethren'.[5]

Bernard broke with the recent tradition of the Order by manifesting himself as a writer and seems even to have opposed Stephan Harding's choice for anonymity. Nothing, however, leads one to suspect that he acted in defiance of his superior. Within a short period and while still a young unknown abbot, he published two works which were soon widely diffused inside and outside the con-

---

by Claudio Stercal, *Stefano Harding. Elementi biografici e testi* (Jaca Book: Milan 1997; translation forthcoming from Cistercian Publications).

[2] In contrast, for example, to the writings of Bernard's friend Hugo of Vitry, first abbot of Pontigny. He left seventy-six sermons (one manuscript), but, apparently, they were collected only after his death. See Charles H. Talbot, 'The Sermons of Hugh of Pontigny', *Cîteaux in de Nederlanden* 7 (1956) 5–33.

[3] See the investigations by Waddell (1999) 230–231 and 273.

[4] Both the *abbatiae Alpensis creatio* and the *Concordia Molismensis* are attributed to Robert of Molesme and have been edited by J.B. Van Damme and Jean de la Croix Bouton in *Les plus ancien textes de Cîteaux* (Achel 1974) 129–130.

[5] *Exordium Parvum* IX: Waddell (1999) 427 (text and translation).

gregation. This would have been impossible without Stephan's explicit consent.[6]

In the *Preface* to his first autonomous work, Bernard expresses the tension which he must have felt as an abbot who had decided to dedicate himself to writing. That first work constituted a commentary on the seventh chapter of the Rule of Benedict, and treated the twelve degrees of humility. In the *Preface* Bernard wonders if he has the right to address the world. Being a monk and an abbot, is he not obliged to remain inside his community and 'to secure myself alone in the port of silence'?[7] In confronting this choice, Bernard poses the crucial question on the fundamentals of monastic life: does a monk strive only for his personal salvation or does he have obligations towards the world outside the monastery?

Bernard deliberately breaks away from the isolation of the monastery. He prefers to step outside and to speak for the benefit of his readers, even when this obliges him to neglect the real task of the monk: living in silence and pondering his own salvation. Bernard

---

[6] Adriaan H. Bredero, *Bernardus van Clairvaux. Tussen cultus en historie*. (Agora Kok – Pelckmans: Kampen–Kapellen 1993) 239–242 [trans. *Bernard of Clairvaux: Between Cult and History* (Grand Rapids: Eerdmans)], on the contrary, wants to detect a sharp rivalry between the older and the younger abbot. More subtle is Auberger (1986) 317–324, who speaks of a different spiritual orientation. For other sound arguments against any competition between Stephan and Bernard, see Jean de la Croix Bouton, 'Negotia Ordinis', *Bernard de Clairvaux* (1953) 147–182; C. H. Talbot, 'The Cistercian Attitude towards Art: the Literary Evidence', in C. Norton - D. Park, edd), *Cistercian Art and Architecture in the British Isles* (Cambridge, 1986) 56–64, 58–60; Martha G. Newman, 'Stephen Harding and the Creation of the Cistercian Community', *Revue Bénédictine* 107 (1997) 307–329, esp. 326–328; Herbert Edward John Cowdrey, 'Stephen Harding and Cistercian Monasticism', *Cîteaux* 49 (1998) 209–219; Charles Dumont, 'Humanisme et rusticité. L'intention et la pratique des premiers cisterciens', *Cîteaux* 31 (1980) 21–34.

[7] *De gradibus humilitatis et superbiae*; SBOp 3:16. Although conforming to the traditional *topos* of modesty, these words have a more important tenor than is usually understood. For when considered in the context as evoked in this preface, the treatise is addressed to Geoffrey de la Roche-Vanneau, recently appointed abbot of Clairvaux's second daughter, Fontenay. The treatise thus is meant for the inner circle of Bernard and his monks. Yet the preface clearly demonstrates Bernard's wish to reach more persons, to break out of the intimate world of Clairvaux.

chooses to 'communicate the fruit of the word' (*communicare fructum sermonis*). Apparently, Bernard wants to go further than just giving an exposition on a certain topic. He wants to communicate not just the word, but the fruit of the word. He wants to share the result of the word: he aspires after the *sermo efficax et vivus*, 'the living and powerful Word'. Only thanks to this fruit of the word does Bernard consider it possible to establish a community between himself and his reader. For the sharing of the fruit, he uses the word *communicare*, a word charged with sacral connotation.[8] In Bernard's eyes, writing and reading become a ritual, almost a liturgical event which creates a spiritual community between the writer and his readers.

This concept of writing must be kept in mind when considering the evolution of Bernard's works. Until the 1130s, he published mostly tracts on monastic subjects: humility in the *De gradibus*[9]; *caritas* in *De diligendo*[10]; obedience in *De praecepto et dispensatione*.[11] In addition, he supported the reform movement inside Cluny instigated by William of Saint Thierry[12] in his *Apologia*[13], and even ventured briefly into the field of scholasticism with his treatise *De gratia et libro arbitrio*.[14]

---

[8] William of Saint Thierry uses the same word in his biography of Bernard when he describes the explanation by his friend of the Song of Songs: *Vita prima* I.59; Patrologia Latina 185:259. For an analysis of this passage, see my book *Een middeleeuws drama. Het conflict tussen scholing en vorming bij Abaelardus en Bernardus* [*A Medieval Tragedy. The Conflict between Instruction and Formation in the Confrontation of Abelard and Bernard*] (Pelckmans-Klement, 2002) 215–217.

[9] *De gradibus humilitatis et superbiae*; SBOp 3:13-59; trans. *The Steps of Humility and Pride*, CF 13A.

[10] *De diligendo Deo*, SBOp 3:119-154; trans. *On Loving God,* CF 13B.

[11] *De preceptione et dispensatione*, SBOp 3:252-294; trans. *Bernard of Clairvaux: Treatises 1* (1970) 103–150.

[12] Stanislaus Ceglar, 'Guillaume de Saint-Thierry et son rôle de directeur aux premiers chapitres des abbés bénédictins (Reims 1131 et Soissons 1132)', in Michel Bur, ed., *Saint-Thierry, une abbaye du VIe au XXe siècle*. Actes du Colloque internationel d'Histoire monastique Reims-Saint-Thierry, 11 au 14 octobre 1976. (Saint-Thierry, 1979) 2:299-350 [trans. *William Abbot of Saint Thierry* (Kalamazoo, 1987) 3–7].

[13] *Apologia ad Guillelmum abbatem*, SBOp 3:63-108 [translated as *Cistercians and Cluniacs: St Bernard's Apologia to Abbot William*, CF 1A].

[14] Perhaps even *De diligendo* must be considered more in the scholastic context than in the monastic. In the same period Bernard also wrote his letter 77 to Hugh

Only two works seem to form an exception to this general rule: the *In laudibus Virginis Matris* (Miss)[15] consists of four homilies, and much of his *De laude novae militiae*[16] reminds one of a sermon. The exception is only apparent, however, *Miss* was indeed initiated as a treatise before it underwent a drastic elaboration and received the form in which it is known today.[17] Moreover, in his prologue, Bernard himself declares that the work was written during his period of illness and seclusion from the monastery. Thus he never delivered these homilies to his community.

The *De laude* text for the Templars may indeed have been delivered by Bernard, although the prologue rather supposes the contrary. Bernard wrote the work at the repeated request of Hugh of Payens, the founder of the military order. Its alternative title, *Liber ad milites Templi*, makes explicit its original purpose as a tractate. Actually, it reminds one of the development of Bernard's first treatise on humility, which was based on the sermons he had preached in front of his monks. That he did not publish them as a series of sermons but instead prefered to rework them into a tract reveals that he had a clear opinion of the objectives of each genre, one to which he was to stick for the rest of his life. Whenever he interprets a biblical passage, he publishes his commentary as a series of sermons. His other writings, however, remain in the more accepted form of the treatise.

Developing a biblical commentary in a continuous series of sermons was, in fact, something entirely new in the beginning of the twelfth century. Homiliary commentaries were known from Late Antiquity,

---

of Saint Victor, known as the treatise on baptism. The reason for Bernard's scholastic concern during these years must have been the competition he experienced from Abelard's success at the Paraclete. For a more detailed analysis of the years 1124–1127, see Verbaal (2002) 253–271 and my article 'Bernardus philosophus' in *Revista Portuguesa de Filosofia* 60/3 (2004) 567–586.

[15] *Homilia in laudibus virginis matris*, SBOp 4:13-58; trans. *Homilies in Praise of the Blessed Virgin Mary*, CF 18A.

[16] *De laudibus novae militiae*, SBOp 3:207-239; translated as *In Praise of the New Knighthood*, CF 19B.

[17] See the Introduction to the edition by Jean Leclercq SBOp 4 (1966) 7–8, where he mentions the existence of a manuscript containing only the first three homilies as a continuous text.

especially those of Origen and of Augustine on the Gospel of John, but the regular form of a biblical commentary in antiquity was the tract. And so it remained until the twelfth century. Jerome, Gregory the Great, Ambrose, the Carolingians and the commentators of the eleventh and early twelfth century—Bruno, Honorius Augustodensis, Anselm of Laon, Rupert of Deutz, Abelard and even Bernard's friend William of Saint Thierry—all prefered the traditional tractate.

Bernard was the first to break with this tradition and to revitalize the commentary by creating sermons, thus also creating a new contextualization of the writing and reading process. The writer is no longer a distant teacher, making the reading into a one-way process. He has become a living voice (a *sermo vivus et efficax*), melding writing and reading into one momentary event in which the text develops in and by the reading.

And yet, the choice seems not to have been self-evident. Bernard was not to revive the experiment of *Miss* for more than a decade, instead concentrating his attention more on moral subjects. Only around 1135, when he began writing his commentary on the Song of Songs, did he return to the exegetical sermons.[18] And during these same years, against this background, the first sermon collections came into being. The *Sermons for the Liturgical Year* would be the result.

Part 1:
The Evolution of Bernard's Liturgical Sermon Collection

LECLERCQ'S CHRONOLOGICAL SEQUENCE

The textual transmission of Bernard's liturgical sermons has been thoroughly studied by Jean Leclercq. His research led him to distin-

---

[18] For the year, see Jean Leclercq in the Introduction to the edition SBOp 1 (1957) xv. Also Jean Leclercq, 'Les étapes de la rédaction' in *Recueil des études sur saint Bernard et ses écrits* [= *Recueil*] 1 (Rome 1962) 213–244, esp. 213; Constant Talbot, 'Die Entstehung der Predigten über Cantica Canticorum' in J. Lortz, ed., *Bernhard von Clairvaux. Mönch und Mystiker* (Wiesbaden 1955) 202–214, esp. 202. Simultaneously, William starts his exegesis of the Song of Songs: as a treatise.

guish four different and successive collections, which he labelled respectively B (between 1138 and 1140), M (around 1140), L (after 1148) and *Pf*, the final redaction.[19] Dom Leclercq thought he could discern a clear evolution from one collection to the next, a gradual development into the perfect form of the final compilation. A closer examination of the actual elements of each collection, however, shows that the correlations are much more complicated.

The earliest collection [B] contains two kinds of texts: on the one hand, commentaries on some liturgical high holy days; on the other, interpretations of biblical passages or chapters of Benedict's *Rule*. Furthermore, these two texts appear, not in separate blocks, but, apparently, in a random order. There seems to be a certain liturgical scheme reaching from Advent to the feast of Saints Peter and Paul,[20] but it is more than remarkable that there is no explicit text for Christmas. An even closer look discloses that the collection more or less answers a spiritual evolution, passing the phases of conversion, entering the community, recognition, the inner struggle between *timor* and *amor*, the sacraments, revelation and *actio*. Bernard's first attempt might thus well be characterized as a moral or thematic collection. Yet the liturgical elements which are already part of it give a hint that the two interpretative approaches cannot be separated in Bernard's view of the liturgical year.

The second collection [M] offers fewer difficulties. Containing fifty-six texts (thirteen more than B), of which three are perhaps unauthentic,[21] it covers the entire liturgical year from Advent to All Saints' Day, and separates the Temporal from the Sanctoral cycle. In all respects, M seems to be an elaboration of the earlier collection with a more acute attention for the liturgical year.

[19] Jean Leclercq, 'La tradition des sermons liturgiques de s. Bernard' in *Recueil* 2 (1966) 209 and 211–222; and his 'Les sermons de Bernard sur le psaume *Qui habitat*' in *Recueil* 2:4–11, as well as his introduction to the edition in SBOp 4 (1966) 127–130.

[20] 29 June.

[21] See SBO 4 (1966) 130 and 133–135. Also Leclercq 'La tradtion' *Recueil* 2 (1966) 214–217.

The third collection [*L*] offers again a completely different image.[22] It is the largest of all, containing one hundred thirty-six texts, and it falls into two truly distinct halves. The first and greater part contains exegetical texts, arranged according to the biblical books, and thematical meditations on moral subjects, on numerical associations and interpretations. The second part is more strictly liturgical, and is divided into a Temporal cycle (extending from Christmas to Pentecost) and a Sanctoral cycle (going from Annunciation to the feast of Mary Magdalen, 25 March to 22 July). There is almost no overlap with the earlier collections, which demonstrates that *L* must be seen, not as their continuation, but rather as an independent collection parallel to the earlier ones. Indeed, this collection rather gives the impression of some organized archives from which Bernard could draw in view of other needs.[23]

The final liturgical series [*Pf*] contains texts from each of the other collections,[24] and often gives a new meaning by putting them into a new context. By comparing the position of the materials in the previous collections, especially in the earliest one, with the place they occupy in the final series we get some indications of Bernard's underlying motivation in creating a new cistercian homiliary for the liturgical year.

REASONS FOR THE CREATION OF A DISTINCT CISTERCIAN SERMON COLLECTION

What could have moved Bernard to give the cistercian congregation a proper and completely new liturgical homiliary? Once again,

---

[22] See SBO 4 (1966) 130 and 135–138. Also Leclercq 'La tradtion', *Recueil 2* (1966) 217–222. The contents of *L* as given in SBO 4:135-136 are incomplete: Adv VII – Circ II have been left out.

[23] The way in which texts for private use were kept and filed in medieval monasteries has not been studied as far as I know. In this respect, Bernard's writings offer an interesting subject, because both the *Sermones de diversis* and the *Sententiae* appear to mirror other, less organized, private archives. I still hope to publish some results of my research on these collections.

[24] See SBO 4 (1966) 121–122. Also Leclercq 'La tradtion', *Recueil* 2 (1966) 223–228.

Bernard was acting contrary to the early cistercian tradition and especially against the spiritual attitude of his abbot-father, Stephen Harding. For if there is one aspect characteristic of Stephen's mentality, it is his acute sense of authenticity. This led him to revise the biblical text with the assistance of jewish scribes, a very successful enterprise.[25] This also incited him to impose on the congregation an entirely new hymnody in accordance with what he thought was the most authentic tradition. This reform proved less fortunate and soon after Stephen's death a second reform was deemed necessary and was assigned to Bernard.[26]

In the light of all this, the period in which Bernard's first liturgical collections were created is telling: they were finished around 1138 and 1140, i.e. four years after Stephen died and the General Chapter decided to revise the cistercian liturgy. It seems very unlikely that Stephen would have agreed with such a reform, which meant a real rupture with his own quest for authenticity. For this reason, he would not have been very open to the replacement of the traditionally used carolingian homiliary by a personal creation of one of the members of his congregation.

This, in turn immediately poses another question: what may have been Bernard's objective in creating a new sermon collection for the liturgical readings? As a matter of fact, it seems rather unlikely that he envisaged the widespread use of his collection in cistercian liturgy, which, in fact, did not happen. The congregation did not abolish the traditional homiliary as it had been used (and would be used thereafter) by most of the medieval Church.

Moreover, it is even more unlikely that the General Chapter would have permitted a similar violation of its own decisions. The *Ecclesiastica*

---

[25] Michael Casey in '*Exordium*, un programme d'étude sur la tradition cistercienne, qui fut proposé aux communautés cisterciennes durant l'année du 9ème centenaire de la fondation de Cîteaux: Unit 2 "The Founders of the New Monastery"' p. 29 (http://www.rc.net/ocso/Exordium/exordium.htm).

[26] Around 1131, the new cistercian hymnody was sharply criticized by Abelard in his letter 10 to Bernard. See Edmé Renno Smits, 'Peter Abelard. Letters IX – XIV. An Edition with an Introduction', Dissertation: University of Groningen (Groningen 1983), esp. 245.

officia clearly restricts the number of occasions on which the abbot is allowed to preach to the community to only sixteen festivals: the first Sunday in Advent, and Palm Sunday; Vespers of Christmas, Epiphany, Easter, Ascension, Pentecost, and of the major feasts of the Virgin (Nativity, Annunciation, Purification, and Assumption), of the Nativity of John the Baptist, Peter and Paul, Saint Benedict, All Saints' and the Feast of the Dedication.[27]

Bernard's collections, however, surpassed these boundaries from the beginning. Not only do they contain several sermons for one and the same celebration, but he also choose to include sermons for occasions on which preaching was not mandated. Normally, scholars refer to the first sermon for Septuagesima [Sept] or to the tenth sermon on Psalm 90 [QH] to explain this transgression of the cistercian regulations.[28] In the first, Bernard attributes his frequent preaching to the spiritual avidity of his listening monks.[29] In the latter, he excuses himself for preaching on so many occasions, even against the customs of the congregation, by appealing to his infirmity, which forbids him from joining in community work. For this reason, the General Chapter would have given him permission to compensate for this failure by his preaching.[30]

Doubt has been expressed on the sincerity of such remarks.[31] Some very simple objections can be made against the accuracy of these

---

[27] See Danièle Choisselet and Placide Vernet, edd., *Les* Ecclesiastica officia *cisterciens du XIIème siècle*, cap. 67; La documentation cistercienne 22 (Reiningue: Abbaye d'Oelenberg, 1989) p. 190. Also Marielle Lamy, 'Introduction' in *Bernard de Clairvaux: Sermons pour l'année I. 1: Avent et Vigile de Noël* (Paris: Éditions du Cerf, 2004) 27.

[28] See Christopher Holdsworth, 'Were the sermons of St. Bernard on the Song of Songs ever preached?' in Caroline Muessig (ed.), *Medieval Monastic Preaching* (Leiden-Boston-Cologne: Brill, 1998) 295–318; and my refutation of his conclusions in Wim Verbaal, 'Réalités quotidiennes et fiction littéraire dans les Sermons sur le Cantique de Bernard de Clairvaux' in *Cîteaux* 51 (2000) 201–218. Our discussion is on-going and I express my profound appreciation for the open-mindedness of Professor Holdsworth who has always encouraged me in his amiable way to push my research always further.

[29] *Sept* 1.2 in SBOp 4 (1966) 346.

[30] *QH* 10.6 in SBO 4 (1966) 447.

[31] See Lamy (2004) 28.

claims. Even if the Chapter had allowed Bernard to compensate for his physical infirmity by the labor of preaching, there is no reason why it would have given him permission to publish these sermons. On the contrary, the Chapter seems to have been very reserved about the publication and dispersion of writings by cistercian monks.

Furthermore, as will in due course become clear, it is no coincidence that Bernard treats this problem in his sermons for Lent. Why did he not do this as well on other occasions? The fact that he returns to the subject twice, both within the same liturgical framework, raising the question of whether this substitution of preaching for manual labor does not rather underline the central theme of these sermons, while this consideration is excluded from other homiletic sequences based on different underlying themes. Raising a similar question, however, means that the structure of the collection has to be taken into consideration: does it present what it seems to present? Once again, the evolution of the liturgical sequence might offer an answer.

THE EVOLUTION IN BERNARD'S VIEW ON THE COLLECTION

In order to understand the evolution of Bernard's interpretation of the liturgical year, one must limit one's attention to the two collections which truly can be labelled 'liturgical': *M* (around 1140) and *Pf* (before 1153). The older one contains fifty-six texts, although the last three probably ought not to be considered part of the actual sequence. There remain then fifty-three texts which cover a large part of the liturgical year—from Advent to All Saint's Day—and these are divided into two parts, the Temporal and a more limited Sanctoral sermon series.

The *De tempore* covers all the high feasts of the year as prescribed by the *Ecclesiastica officia*, but widens its scope broadly by adding to the obligatory feasts two sermons for the Circumcision, five sermons for Lent, a sermon for Maundy Thursday, and another for the Rogation days. Furthermore, various feast days are generously gifted with sermons. The result is the following distribution: Advent, three sermons; the Vigil of Christmas and Christmas, five; the Circumcision, two; Epiphany—including the sermons which were afterwards assigned to the Octave and the first Sunday after the Octave—four; Lent, five; Palm Sunday, two; Maundy Thursday, one; Easter—including two sermons which ended up among the *Sermones de diversis* and two sermons for the Octave of Easter, six; Rogation days, one; Ascension, four; Pentecost, two.[32]

The *De sanctis* remains clearly restricted to festivals prescribed by the Order, with a heavy emphasis on the feasts of the Virgin. The sole addition to the liturgical year is the feast of the Archangel Michael (29 September). This results in the following distribution: a coherent block around Mary, containing sermons which were afterwards assigned to the several feasts: Annunciation, Purification, and Assumption, ten; Archangel Michael, two; Dedication of the Church, three; All Saints, three.

As becomes clear, in this early liturgical collection, Bernard kept himself rather strictly within the boundaries of tradition. In the Temporal, indeed, he allows himself some liberty in expanding the scope, but within acceptable limits. In the Sanctoral, he is even more careful.

When we turn to the final collection then, the talley becomes entirely different. A first remarkable change is Bernard's decision to abandon the division between Temporal and Sanctoral. This meant a revolutionary change of view indeed. All contemporary sermon collections continued to maintain the traditional division as it had been established very early and sanctified by ecclesiastical custom.[33]

---

[32] In considering the older liturgical collections, one has to be very careful not to succomb to the seductions of retrospection. Only internal evidence or the position inside the collection can determine with which liturgical scope Bernard has written and inserted a certain text. Unfortunately, this aspect sometimes seems to be forgotten, which implies that Bernard should have had, from the beginning, a clear view on the purpose of his liturgical collection. As will be demonstrated, the evolution of the collection rather suggests the opposite.

[33] The traditional model is provided by the homiliary as compiled by Paul the Deacon for Charles the Great (782–786), which was widespread and used during the entire Middle Ages in Western Europe. See Pierre Salmon, *L'office divin au Moyen Âge I: Histoire de la formation du bréviaire du IXe au XVIe siècle* (Paris: Les éditions du Cerf, 1967) 28 n. 3. In the cistercian congregation itself the Night Office homiliary

A good example is offered by the homiliary which Peter Abelard composed for the benefit of the Paraclete only a few years before Bernard's first collection. Abelard's collection consists of thirty-four sermons divided into a Temporal cycle (twenty-two sermons ranging from the Annunciation to the *Feria quinta* of Pentecost), and a Sanctoral cycle of (twelve sermons not chronologically ordered).[34] The decision to give the sermons their chronological place within the liturgical year does not seem to have been the most obvious choice, because it had never or hardly ever been made before Bernard.[35]

What is more, the texts Bernard included considerably augmented the usual number. The ultimate collection comprises one hundred twenty-eight sermons for forty-three occasions, more than twice as many as were permitted by the *Ecclesiastica officia*! Sermons were even added which contravened an explicit interdiction against preaching at the commemoration of the dead;[36] Bernard inserted a sermon for Malachy and one for Humbert, a former abbot of Igny. The collection also contains sermons for occasions which can hardly be reckoned as part of the liturgical year: especially the summer sermons *De altitudine et bassitudine cordis* and *De labore messis*, and also the *Sermo ad abbates*.

A third change in the development of the collection concerns the sermons themselves. Most of those texts which had already appeared

was composed on the basis of this very collection. See Chrysogonus Waddell, 'The Liturgical Dimension of Twelfth-Century Cistercian Preaching' in Carolyn Muessig (ed.) *Medieval Monastic Preaching*, Brill's Studies in Intellectual History vol. 90 (Leiden, Boston, and Cologne: E. J. Brill, 1998) 335–349, esp. 342. Also Réginald Grégoire, 'L'homéliaire cistercien du manuscrit 114 (82) de Dijon' in *Cîteaux* 28 (1977) 133–207.

[34] See the only full edition to date by Victor Cousin, *Petri Abaelardi Opera* I (Paris: Durand, 1849) 349–595, reprinted in Migne *Patrologia Latina* 178. To these thirty-four sermons can be added some other texts which did not, however, belong to the Paraclete compilation. See John Marenbon, *The Philosophy of Peter Abelard* (Cambridge: Cambridge University Press, 1997) 78 n. 80.

[35] Bernard might have been inspired by the sermon collections of some of the Church Fathers, notably Gregory the Great and Origen.

[36] *Ecclesiastica officia* 67.5: *In his etiam diebus exceptis festis transpositis. et excepta commemoratione defunctorum habentur sermones in capitulo.* Choisselet and Vernet (1989) 190.

in one of the earlier compilations were entirely reworked. This is especially true for those sermons of which an early version is known. They are often completely different from the ultimate result.[37]

Finally, there is what might be considered the most telling change: sometimes the order of the sermons within the year has been changed. The sermons on the Dedication, for example, are transferred from their initial position between Saint Michael's Day and All Saints' Day to a position after All Saints'.[38] A transfer of the sermons for a specific occasion does not imply, of course, that this ceremony itself was assigned another place in the liturgical calendar.

In the case of the sermons on the Dedication the solution may be found in a transposition of their object. Originally they may have been written to commemorate the Dedication of the monastery church at Clairvaux, celebrated on 13 October, which falls between Saint Michael's and All Saints' Days.[39] In the end, these same sermons, without considerable change, were taken to commemorate the Dedication of the church of Saint John Lateran, that is, 9 November, thus after All Saints' Day. This implies that the same texts were deprived of their local significance and limitation to a specific monastery and given a more universal application, Saint John Lateran being considered the mother of all churches.

On one occasion, Bernard clearly interferes with the chronology of the calendar. His sermon on the death of Malachy, archbishop of Armagh, who died in Clairvaux on the night of All Souls' (2 November), was allotted a place between the sermon for Saint Clement (23 November) and the Vigil of Saint Andrew (29 November). The community, however, commemorated Malachy's death on 3 (later

---

[37] See SBO 4 (1966) 152–153, and other studies by Jean Leclercq dedicated to the problem of Bernard's editorial work, e.g. his 'S. Bernard écrivain d'après les sermons sur le psaume "Qui habitat"', *Recueil* 4 (1987) 107–122.

[38] The respective order in the collections *M* and *Pf.* See SBO 4 (1966) 133–134 and 138.

[39] The construction started in 1135, and the church was finished and dedicated in 1138. See Robert Fossier, 'L'essor économique de Clairvaux' in *Bernard de Clairvaux*. Commission d'histoire de l'ordre de Cîteaux (Paris: Editions Alsatia, 1953) 95–114, esp. 101–103; as well as the 'Tables chronologiques', 592 (1138).

5) November,[40] but apparently, this position of the text did not suit Bernard's aims for his collection.[41]

The introduction of these changes can lead to only one conclusion: the sermon collection for the liturgical year did not come into being in an organic way. It is much more than just a compilation of liturgical sermons preached (or even written) by Bernard solely within a monastic liturgical context. Not only does the compilation not conform to the customs of the first cistercian generation, it even runs counter to the explicit prescriptions of the cistercian customaries. It could never therefore have played an official part in cistercian liturgy, in which there is no place for a similar expansion of homiletic activity.

What then might have been Bernard's intention? When the collection cannot be attributed to liturgical use, it seems to have no other place within cistercian community life than private reading, *lectio divina*. If so, the collection becomes one of the important elements in Bernard's attempts to transform the cistercian congregation into a textual community.[42] Yet, on the other hand, the scope of the

---

[40] David Hugh Farmer, 'Malachy' in *The Oxford Dictionary of Saints* (Oxford: Clarendon Press, 1980) 257–259, esp. 258. Also Jean Leclercq, 'Documents on the Cult of St. Malachy' in *Seanchas Ardmhacha* (Journal of the Armagh Diocesan Historical Society) 3 (1959) 318–332; reprinted in Leclercq, *Recueil* 2 (1966) 131–148, esp. 131 and 142–143.

[41] As I already suggested elsewhere the same must be implied for the sermon on Humbert's death which closes the final collection. On the date of Humbert's death a double tradition survived within the cistercian congregation. His death was dated 7 September or 7 December. See Elphège Vacandard, *Vie de saint Bernard abbé de Clairvaux* 2 (Paris: Librairie Victor Lecoffre, 1895) 392 n. 1; and Gerhard Winkler, *Bernhard von Clairvaux. Sämtliche Werke Lateinisch/Deutsch,* 8 (Innsbruck: Tyrolia, 1997) 26. The last date, however, could be a later correction to make the sermon fit in the chronological sequence.

[42] See for the introduction of this crucial concept in literary critics, Brian Stock, *The Implications of Literacy. Written Language and Models of Interpretation in the Eleventh and Twelfth Centuries* (Princeton, 1983), esp. chapter 2: 'Textual Communities', 88–240. On page 90 the textual community is described as follows: 'What was essential to a textual community was not a written version of a text, although that was sometimes present, but an individual, who having mastered it, then utilized it for reforming a group's thought and action.' On Bernard's use of the recently developing

collection as a whole, as well as the length of the individual sermons raises doubts concerning the suitability of the collection for meditative reading. They are simply too long to be fruitfully ruminated.

In this respect, they come close to the Sermons on the Song of Songs, which were started and completed in about the same period (from 1135 till after 1148). Neither collection allows an immediate access to the intention of the author. Both collections demand a prolonged and continuous attentive reading in order to master the underlying meaning of their complex construction. During the last decade, after the commemorative studies of the early 1990s, Bernard has been shown to have been a master in allusive writing—causing a perpetual uneasiness in his careful readers who never quite get a hold on the true significance of his torrential flood of words, images, figures.[43]

Despite the still widespread image of Bernard as a rather baroque and organic writer who has to be taken at his word, the time now seems ripe to consider him as the true organizer he was, someone who did not allow a single word to be casual or the least figure and image to be superfluous. If Bernard arranged and rearranged his liturgical sermons continuously in order to arrive at the collection's ultimate, truly perfect form, then readers ought to feel obliged to penetrate to the very heart of the message conveyed by the text. They must learn to read the sermons in function of the liturgical year as it was seen and reinterpretated by Bernard.

---

attitude of silent reading, see Wim Verbaal, 'The Writer's Love. Love and the Act of Reading: Plato, Augustine and Bernard of Clairvaux' in Geert H.M. Claassens and Werner Verbeke, edd., *Medieval Manuscripts in Transition. Tradition and Creative Recycling* (Leuven: Leuven University Press, 2006) 323–336. Also Wim Verbaal, 'The Preaching of Community: Bernard of Clairvaux's Sermons and the School of Experience' in *Medieval Sermon Studies* 48 (2004) 75–90.

[43] Pioneering work on Bernard's writing style has been done in the now indispensable book of Marinus Burcht Pranger, *Bernard of Clairvaux and the Shape of Monastic Thought. Broken Dreams* (Leiden–New York: Brill, 1994). In this line also lies the excellent work by Mette Birkedal Bruun, see her *Parables. Bernard of Clairvaux's Mapping of Spiritual Topography* (Leiden–New York: Brill, 2007).

THE ORGANISATION OF BERNARD'S LITURGICAL SERMON
COLLECTION

The Cyclical Reading: The Liturgical Year [44]

The first and most evident reading of the collection remains, of course, the liturgical one, the interpretations of the sermons as a textual commentary on the successive ecclesiastical high holy days. The story told by the sermons, then, is the liturgical story of Christ, a commemoration of the earthly life of the Redeemer. As such, it covers, in fact, the old Temporal cycle as it appears in Bernard's earlier compilations.

The final collection, however, does not break off after the Temporal cycle. Neither does it go back in time to take up liturgical festivals belonging to the Sanctoral cycle but celebrated during the timespan covered by the Temporal. In this respect too, the final collection differs from the earlier one.

While Bernard does not break entirely with the traditional reading of a homiliary, he nonetheless knows how to give it a revolutionary turn. The liturgical year is taken as a single continuum coinciding with the calendar year. Thus, Bernard brings about an identification of liturgical with secular time, of the time sanctified by the commemoration of Christ with the time of the year by human time-reckoning.

This may have a double consequence. At first sight, liturgical time seems desacralized, losing its consecrated character by being equated with chronological 'working' time. Of course this would not have been Bernard's purpose, and for this reason it is good to recontextualize the sermon collection within the monastic scope. In the monastic experience of time, human time-reckoning in calendar years coincides with the liturgical time-cycle. In the monastery, the natural cycle of the year is sacralized and transposed on to a more spiritual level. But

---

[44] The following is an elaboration of my earlier statements in 'Bernard of Clairvaux's Sermons for the Liturgical Year: A Literary Liturgy' in Nils Holger Petersen, Mette Birkedal Bruun, Jeremy Llewellyn, and Eyolf Østrem, edd., *The Appearance of Medieval Rituals. Disputatio 3* (Turnhout: Brepols, 2004) 49–66.

in the end, even at this spiritual level, the corresponding time concept is cyclical and based on repetition and return. At the end of each year the cycle closes to start once again from the beginning.

When the sermon collection is considered from this perspective, its reading will be cyclical too. On this level, Bernard's purpose will have been to provide the monk with an accompanying reading during the year, a meditative reading to be taken up again year after year. Thereby laying the foundation for a kind of rumination over the years, he is not addressing himself to the short-term memory as it is stimulated by ruminating easily comprehensible texts. He aims at the *mémoire de longue durée*, the long-term memory which offers the monk a spiritual framework for his natural time-cycle and obliges him in some way to lift his experience to the level which conforms to the liturgical signification of the year which is bestowed by the repetitive reading of the sermons. The collection serves as a kind of *aide-mémoire*, helping the reader to sanctify time by giving the year its liturgical points of meditation.

The Linear Reading: Man's Life

Out of this first level of reading, a second will immediately arise. The liturgical year is equivalent not only to the earthly year but even more to man's earthly existence.[45] The sermon collection cannot therefore limit itself to providing a frame to the natural cycle of the year; it must also tell the story of man's life on earth from conception and birth to death, from the time of expectancy (Advent) to the time of commemoration (Humbert).

By a transformational process similar to that seen on the cyclic level, however, this aspect is raised to a more spiritual level as well. A monk's life is sanctified by his choice to live the perpetual sacrifice

---

[45] See Mario Righetti, *Manuale di storia liturgica* 2 (1969) 1. As a matter of fact, the interiorization of the liturgical year as an individual experience fits in perfectly with the well-known spiritual current of the eleventh and twelfth centuries. See Chrysogonus Waddell, 'The Reform of the Liturgy from a Renaissance Perspective' in Robert Benson and Giles Constable, edd., *Renaissance and Renewal in the Twelfth Century* (Oxford: Clarendon Press, 1982) 88–109, esp. 98–99.

of Christ, because that life is the re-enactment of the earthly life of the Redeemer. The story of Christ's life is the story of each monk's life. The story of man's life then becomes a story of a monk's spiritual life: from his conception and birth, viewed as the spiritual re-birth by *conversio*, until his victory over death by his awakening and eternal birth in the Spirit.

This story, however, has an end and a beginning. Its time concept is linear and progressive, allowing no return. Its reading therefore has to be linear, too, progressing from the starting point to the final pages, and avoiding any regresssion to earlier stages. At this level, Bernard's often repeated warning not to return to an earlier stage has to be taken into consideration. Or, as he states so aptly in the sermon on the Purification:

> In all these matters, if anyone pretends to make progress or to progress from strength to strength, anyone like this should know that he is standing still and not in the procession – in fact, that he is in regression; for in the path of life, not to make progress is to make regress. Nothing ever continues in the same state. Indeed, our progress lies in this – as I remember having said quite often – that we should never think that we have 'made it', but should always strain forward to what lies ahead. We should strive unceasingly to become better and we should leave our imperfect being constantly open to the oversight of divine mercy.
>
> *Purification* 2.3

This level of reading approaches the sermon collection as if it were a mirror for living the spiritual life according to Christ's earthly existence, as it is represented by Bernard. The reading must be one which incorporates into the life of the reader Bernard's written interpretation of the life of Christ. Reading the collection as a mirror for life means living its reading.

The Punctualized Reading: The Power of the Word

A third level is less apparent and results from internal elements which have often been noticed but from which no conclusion has yet been drawn as to the concept of time and its consequences for reading. Bernard's liturgical sermons contain continuous cross-references to liturgical events celebrated at other moments in the year. Augmenting the basic liturgical intertextuality, he continuously links the various ceremonies during the year by citing texts from their particular liturgies. The sermons on the Ascension, in particular, are closely connected with the events of Advent and the Nativity. The ascent and descent of Christ are presented almost as one and the same event, the Nativity implies the Passion and the Resurrection, just as the Ascension implies the Nativity.[46]

The story of the Divine Word and its Incarnation encompasses the entire existence of Christ, each of whose words and deeds evokes all the others, just as there can be no division possible in the divine nature of the Son, not even a division in time. At the level of the divine Word, time has disappeared and been replaced by eternity, which may be considered as the simultaneity of all events.

By this procedure, Bernard succeeds in breaking the two-dimensional textual space and building into the reading a multiple perspective. Each event within the liturgical cycle evokes others and overlaps with them. Each liturgical event contains all the others.

Both cyclical and linear time-reckoning become neutralized by this punctiliar experience. The reader is lifted out of his momentary reading of a repetitive or linear pattern and forced into an all-embracing reading capable of comprehending at one time the entirety of the year and of human life. He is no longer subject to the natural cycle or to the linear progression from birth to death; he is instead elevated above them. He is granted the perspective of the divine Spectator who comprehends the entirety of time in all its aspects—repetitive,

---

[46] Cf. John 3:13: 'No man hath ascended up to heaven, but he that came down from heaven.' English translations of the Bible are quoted according to the King James Version which comes closest to the Latin text used by Bernard. See Righetti, *Storia liturgica* 2 (1966) 5, where he stresses that the entire liturgical year centres around the mystery of Easter: 'Si potrebbe anzi dire, che la celebrazione del mistero pasquale forma un unico ciclo che abbraccia l'intero anno liturgica.' ('One could also say that the celebration of the Easter mystery constitutes a unique cycle which encompasses the entire liturgical year.')

linear, universal, individual. The reader is transported into a timeless, eternal presence. His reading has become a sanctifying reading, bringing about the genuine, albeit momentary, enactment of the divine Word.

THE COMPLEXITY OF THE COLLECTION

To understand Bernard's organization of the sermon collection, we must keep in mind the three structural elements mentioned above. Bernard manages to fuse these three reading perspectives into a coherent, but multi-leveled, unity in which each strand merges with both the others to give a single but multi-dimensional narrative line. This has to do with the particular interpretation Bernard gives to his writing activity.

As a writer, Bernard positions himself even above the last mentioned level. He is not only presenting himself as looking from above, as does the divine Spectator. As a writer, he is even on a level with the divine Creator, having the power to influence the human way of experiencing time, place and space. He is a mediator of the divine Word which has the power to create or to adapt the universe according to the Word's plans. Only because of this coordinating capacity does he prevent the various interpretative layers in the text from falling apart. And in this approach, it is neither nature nor man, nor even God, but the author and his writing skill which have the power to create. Remember that the liturgical collection was presented as a *written* work in the first place. The way one reads it, the way the solemnities are presented, the references made to other liturgical events or to human life are all directed by the writer, who has complete freedom to arrange everything according to his wishes.[47] This creative freedom gives him the opportunity to approach time entirely

---

[47] This may be seen clearly in the Annuciation sermons, see my analysis in Verbaal 'Literary Liturgy' (2004) 60–62. See also my analysis of Bernard's 26th *Sermon on the Song of Songs:* 'Preaching the Dead from Their Graves: Bernard of Clairva's Lament on His Brother Gerard' in Georgia Donavin, Cary J. Niedermann, and Richard Utz, edd., *Speculum Sermonis, Disputatio* 1 (Turnhout: Brepols, 2003) 113–139.

in his own way. For at the divine level, time can be considered as a point enclosing everything simultaneously. Time can then also be rearranged in view of the writer's purposes, as long as he does not diverge from the story of the Word. The time concept becomes non-chronological, even anti-chronological, though it remains enclosed within the story as it is told and, for this reason, it obeys the claims of the text, i.e. of the author.

What does this mean, then, for the organization of the collection? The first organizing principle and somehow the framework for all the others is, of course, provided by the liturgical year. On the factual level the succession of solemnities constitutes a set pattern that does not allow Bernard much latitude. But what it does offer, he knows how to take advantage of! I have already mentioned how he moves the sermons for Malachy, Dedication of the Church, and probably also for Humbert, to other places within the collection, thus fitting them better into the story he wants to tell. Similar reasons will have moved him to insert the sermons for Palm Sunday after Saint Benedict and the Annunciation.

With the exception of Malachy and Humbert none of these insertions and transpositions really alters the liturgical accuracy of the collection. One of the aspects of Bernard's genius which still has not been well understood is his capacity to give traditional forms and rules an entirely new content and interpretation. He makes them say what he wants them to say—something not true only of the Bible, as Geoffrey of Auxerre noticed.[48]

The liturgical year retells the story of Christ. A second organizing principle therefore becomes clear when we consider the fact that Bernard does not end with Pentecost. For Bernard, the story of Christ is primarily the story of the divine Word. And in this story two parts can be distinguished: the material existence of the Word (the earthly life of Christ, covering the period from Advent until Ascension); and its spiritual existence (the workings of the Spirit, starting at Pentecost). This story does not end with Christ's return to heaven. It continues after Pentecost as the story of the Church—as

---

[48] Geoffrey of Auxerre, *Vita prima* 3.7; PL185:307B.

well as that of every human being—unfolds.[49] For this reason, the collection of liturgical sermons had to continue beyond the limits of the first compilation.

In the final collection many texts are introduced which treat the textual significance of the Word not only as the initial expression of God's will, incarnate in the person of Jesus Christ and later withdrawn into heaven, but also as the inspiring force of the Spirit, still and always working through and in the Church and even more effectively in the Bible. Texts such as the sermon for the feast of Saint John the Baptist, the first sermon for Peter and Paul, the sermons for the fourth and sixth Sundays after Pentecost—all introduced immediately after the conclusion of the story of the Word incarnate—treat the question of how human beings have to act to live according to the Word. In this way these later sermons intensify the themes developed in the first half of the collection.

A double structure thus becomes visible, making the sermon series comparable to the *Sermons on the Song of Songs*. In the first half of the Canticle commentary the marriage is treated, i.e. the joining of the Groom with his Bride. Liturgically, for Bernard, this signifies in the first place the re-incarnation of the Word, its descent into the soul of the reader, i.e. the long and painful preparation of the soul to host the divine Word. In the second half the resultant motherhood is treated, i.e. the fertility of the Bride and Mother, when the Word, no longer the sole center in the life of the reader, radiates out; when, that is, the reader has become fruitful in the Word thanks to his reading and incorporating it. The pivotal point between the two parts seems to be the sermon for Saint John the Baptist.

The links between both collections thus appear to be much closer than has hitherto been supposed. In fact, both address what may be characterized as the central concern of Bernard's writing: how to

---

[49] A similar narrative line can be distinguished in the first collection, *B*, in which the liturgical element somehow seems to have been less decisive than it is in the second revision, *M*. *B* demonstrates a clear will to evoke by the succession of sermons a spiritual developement, an education in the Spirit. The basic lines are largely the same as those which govern the final liturgical collection, as I hope to demonstrate in a separate article.

make fruitful the re-wording of the Word, how to pronounce the *sermo vivus et efficax*, 'the living and powerful Word'?

This two-sided structure is important not only for the liturgical collection as a whole; it can be recognized also on a smaller scale in the organization of smaller 'blocks' within the compilation. For a certain rhythm is discernable in the succession of the sermons. Actually, the one hundred twenty-eight sermons can be divided into smaller groups, organized according to a similar pattern. Each smaller unit opens with a sermon or a group of sermons dedicated to the Virgin or attachable to the Virgin: Advent, Purification, Annunciation, and the homiletic block around the Assumption and the Nativity of the Virgin. These sub-units then end with a sermon on the human level: the Conversion of Saint Paul, Saint Benedict, On the labour of harvest, or Humbert. Thus, each sub-unit mirrors the two-sided structure of the entire collection: each starts with the Virgin as the outstanding model for humanity, the person in whom the Word was truly incarnated, and each ends with the Word's activity through an individual human being.

Now these smaller sub-units in their turn all recapitulate the linear narration of man's spiritual life. The theme of each group is singularized by the last sermon, which illustrates the earthly, human counterpart of the central idea.

> The first group, from Advent to the Conversion of Saint Paul— the Christmas-group in a broad sense—treats the way to conversion as man's spiritual rebirth.

> The second group—Lent, from the Purification (2 February) to Saint Benedict (21 March)—treats discipline, i.e. the purification of life attained by submission to the divine commandments and the Rules of the monastic legislators. This second entity mirrors man's education in the Spirit.

> Then follows the Easter and summer group, from Annunciation (25 March) to the Harvest sermon. This larger unit first treats the last part of Christ's earthly life—his Passion, Resurrection and Ascension—and then in the second part starts with the descent of the Spirit and its working through human beings. On the human level, this group can be characterized by agricultural work, i.e. the sowers and harvesters.

The final unit—on death and the victory over death—opens with the larger block around the Assumption and Nativity of the Virgin, stressing the conviction that death is not the end but rather eternal rebirth in the Spirit. This theme is elaborated as a spiritual descent which ends in the life and death of the all-too-human monk Humbert with his strengths and his weaknesses.

The division of the collection into these four sub-groups casts light on Bernard's organizational skills as well as on the motives he had in making the compilation. In its structure, the entire collection now obviously consists of four groups of, successively, twenty-nine, twenty-nine, thirty-six, and thirty-four sermons, demonstrating Bernard's meticulous care for creating inner harmony.[50]

In addition, these four groupings mirror the fundamental message of the Sermons on the Song of Song that man has to live with the coming and the going of the Word. In the first and the third groups—Christmas and Easter—man is confronted with and inspired by the earthly presence and working of the Word. In the second and the fourth, however, in which daily life and death become the central themes, man stands alone; that is to say, the Word seems absent and works only through the intermediation of his material counterparts: the written word (Psalm 90); and the Church of the Saints.

Two of the three narrative lines we have marked out can be discovered in Bernard's organization of the collection. The cyclical strand is mirrored by the return of the same organizing principle for the entire collection as well as for the smaller sub-groupings. The linear movement is developed by the liturgical organization and its redivision into four sections according to man's spiritual growth—rebirth (conversion); education (discipline); work (sowing

---

[50] A similar numerical harmony was striven for in the sermons on the Song of Songs, which are composed according to the structure of the *Rule*. The *Rule* contains a prologue, an epilogue and 72 (6 x 12) chapters; Bernard's *opus magnum* consists of a prologue (SC 1), an epilogue (SC 86), and 84 (7 x 12) sermons. This analogy was pointed out to me in a letter of 24 November 1999 by the late Michel Coune OSB, probably one of the greatest authorities in the field of Bernard's writings, although he almost never published his views and insights: he preferred instead to live them.

and harvesting); and death (overcoming death). Moreover, both movements will reappear within each thematic sub-grouping.

Only the third narrative line, the punctiliar time experience, cannot be clarified in an overview of the totality of the collection. To lift oneself up to this level, one can no longer rely on a somewhat abstract analysis of Bernard's corpus. From now on, he must be read, and very carefully read!

SUMMARY

The somewhat technical approach of the preceding pages was meant to open readers' eyes to a still all-too-undervalued aspect of Bernard's writing. Bernard was an artist—as Dom Jean Leclercq rightly pointed out in several of his articles. Bernard had a keen sense of beauty and harmony, but he never cultivated the principle of art for art's sake. First and foremost he remains an abbot, a spiritual teacher, and by the attention he paid to every detail he made it clear that he wanted only to get an inescapable grip on the reader.

This made him ponder for many years the most suitable way in which to organize his liturgical sermons. The three compilations known to have preceded the ultimate collection demonstrate the care and the long preparation Bernard took in achieving his aim. They also show the way his interpretation of the liturgical year changed over time, causing him to renew entirely the traditional genre of the homiliary.

In the final collection, various narrative strands can be distinguished which mirror equivalent concepts of time within the liturgical year. Each had its own impact on the structuring of the entire compilation, each needs to be reckoned with in reading the sermons one by one. Taken together, they assign to each individual reader his proper place within the universe as it is mirrored, or rather constructed, in the collection: man's life breaks through the natural cycle of the year while overlapping with it, just as God's eternal *Now* breaks through both natural and human time because it overlaps and absorbs them.

Bernard was an innovative writer and thinker, although he preferred to remain within the boundaries of tradition and to realize his sometimes revolutionary insights within these limitations. They must have offered him a challenge, not an obstacle. Even now, the careful reading of Bernard's texts may discomfit the reader, because Bernard never allows his readers to feel they are on solid ground.

Part 2:
The Message within the Sermons

BIRTH, GROWTH AND RECOGNITION OF A CONCEPT

Before we enter more in depth into the sense of the first block of sermons, going from the Advent to the Conversion of Saint Paul, it will be illuminating to follow the successive steps which gave birth to Bernard's final version of these sermons. Not only does this demonstrate that Bernard had, from the beginning, a very clear concept of his aim for the entire collection, but an examination of the earlier versions may also throw light on the underlying themes that led to the final scheme.

Deliverance of the Soul: The First Version [B]

In collection B, Bernard's first arrangement, the block corresponding to the sermons translated here contains approximately twenty-two texts; of these the largest part was ultimately eliminated. Most of those cut became part of the collection known as the *Sermones de diversis* (*Miscellaneous Sermons*) or of one of the three collections of *Sententiae*.[51] Many of them remained nothing more than a draft or a rough reflex of some idea. They demonstrate the preliminary

---

[51] The collection B contains the following texts, indicated by the sigla they received in the final edition: *1.* Div 14; *2.* Adv 4; *3.* Adv 5; *4.* VNat 2; *5.* Div 85; *6.* Sent 3.15; *7.* Sent: *Laqueus* (edited as an appendix to QH 3); *8.* Div 75; *9.* Sent 1.5; *10.* Sent 1.6; *11.* Sent 1.7; *12.* Circ 3; *13.* Sent 3.16; *14.* Sent 3.17; *15.* Div 73; *16.* Epi 1; *17.* Epi 2; *18.* Div 29; *19.* OEpi; *20.* Div 86; *21.* pEpi 1; *22. De voluntate* (Sermones varii VI). Most of these texts are written in a first editing. For the entire collection B, see SBOp 4 (1966) 130 and 133-135. Also Leclercq 'La tradtion', *Recueil* 2 (1966) 214–217.

character of the entire collection, which Bernard probably never planned to circulate.

Yet the grouping of these texts was far from arbitrary.[52] In the succession of those twenty-two texts in B a clear order is recognizable, and gives expression to a spiritual progress, or even better: to the process of spiritual liberation.

The first text, now Div 14, functions as an introduction to the entire theme of the block that follows. It treats a subject dear to Bernard, the exegesis of Wisdom 7:30–8.1: 'Wisdom shall beat vice. She reacheth from one end to another mightily: and sweetly doth she order all things'.[53] In the wording of B, this exegesis takes on the form of a psychomachia between the forces of Wisdom and those of Vice.[54] Nonetheless, the aspect of battle, which was to be elaborated more fully in the later versions, is not yet emphasized. Man is not represented by Bernard as besieged by the vices which are auxiliary to Evil: each of the vices is instead generated out of another in a natural way: 'If neglect prevails, it begets curiosity. . . . If curiosity will not be vanquished, it gives birth to the experience of vices. . . . But if experience prevails, it begets concupiscence so as to passing over into an affection of the heart. . . . But if concupiscence will not be quenched, from it will be born habit.'[55]

This somehow natural development of the vices does not, however, change the final result: the captivity of man's soul which leaves

---

[52] In any case, Bernard's mind did not lend itself very much to a random ordering, as will be demonstrated by the liturgical part of the penultimate collection.

[53] Translation according to the King James' Bible, with adaptations in order to make the English conform to Bernard's text. *Sapientia* 7.30–8.1: *Sapientia vincit malitiam. Adtingit enim a fine usque ad finem fortiter et disponit omnia suaviter.*

[54] Bernard treats the same theme elsewhere and the version of B appears to be already a second elaboration. I have studied the evolution of the idea and its wording in Bernard's œuvre in my Ph.D. thesis, Gent 2000.

[55] Div 14 (P) 2 (SBOp 6/1:138): *Porro negligentia, si praevaluerit, generat curiositatem. 9.9 Curiositas, si non fuerit superata, parit experientiam mali.* (SBOp 6/1:135); 3: *Si vero praevaluerit experientia, generat concupiscentiam, ut transeat iam in affectum cordis . . . 9.9 Alioquin, si concupiscentia exstincta non fuerit, nascitur de ea consuetudo.* (SBOp 6/1:136); 5: *Haec consuetudo, si victa non fuerit, parit contemptum; 6: Si ergo non praevaluerit intelligentia reducere animum ad spem, contemptus deicit in malitiam.*

him longing for deliverance.[56] It is important to keep this point of departure in mind, because in B the following texts (2–10) focus attention on the importance of desire—man's longing to be delivered from the power of Vice—and on reason's struggle with the contaminated human will. This inner strife ends with the conversion of the will, which in turn leads to compunction and the sincere wish to repent by humiliating oneself before God. Only out of this humiliation is real recognition of God's true character possible, for it produces the tension between *timor* (awe) and *amor* (attraction).[57]

The entire development thus falls roughly into two movements: a period of tension between good and bad desires; and a slow growth toward recognition and knowledge of God's eternal elusiveness. The central moment is constituted by text 11 (Sent I.7), treating of the *piger*, the man who is slow to take up the burden of spiritual exercises.

The reader may, however, distinguish a threefold movement consisting of the slow purification of the three forces of the soul. First (texts 1–11), the *ratio* is central in its attempts to get the upper hand on the weaknesses of the body. Then (texts 12–14), the *voluntas* learns to postpone its own desires and to submit to a spiritual superior. Finally, by the combined efforts of will and reason, man gains his first view of God's true nature, which then begins to purify the memory. This threefold movement can also be taken as evoking the inner conversion of the individual personn, his outer conversion in the act of entering the community and his inner purification by externally living a community life.

Obviously, the succession of texts in B responds to a clear concept. As we mentioned, most of the texts remain in an unfinished state, but some of them were destined to find their places in the eventual

---

[56] This aspect is repeated and accentuated in the conclusion of Div 14 in its primary version (P) as it is edited in the Apparatus of SBOp 6/1:134-139.

[57] Texts 2–5 describe the possibility of spiritual and corporal renovation, 6–10 evoke the struggle between *ratio* and *voluntas* and the temptations of the will and the flesh, 11 describes the delay of true repentance, 12–14 voluntary humiliation, 15–19 the slow recognition of God's true nature in humility, love, justice and its unknowability, 20–22 God's love and will and the start of man's purification. For the correspondence of the place-numbers with the actual sigla of the texts, see above, note 2.

liturgical collection: Adv IV and V (B2 and 3), VNat II (B4), Circ III (B12), Epi I and II (B16 and 17), OEpi (B19) and pEpi I (B21). By the place they occupy in B, they thus give some indication for the way the final collection may be read.

Renovation of the Soul: The Second Version [M]

In the second version, M, the block before Lent contains fewer— only fourteen—texts than the corresponding texts in B. All of them were to be inserted into the final liturgical collection and the succession of the sermons obeys the chronological sequence of liturgical feasts during the year. M has one important difference from B: in M, a group of sermons is explicitly dedicated to the Nativity. That no text in B treats the Christmas-event seems to prove its thematic rather than its liturgical character.[58]

In spite of the stronger liturgical emphasis in M, the thematic bases within the block remain largely the same. The movement opens with preparing man for his inner renovation and, as in B, closes this first part with the restoration of the new Jerusalem (M4: VNat 2). Remarkably, the sequence does not open, as does B, with man's captivity. Instead, Bernard immediately introduces the theme of Advent by the long, rhetorically superb construction of Adv I, posing six questions: who comes, and whence, whither, why, when, and by what means he comes.[59]

By this different beginning, a switch of perspective is introduced. Man is no longer presented as besieged and conquered by the forces

---

[58] M consists of the following texts: *1.* Adv I; *2.* Adv II; *3.* Adv III; *4.* VNat II; *5.* VNat I; *6.* Nat II; *7.* Nat III; *8.* Nat IV; *9.* Circ I; *10.* Circ III; *11.* Epi I; *12.* Epi II; *13.* OEpi; *14.* pEpi I.

[59] During the sermon itself, however, Bernard does not keep to this plan, substituting for the question 'who comes' the declaration 'how great he is who comes' (Adv I.2-5); splitting up the question 'why' into two questions 'for what purpose' and 'why he to us and not we to him' (Adv I.7-8), and, finally, replacing the question 'by what means' with a repetition of the question 'by which way' (Adv I.end of 6 and 10-11).

of Evil;[60] he is instead immediately introduced in his confrontation with the coming Word. A second difference with B is the stronger emphasis put in M on Christ as the living Word of God. Man's renewal as it takes form in the Nativity is seen as being centered on the 'commingling' of the apparently incompatible, the union of earthly dust and divine spirit in man's creation and the indissoluble union of flesh, soul and Word in man's recreation (Nat II.4).

True human deliverance then is explicitly attributed to the descent of the Word into the human soul. Before that can happen, soul and body have to be prepared to receive the Word (texts M1-4). Next, Bernard describes God's descent as the union of the Word with man's being (M5-8). Finally, by this union, man begins to acknowledge the true nature of God and to attempt to conform his outer deeds with this inner recognition (M9-14).

The double movement we saw in B thus appears again, but in a slightly different form. First, a movement in two parts can be distinguished: it opens with the *renovatio hominis* in the sermons for Advent and the Nativity and continues in the *agnitio Dei* of the Circumcision and Epiphany sermons. The pivotal point occurs in Circ 3, in which the understanding of the Word in its signs and names leads to humble submission to a spiritual leader, a member of a community.

Also recognizable in M is the triple segmentation of B: an opening to the Word (the inner conversion of M1-8); the submission of oneself to the will of the Word under the direction of a spiritual master (the outer conversion of M9-10); and the union of inner and outer conversion in humility born out of recognition (M11-13), leading to the inner purification as the transition to the sermons for Lent (M14).[61]

---

[60] Although this aspect does not completely disappear, as will be demonstrated in the last collection.

[61] The guiding principles of B still appear in M but less explicitly. Desire, for example, remains the most important force with respect to the inner conversion. Although Bernard touches its importance rarely in a straightforward way, he concentrates his vocabulary of desire in the sermons for Advent, Christmas Eve and Nativity itself. The vocabulary of conversion and mutation, on the contrary, is

The combination of the thematic strand in B with the strongly liturgic perspective of M shows the multi-layered construction of the entire block. Both approaches are linked by the central position occupied by the Word in the descriptions of the events and participants, in the naming of all those involved in the actions and, above all, in the words with which Bernard, the writer, the preacher, interprets the Word. Because, as Bernard wrote elsewhere, 'the Angel Gabriel announces to Mary that she will conceive Jesus, that is, whichever preacher to whichever sinner. By his preaching, the sinner conceives, when he proposes to convert himself to God' (Sent 3.11). It is this paradigm of the Annunciation of the Word to the reader by his (written) preaching which was to direct Bernard's choices in composing the ultimate liturgical collection.

The Liturgical System: The Third Version [L^B]

Between the two liturgical collections M and Pf, Jean Leclercq placed another which he labelled L. Actually, only the last part of this collection, hereafter labelled L^B, can truly be called 'liturgical'; the first ninety-four texts show no link at all with the liturgical year. The liturgical part of this intermediate collection consists of forty-two texts and in some manuscripts, these are preceded by the mention of an *Explicit liber primus* for the first part of *L*, thus indicating clearly their erstwhile independent status.[62]

As will be demonstrated, they never were meant to form a separate series alongside the other two, nor may they be considered some kind of transition between the earlier collection, M, and its future replacement, Pf, as might be concluded from the way they were presented by Jean Leclercq, who accordingly concluded that L^B,

---

concentrated in the second half of the movement: in the cycles of Circumcision and Epiphany.

[62] SBOp 4 (1966) 130 and 135–138. Also Leclercq 'La tradition . . .', *Recueil* 2 (1966) 217–222. Of course the independent status of both parts of L does not exclude the possibility that some of the texts in the first part ultimately found their place within the liturgical collection, for example, the exegesis on Psalm 90, the first ten sermons of which open the entire collection L.

when compared with M, represented more or less a regression. In order to prove that L^B is of less importance to a good understanding of Bernard's intentions with the liturgical sermons, we need to deal briefly with its composition, which offers a surprising insight into Bernard's mind.

The part of L^B corresponding to the first liturgical block before Lent in the final redaction, consists of twenty texts, almost half of the entirety.[63] Many of these texts were indeed to be included in the eventual collection, but their composition in L^B seems to be guided only partly by the liturgical sequence. In fact, the liturgy appears to offer only the framework within which the sermons are grouped according to subject or applied method. Thus, L^B1-3 each consists of the exegesis of a text linked to Christmas Eve: successively the *Invitatorium* and the *Responsorium* of the Mass and the concluding verset of the chapter-reading. L^B4-6 treat of human needs in the various tensions between body and soul or hope and reality. L^B7-9 center on God's mercy (*misericordia*) and L^B10-12 on the two visits to the temple for the Circumcision and the Purification. L^B13 treats the spiritual duties of the pastor; L^B14-15 the spiritual sense of the Circumcision. L^B16-17 enter into the spiritual sense of the gifts of the Magi and, finally, L^B18-20 explain the meaning of the jars at the marriage of Cana.

A transparent systematization thus becomes clear. Texts treating a similar subject from different perspectives are put together in such a way as to form small groupings of, mostly, three texts. This subdivision into groups of three can also be recognized in the first and larger part of L, which consists of purely thematical or exegetical texts. When considering the importance of the number three in Bernard's textual compositions and exegetical method, we need not be surprised at this. It illuminates how, even in his personal archives, he chose a strict systematization which enabled him to discover in

---

[63] L^B contains the following texts concerning the period before Lent: *1.* VNat III; *2.* VNat V, *3.* VNat VI; *4.* Adv VI; *5.* Adv VII; *6.* VNat IV; *7.* Nat I; *8.* Nat V; *9.* Innoc; *10.* Div 51.2; *11.* Div 53; *12.* Div 51.1; *13.* Sent I.11; *14.* Circ II; *15.* Sent I.14; *16.* Sent I.15; *17.* Epi III; *18.* Div 55; *19.* Div 56; *20.* pEpi II.

a short time the texts he needed.[64] In this respect too, Bernard proves to be a child of his own time, an age in which the organization of knowledge and of the sources of knowledge (books and texts) reached a true culmination point.[65]

In any attempt to trace the development of the liturgical collections, L^B proves much less interesting than B and M because its organization answers a purely pragmatical concern and teaches us almost nothing about the guidelines of Bernard's spiritual concept.

SUMMARY

From this description of the various preliminary versions of the liturgical block around Christmas and Epiphany, it may have become clear that Bernard did not simply collect sermons in order to comment on the liturgical solemnities of the year. He had a definite but very complex concept of the messages which he wanted his collection to convey. Several strands had to be connected. The first of these were the liturgical high days, which in this block concentrate on three events in the life of Christ: Nativity, Circumcision and Epiphany.

To these three liturgical feasts are linked the working of the living Word, both in its historical form as the incarnated Son and in its concrete material form as the words of Bernard's texts transmitting the Word. I hope this makes the idea more transparent which underlies all of Bernard's writing: the Word became incarnate once in the historical person of Christ, but he immaterializes continuously in the written words that speak of Him, i.e. the words of the Gospels

---

[64] In the section under discussion only L^B13-17 form an exception, but in fact they all treat the spiritual sense of concrete aspects or texts, thus constituting a systematical group on its own.

[65] Paul Saenger, 'Lire aux derniers siècles du Moyen Âge', in Guglielmo Cavallo and Rogier Chartier, edd., *Histoire de la lecture dans le monde occidental* (Paris 1997) 147–174; and Saenger, *Space between Words. The Origins of Silent Reading* (Stanford, 1997). See also Jacqueline Hamesse, 'Le modèle scolastique de la lecture', in Cavallo and Chartier, *Histoire de la lecture,* 125–145, and the bibliography of Richard Rouse referred to by Hamesse on p. 444, n. 20.

but also the words of those writers who talk about Him, being the Word which wants to re-incarnate in the reader by means of the words he is reading. In this way the sermons successively evoke the inner conversion of a human person who opens himself to the Word/words, the external translation of this inner conversion in his decision to submit to the obedience of community life, and, finally, his recognition of the true nature of the divine Word. These three events were linked by Bernard to the three augustinian faculties of the soul: reason, will, and memory. Each of them has to pass through a period of tension and strife in order to achieve its own purification.

Simultaneously, the threefold partition of the block corresponds to a twofold partition between man's restoration, founded on his desire for deliverance of Evil, and man's recognition of God's appearance in the world through the divine Word. Once more, the pivotal point is man's conversion, as evoked in the sermons for Circumcision. In the final version of the sermon collection, all these differing (and sometimes diverging) lines had to be brought together. In what follows, we will demonstrate that Bernard not only succeeded in attaining this objective but that he managed to introduce even other narrative strands.

COMPOSITIONS WITHIN COMPOSITIONS

General Aspects

Nowadays, following the work of Jean Leclercq, it is hard to imagine, when reading the liturgical sermons in their modern editions, that this neat succession of texts is the result of so long and meticulous a process. Bernard's organizational genius did not express itself only in the growth and development of the Clarevallian congregation. It can be recognized as well in the structure and composition of his written works, and of this the liturgical sermons offer an exemplary illustration.[66]

---

[66] We pass over the way in which Bernard managed to fuse different existing sermons into one coherent and consistent text. It can be proved that several liturgical

When considering the first block of sermons, from Advent to Epiphany, in the final collection against the background of the other, preliminary compositions, one cannot but admire Bernard's perspicacity as a writer and as an editor with spiritual objectives. The entire sequence now counts twenty-nine texts; of these only the last one, the Sermon on the Feast of the Conversion of Saint Paul, did not appear in one of the earlier collections. All the other sermons are reused, sometimes largely rewritten, yet often they derive their new sense uniquely from the new place they occupy inside the final structure.

Just one example may throw some light on Bernard's compositional talents. The six sermons for Christmas Eve appear in all three preliminary collections. In the first one, B, VNat 2 consituted—with the preceding Adv 4 and 5 and the succeeding Div 85 and Sent 3.15—a thematic unity on man's longing for spiritual renewal as it is linked to the events of Advent and Christmas Eve.

In M, VNat 2 was linked to VNat 1, but in reverse order, thus creating a stronger liturgical accent because both sermons contain exegeses of texts which were read or sung during the Vigil of Christmas. Their order may have been inspired by the liturgical chronology, VNat 2 treating the responsory of Vespers, VNat 1 the closing verset of the morning reading in chapter.

Subsequently, in L, all the other sermons appear but not in their final sequence. VNat 3, 5, and 6 constitute a distinct exegetical group of liturgical texts belonging to the Christmas Eve, respectively the invitatory and responsory of the Mass, and once more the closing verset of the morning reading in chapter. VNat 4 forms part of a thematical group together with and following Adv 6 and 7, treating the tensions by which man suffers.

---

sermons are actually compounds consisting of elements which may have been written for different occasions, sometimes even without the slightest inner connection. The transitional phrases Bernard inserted in some of his sermons has already been pointed out, but, of course, the exact delimitation of these kind of transitional sentences constitutes a very problematic subject to deal with. Nonetheless, especially the *sermones de diversis* and the *sententiae* offer some interesting examples of Bernards reworking of existing texts.

The final arrangement of these six texts takes the preliminary contexts only slightly into consideration. Instead, a new governing principle is introduced, one based on the exegetical character of most of the sermons and resulting in a very strong composition:

1. VNat 1 treats the closing verset of the morning reading in chapter (with the first paragraph as a general introduction);
2. VNat 2 examines the Vespers responsory;
3. VNat 3 starts from the invitatory of the Mass;
4. VNat 4 is based on the exegesis of a verse from the Song of Songs (2:6);
5. VNat 5 makes the responsory of the Mass its point of departure;
6. VNat 6 returns to the morning reading in chapter.

The result is partly a circular construction—central to which is the exegesis of the Song of Songs—and partly a linear, liturgical composition—based on Vespers, the Vigils invitatory, a responsory with, once again, the exegesis of the Song of Songs in a central place. The combination of both organizational patterns gives a special meaning to the second exegesis of the chapter lection; this strengthens the sense of circular movement within the entire block, closing it, so to say, at its beginning; yet simultaneously the linear, progressive movement from sermon to sermon prevents the exegesis from remaining on the same level. The reader of this unified block centered on Christmas Eve ends at exactly the same point where he started, only to realize that it is no longer the same point.

This coincidence of two apparently irreconcilable inner movements is not limited to the Christmas Eve sermons. Both are characteristic of the liturgical collection as a whole. Their reappearance on the smaller level of the unity of a liturgical feast only underlines the coherence of the entire concept. No less important are they on the intermediary level of the first sermon block from Advent to the Conversion of Saint Paul, or even on the smallest level, that of the single sermon itself; they appear as fundamental elements in Bernard's discourse.

Linear Experiences

The first expectation in any reading is based on an experience of progress: every reader expects his reading to produce a forward movement, that is, a kind of linear experience moving from a beginning toward an end. Thus the reader of Bernard's liturgical sermons, commencing with those for Advent, will anticipate their introductory status. And, indeed, Bernard does not mislead his reader. For in several aspects these opening sermons retake themes and elements known from other bernardine works, and especially from those parts of them which somehow treat an initial phase in the spiritual way.

When setting out to answer his first question in Adv 1, 'who it is who comes', Bernard immediately deviates, as we have said before, treating not so much 'who it is who comes' but rather 'how great he is who comes'. Stating that the Son of God is utterly as high as God himself, he starts to adapt his opening question even more, changing it into 'why it is the Son who comes' (Adv 1.2). Then Bernard launches into a rather long digression on the revolt of Lucifer and his downfall, dragging along the first humans (Adv 1.2-5).

The liturgical collection thus opens with the same subject which Bernard treated at the start of the scale of humility or pride in his first treatise (Hum 31-37). There Lucifer illustrated the dangers of *curiositas*, the beginning of pride. Now, once more, Bernard warns against pride (Adv 1.3), but more important to his point of view this time is man's consent to Lucifer's seduction, allowing himself to be 'cast into the pit' (Adv 1.5). This last image recalls the opening sermon of the first collection B (Div 14), where the forces of Evil were each generated out of another so as to get hold of man and imprison him.

Without directly quoting himself, Bernard remains faithful to the plan he set out at the beginning. Man is captured by sin as a result of his own neglect, but, against the background of the liturgical year, what counts most is that the ultimate cause for his fall is not his own action but some kind of pre-history in heaven, the malicious example of the Morning Star. For this reason, man cannot be damned irrevocably provided that someone else, untainted by Lucifer's seduction, can be found to take upon him mankind's guilt and thus deliver humanity. This project can only be conceived, however, in the mind of supreme Wisdom, that is, the Son, who is the Wisdom of the biblical book of that name, as Bernard explains in the opening text of B.[67]

Yet the consistency of Bernard's thought even goes further. The second half of Adv 1 and the largest part of Adv 2 recall the second of Bernard's early works, the homilies in praise of the Virgin-Mother, especially the first two of them. The same images and metaphors return and culminate, in Adv 2.4, in almost a *verbatim* quotation of the earlier work, the evocation of the theme of the *Virgo-virga*.[68] Even more important, however, is Bernard's emphasis on *devotio,* which constitutes something like the leitmotiv in the earlier work.

This reminiscence of Miss continues in the following sequence for Christmas Eve. Here this reminiscence becomes even more open and undeniable. When Bernard urges the monks to run by evoking all those who are waiting for them: the world, the saintly martyrs, the angels, the threefold Godhead (VNat 2.4-7), he almost literally repeats his earlier exhortation to the Virgin (Miss 4.8). This parallel cannnot be taken lightly: when Bernard exhorts his readers in the same way and in almost the same words as he does the Virgin in his homilies, this indicates that he wants those reading his liturgical sermons to be not just equal to the Virgin of the Annunciation but rather actually to be her. Reading the sermons for the liturgical feasts of Advent and Christmas Eve, according to Bernard, means *becoming* the Virgin waiting for the birth of the Word.[69]

---

[67] In his first sermon for the Annunciation, Bernard will come back upon this subject, expliciting the connection with the verses from the book of Wisdom.

[68] Compare Adv 2.4 with Miss 2.6.

[69] See my earlier articles in which I have elaborated this point in Bernard's writing and reading technics, esp. 'Annoncer le Verbe. Les homélies sur le *Missus est* de saint Bernard' in *Collectanea Cisterciensia* 65 (2003) 111–136 and 193–221. Also '*Sacra Pagina*. De taalmystiek van het Woord en zijn lezer' in B. Biebuyck, K. De Moor, B. Keunen, G. Martens, D. Praet, A. Roose en W. Verbaal, *Negen muzen - tien geboden. Historische en methodologische gevalstudies over de interactie tussen literatuur en ethiek.* (Gent, 2005) 47–84.

The final collection [Pf] thus corresponds to the same scheme discovered behind the organization of M: the conception and birth of the living Word within the believer. Once more, the double movement can be recognized: a movement of preparation—this time characterized as a *sanctificatio*—which extends from Advent to the feast of the Holy Innocents; and a movement of recognition or *agnitio*, culminating in the recognition of Christ's Lordship by Saul, who becomes Paul. As in M, the first movement is driven by the force of desire, the vocabulary of desire being once more concentrated in the sermons around Christmas. The second half concentrates more on the understanding of the Word, i.e. the translation of the Word's inner sense into outward action, into a conversion of life.

The difference between the final and the earlier collection, however, lies chiefly in Bernard's choice of the specific pivotal point between these two movements. In M, the point of transition occurred at man's actual conversion, at the submission of his own will to the will of a spiritual guide and his entry into community life—as enunciated in Circ 3. Now, in the final collection, this turning point is moved forward to explain the true sense of the Christmas event. We noted above that a peculiar aspect of the earliest collection, B, was the absence of any specific text dedicated to Christmas. Even in M, attention to Christmas itself remained rather restricted to a descriptional exegesis. In the final collection, however, a new and illuminating sense is provided by the opening sermon [Nat 1] on the *Verbum abbreviatum*, the divine Word in its most humble form, the *Verbum infans*, the Word as a child, or better: the Word without words.[70]

A short review of the new arrangement in the final liturgical collection may perhaps clarify Bernard's overarching concept. When it is compared to the preliminary collections, only the first half of the block has significantly changed. The sequence of Advent to Christmas was extended from eight sermons (in M) to nineteen (including Holy Innocents), whereas the sequel, from Circumcision to Epiphany, was increased only by four sermons (including the Conversion of Saint Paul). Bernard clearly wanted to put more emphasis on the

---

[70] The combination *Verbum infans,* rare in christian literature, appears only four times in Bernard's works, three of them in the liturgical sermons for Christmas Eve and Christmas. Elsewhere it appears only in Miss 2.9.

preparatory parts of his collection. The expansion of the first half is principally due to the extension of the Advent and Christmas Eve cycles, which increase respectively from three to seven and from two to six sermons.

What were the results? In the Advent sermons, the final arrangement adds new accents within the sequence as a whole. Originally, in M, the Advent sermons ended with the preparation of the soul's house with its seven pillars (Adv 3), closing the season on a somewhat moral plane. In the continuation in Adv 4, however, the earlier theme—the way by which the Word is coming—is taken up again and elaborated, becoming more an inner evolution of the renewal of one's own affectivity. This affective, inner conversion then continues in the fifth sermon, whereas the sixth turns its attention on the renewal of the body, which can now be understood only as the result of this inner conversion. In the seventh sermon, the entire movement is shortly reviewed but with the purpose of inciting a new movement, of hastening towards the great Teacher at every decision, a theme very reminiscent of Bernard's invocation of the Virgin in Miss 4.8. Central in the cycle of Advent therefore is the reception of the Word, an exhortation to the right way of listening to the Word, that is, listening with the devotion which incites desire.

The sermons for Christmas Eve, as we have already shown, constitute a beautiful exegetical unity, concentrated as they are on texts drawn from the solemnities of the day. This section is not, however, simply a self-contained entity. After having prepared his readers to listen in the sermons of Advent, Bernard then takes up the logical sequel, the preaching or annunciation of the Word itself. The liturgical framework offers the most concrete manifestation of the Word becoming matter, i.e. becoming reality in the audible words which evoke the human images of Christmas.[71]

These images, then, have to be understood as a language on its own, as *signa* that need to be interpreted. A mediator is needed, someone who is able to open the secrets of these signs and give them their true meaning, in this way teaching the reader how to read these

---

[71] This explains also the entire exegesis of the names in VNat 1, which largely is a retake of Miss 1-2.

signs, this Word without words. The reader will be able to enjoy the heavenly bread if it is broken for him, and this only the Lamb can do (Nat 2.4).[72]

The sermons for the feasts of the Holy Innocents, Saint John, and Saint Stephen form the human counterpart to the desire for a life sanctified by the Word. With the Circumcision sermons emphasis is shifted from the divine Word in its activity to the necessary human response. First, man accepts the consequences of having conceived and given birth to the Word in his own life by submitting to the divine will and dedicating himself to life within a spiritual community.[73] Next, he begins to acknowledge the rightness of his choice by recognizing the presence of the Word in his own inner and outer life.

Originally, in M, this recognition passed by the smooth transition made in the sermons OEpi and pEpi to the succeeding road of purification as it was elaborated in the sermons for Lent. In the final collection, however, Bernard chose to break this passage by the insertion of the sermon for the Conversion of Saint Paul, thus obliging the reader to pause and even to turn back. What reason might there be for an image of conversion after the conversion of the reader ought already to have been effectuated? In order to understand this aspect of Bernard's writing, we must call in mind the other movements implied in his sermons.

Circular Experiences

The sermon on the Feast of the Conversion of Saint Paul (Pl) is the only text which does not appear until the final collection. This earlier omission had not been due to Bernard's forgetfulness; the feast of Paul's conversion was not a solemnity on which the abbot was permitted to preach in the cistercian congregation. Bernard's

---

[72] This same image Bernard uses in the opening of his sermons on the Song of Songs (SC 1.4), creating once more a link to the initial state of one of his other works.

[73] Compare *Sentences* 3.11 with its equation of the Annunciation event with the preaching of the Word: see above, page xxxviii.

insertion into the collection of a sermon for this occasion enlarges the gap between the liturgical year as set out and as practised in the monastery. The reasons for its insertion thus have to be found elsewhere.

Reading the sermon for Saint Paul makes it immediately clear that this text constitutes something of a recapitulation of the entire preceding block. The sermon falls into two sections which, taken together, illustrate within the life of Paul almost the entire movement from Advent to Epiphany. The first moment (Pl 2-5) concentrates on revolt and aversion to the spiritual life of Christ. The second moment tells the story of Paul's submission, first to the will of Christ, then to the will of his representative (6-8). The whole sermon thus becomes a story of conversion as the story of an inner change from following one's own will to obeying the will of someone else. The story ends with Paul waiting for Ananias to lay his hands on him, an image which Bernard transposes to fit his readers, refusing them the responsibility of leadership before it is officially imposed upon them (Pl 8). The sermon for Saint Paul thus recalls the movement from Advent to the Circumcision. In Circ 3, the reader is exhorted to submit himself to a spiritual leader and to community life, just as Paul had to be led into Damascus and wait for the healing hands of Ananias (Pl 7 and 8).

While it may seem only a small detail, it is quite remarkable that Bernard ends his sermon not with Paul's healing but with his waiting for healing. The last image he gives of Paul is his having 'foreseen, perhaps in a dream, that a man was going to come to him who would lay his hands on him that he might regain his sight' (Pl 8). Bernard does not allow the reader to see Paul regaining his sight and coming to true recognition. That is: he eliminates the theme of Epiphany and leaves the reader with the image of a Paul in expectation, longing to be delivered from his blindness. The final image is thus the image of man in captivity; the reader has been returned to the beginning where man was imprisoned by his own sin.

In the sermon for Paul's conversion, the reader is thrown back, made to realize that he has not after all escaped, that Wisdom still has not delivered him, that his desires for freedom are not yet fulfilled. He returned to the point where he started.

Yet it is not exactly to the same point from which he started, because in the mean time he made progress. The linear movement is not canceled by the impression of circularity. The repeated circular movement has instead allowed him to progress. In sermon after sermon Bernard has given the reader the impression of turning him around, of causing him to circle, of leading him back to points and themes already covered. The first sermon of Advent closes on the same question which had been answered halfway through it: what is the way by which he comes (Adv 6 and 10) and this same question is taken up again in Adv 5, just as Adv 6 and 7 take once again into consideration all that has been said in the third and fourth sermons.[74] In its turn VNat refers constantly to the Advent sermons, while VNat 1 itself is taken up again by VNat 6 and 7. And so on.

When taking all these internal connections and references into consideration, the reader starts to feel dizzy in the face of the complex web woven by all the sermons. Each text is connected to a number of other texts and nothing is allowed to stand on its own. Yet only by doing so will he grasp the ultimate sense of the final image of Paul longing for deliverance: man will never be able to liberate himself completely from his incapacity to comprehend the true meaning of the living Word. Conversion is perpetual, man is repeatedly thrown back into his own blindness.

This cyclical movement, with its perpetuously returning plight of conversion, implies even more, however. When the reader has truly come full circle, his conversion must surely be complete. The circle he has described can never comprise more than it already contained. The journey can never convert more of him, it can only take his conversion to a higher level. Or, to use the image of a spring, the movement is spiral; what changes is not the diameter of its spiraling but the direction (or, in Bernard's image the height) of its motion.

Encapsulated between Advent to Epiphany, then, is the spiritual sense of the entire liturgical year. The sermon for Paul's Conversion

---

[74] Besides, the Advent sequel ends with man's running in renewed desire, thus once more returning to the point of departure as man longed to receive the Word in his life and body. See above p. xlvii for the circular movement of the Advent sermons in their linear evolution.

recapitulates this process by showing how the totality of the soul is involved in the movement of conversion. Three stages can be discerned which correspond to the three faculties of the soul. First, memory—depicted as the source for hope and repentance as well as the origin of 'the pattern (*forma*) of perfect conversion' (Pl 1)—has to be converted by remembering Paul's conversion. Next after memory, reason must be converted so that the brightness of truth will no longer blind us but will become within us the light of understanding (Pl 3-5). Finally, the will must convert in order truly to achieve 'the pattern (*forma*) of perfect conversion', which is the same as 'the pattern (*forma*) of perfect obedience' in which man renounces his own will (Pl 6).[75]

In the first section of these sermons, extending from Advent to the Nativity, Bernard concentrates on the conversion of memory; his vocabulary of remembrance peaks in Adv 3. From the Nativity to the Circumcision, Bernard is more concerned with the will and its proper direction. Finally, in the Epiphany and later sermons, cognition and understanding are central in Bernard's discourse.

Between the sermon on Saint Paul and the order followed in the entire block there seems to be a contrast. Whereas in the sermon for Saint Paul, will is the last to convert, in the entire sermon sequence will appears in the second position, before cognition and understanding. This discrepancy, however, is only apparent. In the sermon for Saint Paul, the reader is not brought to knowledge and understanding. He, like Paul, is left imprisoned in his blindness; true understanding has not yet been achieved.

---

[75] The word *forma* is one of the most fundamental concepts in Bernard's thought. It does not only mean 'example' or 'pattern', as here, but instead refers to something akin to the platonic idea: a higher, more spiritual signification of being in the mind of God to which man has to conform. Thus, we see the importance of what may be labelled the compelling motto in reading Bernard: *Transformamur cum conformamur* (SC 62.5). We will be transformed [into the higher spiritual truth of our being in God] as soon as we conform ourselves [to the spiritual image of us as it is presented in Bernard's words]. In this sense Saint Paul is more than just an example to Bernard: he is the *forma*, the higher spiritual truthful being to which he wants to be conformed.

Throughout the conversion process, moreover, reason appears as an important condition. It is by reason that will can be converted, just as memory can be healed only under the influence of directive reason. Reason is the faculty that points out that the soul is not yet capable of grasping the brightness of truth, because although the understanding may have foreseen (perhaps in a dream, Bernard significantly says), it has not yet been enlightened. Memory, although converted, is not yet filled with the brightness of truth. The three faculties of the soul have been converted, but only to realize the necessity of ever renewed conversion. Once more, the circle is closed.

Punctual Experiences

The web of connections and interconnections, of crossing and converging movements, of simultaneous impressions of progression and regression, which characterizes the block of sermons from Advent to the Conversion of Saint Paul, illustrates one part of what I have elsewhere called a punctiliar or punctual experience.[76] The reader has the impression that all contains all, that each sermon contains all the other ones, just as each solemnity compasses all the others.

This impression is strengthened by the liturgical resonances in several sermons. While often refering to liturgical variants instead of the biblical sources, Bernard seems very well aware of when he is allowing himself such freedom. Liturgical echoes are remarkably rare in the Circumcision and Epiphany sermons and when they appear they refer mostly to the proper or preceding solemnities.[77]

---

[76] Wim Verbaal, 'Bernard of Clairvaux's Sermons for the Liturgical Year: A Literary Liturgy' in *The Appearances of Medieval Rituals: The Play of Construction and Modification.* Nils Holger Petersen, Mette Birkedal Bruun, Jeremy Llewellyn, and Eyolf Østrem, eds., *Disputatio* 3 (Turnhout, 2004) 49–66, esp. 59–60.

[77] For the liturgical resonances, I base my discourse largely on the excellent work done by the german and french editors and translators. See Gerhard Winkler, ed., *Bernhard von Clairvaux. Sämtliche Werke lateinisch / deutsch* VII (Innsbruck 1996), and

In the sermons for Advent, Christmas Eve and Christmas itself, by contrast, the entire liturgical year can be heard. We noted earlier that the Easter liturgy in particular is echoed in the Nativity sermons, and this reverberation is strengthened by explicit references to Easter in several sermons (VNat 5.4, Nat 1.8, 2.5, 3.4). The same liturgical resonances appear in the sermon for Paul (Pl 2 and 6).

Thus an even more complex web of interconnections appears, linking the major feasts of the liturgical year and even suggesting a certain overlap. Birth, suffering, resurrection and the events marked by other festivals constitute one and the same event. The descending movement of the Incarnation coincides with the ascending movement of the crucified and risen *Redemptor*. The Ascent to heaven does not differ at all from the Descent into human flesh, because he 'who descended is the same as he who also ascended that he might fill all things' (Adv 1.6).

Later in the collection, Bernard will play more overtly with the punctuality of his writing, not only causing the reader to experience a circularity in his reading but even bringing about his complete disorientation.[78] For the moment, it is enough that the reader, still in the initial phase of his spiritual progression, has this feeling of instability, of turning around to find himself back at the point of beginning, which, however, can no longer be that same point of departure.

COME, YE DAUGHTERS, AND SEE!

Let us, to conclude, take a closer look at one of the sermons without taking into account its development, its change of position inside the collection, its reworked character. Let us simply concentrate on one sermon as it appears to the modern reader in its final form. And let us take one of those sermons which have perhaps been

---

Marielle Lamy, Marie-Imelda Huille, and Aimé Solignac, edd., *Bernard de Clairvaux. Sermons pour l'année* I.1 & 2 (Paris 2004) with liturgical notes by Jean Figuet.

[78] See my interpretation of the Annunciation sermons in Verbaal (2004) 60–64 (supra note 27).

a bit neglected until now: a sermon on Epiphany, the second, the central sermon in the group.

In its largest section Epi 2 contains an exegesis of Sg 3:11: 'Come out, O daughters of Zion, and see King Solomon in the diadem with which his mother crowned him'.[79] In treating a verse of the Song of Songs, this sermon already receives a special emphasis, because only two other sermons in the entire block deal with this biblical book, which Bernard—as is well-known—considered of a very special importance. Moreover, each of the sermons which cite it occupies a remarkable position.

For VNat 4, this has already been demonstrated. The sermon occupies the central position in a strongly liturgical construction. It is preceded by the invitatory to the Mass and followed by the responsory, thus giving the impression that VNat 4, with its exegesis of Sg 2:6, somehow contains the very essence of the Mass itself. The other sermon is Adv 4, which also explains Sg 2:6, but this time against the background of Christ's twofold coming and man's obligation to trans-*form* (*reformare*) his heart in order to be trans-*form*-ed and con-*form*-ed (*configurare*) in his body. Linked as it is to these other *Canticum* sermons, Epi 2 in its turn becomes a central text within the group to which it belongs.[80] This may be enough reason to look a bit closer to this text.

'We read of three appearances of the Lord': *Tres apparitiones Domini legimus*. Bernard's opening words direct the attention of the reader. Three elements are given: the number three, the appearances of the Lord, and our reading. The number three will in fact reappear continuously in this sermon: besides the three appearances, there are the three gifts of the Magi (who are themselves three, as everyone knows, although this is not elaborated by Bernard). We will have to deal with three forms of *egressus* (coming out), of angelic powers, of us, and of worldly souls. We will encounter three names of the Lord,

---

[79] Cant 3:11: *Egredimini, filiae Sion, et videte regem Salomonem in diademate quo coronavit eum mater sua.*

[80] Not only as the second of three Epiphany sermons but also in the entire movement after Christmas; Circumcision counts three sermons, as does the post-Epiphany group.

his threefold kingship, three models of faith, a three times threefold recognition and acknowledgement, as well as the three benefits we enjoy.

As for the appearances of the Lord, Bernard does not dwell long in this sermon on their traditional interpretation during Epiphany (adoration, baptism, and the marriage at Cana). They are mentioned in the opening paragraph but never again. Apparently, he wants us to understand something different by them now. And this might have to do with the third element in the opening sentence: our reading. We *read* that the Lord 'appeared' in three forms: 'all on the same day, but not at the same time'. By mentioning the three appearances, however, Bernard obliges the reader to link them, to make them coincide, to experience them as being one, as realized, perhaps not at the same historical time, but at the same reading time. In reading, the difference in time no longer exists. This is true of each reading but even more specifically of those words which tell 'the sacred story of the Word' (Miss 1.1), because the Word has the power to annihilate time.

As a narrator of the story of the Word, Bernard has no need to confine himself to historical, chronological time. And so he continues: 'The second is surely wonderful, the third is wonderful, but the first, still more wonderful, is to be admired.' He disturbs chronology even more in continuing with a second recital, this time enumerating successively the third, the second, and the first appearances. Only the first appearance to the Magi remains fixed, in the final place, thus achieving a primacy above the others as if comprising them all.

It is not only place which gives this primacy to the first appearance, but also its elaboration. Wonderful was the changing of the waters (*aquarum* mutatio), wonderful the testimonies of John, the dove and the voice (*Ioannis et columbae pariter et paternae vocis* attestatio), but more wonderful was his recognition by the Magi (*quod* agnitus *est a Magis*). And that they recognize God (*quod Deum* agnoscant), is shown by their worship (*adoratio*) and their offering of frankincense (*thuris* oblatio).

Bernard plays with his words, creating a rhyming rhythm of the central terms: *mutatio – attestatio – adoratio – oblatio*. But in the middle the pattern is harshly broken and replaced by another word play on the parented words *agnitus est – agnoscant*, taken up again in the subsequent sentence where the Magi recognize not only God but also the King (*et Regem agnoscunt*). In this way the wonder of the Magi's recognition is stressed above the two other apparitions.

Within the Epiphany sermons which have to be placed in the recognition phase of the first block, this emphasis on the recognition, the *agnitio*, is only to be expected. The wonder of the Magi's recognition, however, lies in the fact that nothing points toward a similar understanding. In the other two appearances, wonderful things happened, but where is the wonder now? 'Where is the royal purple of this King? – Where is his diadem?' The purple is 'in those shabby swaddling clothes in which he is wrapped', his diadem is 'the sackcloth of mortality'. It is in the poverty of mankind that the God and King is recognized. In an infant, still 'suckling the breast of his mother', they recognize the powerful King. In a baby that still needs the loving care of his mother, they recognize 'the great mystery of loving-kindness'. In its mortal fragility, they recognize God. How can this be? What makes people stray so far from the ways other people think and look that they 'see him truly' there, where there is no reason to see him this way?

With this amazed question, the reader is left at the end of the introduction. And Bernard seems suddenly to turn to completely different subjects. He launches the verse of the Song of Songs: 'Come out, O daughters of Zion, and see King Solomon in the diadem with which his mother crowned him'. Come out, ye angelic powers, to see your King in his lowliness. Come out, ye inhabitants of the heavenly city, and see King Solomon in our crown, in 'the sackcloth of mortality'. Whence do the angels have to come out? From where else than from heaven? And whither do they have to come out? To where else than to earth, to mortality?

'But they have no need of our exhortation, because they are the ones who long to gaze upon him.' The angels do come out, spontaneously, because they long to see him in his lowliness as much as they already know him in his loftiness. They come out because they feel the force of desire (*desiderant*). It is to us that they come out, to exhort us just as the angel came out to proclaim great joy to the shepherds, 'and with him was a great multitude of the heavenly host'.

Bernard exhorts the angels to come out, but they anticipate him, coming out on their own, thanks to the force of their desire, in order to exhort 'us'. 'To you, then, daughters of Zion–you wordly souls, feeble, pampered daughters and not sons, who possess no fortitude, no virility of spirit–we say, *Come out, daughters of Zion.*' The angels exhort 'us' to come out and 'we' exhort 'you', 'wordly souls', to come out. 'Our' coming out, Bernard seems to say, is our exhortation to you, the reader, our address to you in the repetition of the biblical words containing the Word as it came out from heaven to dwell among men. 'We' are the shepherds, those immediately addressed by the angels who came to proclaim great joy. 'We' are the spiritual writers, the monks, the abbots, those who, like Bernard, have conceived and given birth to the Word, so that it may speak to 'you', to those who have not yet given birth and perhaps not even conceived.

'Come out, ye feeble souls, daughters and not sons.' But whence? And whither? From 'the sense of the flesh', because you are not dwelling in heaven, and to 'the understanding of the mind', because you do not see the loftiness in its lowliness. From 'the slavery of fleshly cravings', because you are not driven by the longing to gaze upon him, and to 'the liberty of spiritual insights', because you do not feel how precious and lovable is his lowliness. From earth where you dwell, to heaven to which you are destined—a movement opposite to that of the angels.

Come out, then, because until now you have not been capable of true recognition. Come out, leave all behind what may hinder you–country, kindred, father's house, that is, cravings of the flesh, curiosity, pride[81]—and see King Solomon. See him truly as the Magi see him, as the Word in exile, mild and lovable; as the judging Word just and terrible; as the reigning Word, glorious and wonderful. Come out and see that the Word is king, everywhere.

Come out and see, because true recognition consists in seeing the truth, in recognizing divinity in a humble, mortal infant; it is recognition of the fact that the Word has come out to be proclaimed by

---

[81] See Sent III.109 in SBO VI-2 (1972) 184.

the angels and by Bernard and to become flesh in 'us', the readers. And see him then in his crowns, the crown of our own miserable human flesh, of his suffering, righteousness, and glory which are all ours. Because when you have truly seen him in recognition, you will come out and 'take up the crown of a child, for your sake, your King'.[82] You will take up his crowns yourself, the crowns of misery, righteousness and final glory.

But you will do this only when you come out and see as the Magi see, as the thief and the centurion see. They offer three models of the faith which sees and by seeing enables true recognition. Like the Magi, the thief, and the centurion, recognize him and yet have no reason to do so. How would the thief know that only by suffering is the way to the kingdom open? How would the centurion know that this dying man truly was the Son of God? Yet they recognize him in what they see: the power of God in the weakness of a vulnerable body, the spirit of life in his last breath and death. They recognize the miraculous union, the conciliation of the irreconcilable, brought about by the coming out of the Word of God in a speechless baby, the *Verbum infans*, recognized by the Magi.

Finally we readers get the answer to the question Bernard left us with at the beginning. The Magi returned in the company of the thief and the centurion to teach 'us' readers the recognition of faith, seeing the truth where no obvious signs are present, reading the truth where the meaning of the Word remains hidden in words. Only now does Bernard close his speech with a direct exhortation to his readers. 'We therefore pray, dearly beloved, that these may benefit you: such a great love as the God of majesty has shown you, such a great humility which he took on, such a great graciousness which appeared to you in the humility of Christ.'

Bernard does not order his readers, nor does he literally exhort them. Rather he prays that they may benefit from what has passed in the sermon; that we may benefit from the love (*caritas*), which he,

---

[82] Epi II.3: *Suscipite coronam parvuli propter vos Regis vestri.* Consider the careful construction of this sentence: 'Take up the crown of a child—for your sake—your King'. It is the child which gets primacy and it is the child which—for your sake—is your King.

abbot, angel, and writer of God's Word addresses to us, his 'dearly beloved' (*carissimi*); that we may benefit from the humility which he took up, that is: which the Word took up, but which 'we', the readers, have also been asked to take up as 'the crown of a child, for your sake, your King'; that, finally, we may benefit from the graciousness (*benignitas*) which appeared in Christ's humility, which is the meaning of all appearances that have been touched upon in the course of the sermon. The three gifts of the Magi prove in truth to be gifts of the Word to 'us'.

Although none of the three biblical appearances was dealt with, in each word in the sermon, in each image evoked, the Word appears and comes to the reader because each word gives expression to the coming out of God's love to us by the Word that comes out of his heart.

Thus, the reader is entreated to recognize what he sees and to show his recognition by 'running, not as at an uncertainty', but by coming out in giving thanks to his Redeemer and Mediator, to him who has mediated the Word by his own words and images, coming out to him in order to make him coming out and see.

University of Ghent
Department of Greek and Latin

Editorial Note

BEFORE E-mail was ubiquitous, in the not too distant days when trans-Atlantic communication proceeded at a leisurely pace, two translators enthusiastically—but one of them mistakenly—set out to translate Bernard's Advent and Christmas sermons. The duplication of effort was not caught until both versions were nearing completion. Finding strengths in both translations, the editor of Cistercian Publications asked yet another veteran translator to go through the texts and create a single translation out of both. Before long a third translation, incorporating some of each and a great deal of new material, arrived on her desk. Now there were three translations, each having its strong points and its weak. Against this unanticipated embarrassment of riches foundered editorial hopes of having all the liturgical sermons of Saint Bernard in print by the noncentenary of his birth in 1990.

Not wanting to choose among them, the editor then persuaded John Leinenweber to create the 'master translation', a task which he graciously accepted and gracefully executed. Drawing on the strongest aspects of the three existing translation and on some points consulting the translation published by 'A Priest of Mount Melleray' in the 1920s, he produced the text which is printed here, edited only at minor points for consistency in terminology.

To John Leinenweber and to the translators, the late Irene Edmonds, Sister Wendy Mary Becket, and the late Conrad Greenia OCSO, the editor and the board of Cistercian Publications are deeply indebted. To have three very talented translators work on a single text is perhaps prodigal in an age in which qualified latinists are increasingly hard to find, but their individual insights, masterfully combined by a fourth fluent translator, have produced an English version of these sermons which is, if someone with a vested interest may say so, very nearly worthy of the stirring and polished Latin of the Last of the Fathers.

THE SCRIPTURAL REFERENCES

To make clear how steeped Saint Bernard was in Scripture, scriptural quotations and allusions are set in the margins, with the corresponding phrase noted in the text. For the abbreviations, see pages lxiii–lxiv.

Citations in square brackets refer to the Vulgate text. In some instances the phraseology of the Vulgate text is not replicated in modern english translations. When this happens, only the Vulgate text, in square brackets, is cited. Otherwise, scriptural references are cited according to the enumeration of the Jerusalem Bible, with Vulgate variations—chiefly occurring in the psalter—set in square brackets. VL following a scriptural reference indicates that Bernard cited the passage from the *Vetus Latina*, the pre-Vulgate latin translation which he would have known chiefly through passages quoted by the Fathers of the Church. LXX indicates the Septuagint text.

Direct scriptural quotations, even those containing a minor variation from the Vulgate text, appear in italics. Phrases and allusions taken from Scripture, but not quoted verbatim, are noted, but not italicized. A very few allusions to the Latin Bible which were noted by Jean Leclercq and his co-workers in the critical edition have not been cited here, either because only a single word is quoted or because the phraseology in English simply does not, and cannot, sustain the allusion. To appreciate the manifold borrowings, as well as to enjoy Bernard's eloquence, readers need to consult the latin text, which is published in the *Sancti Bernardi Opera*, volume 4.

ERE

Table of Abbreviations

BOOKS OF THE BIBLE

Gen	Genesis	Si	Ecclesiasticus, Sirach
Ex	Exodus	Is	Isaiah
Lv	Leviticus	Jer	Jeremiah
Nm	Numbers	Lam	Lamentations
Dt	Deuteronomy	Bar	Baruch
Jos	Joshua	Ez	Ezekiel
Jgs	Judges	Dn	Daniel
1 Sm	First Samuel	Hos	Hosea
	[First Kings, vulgate]	Jl	Joel
2 Sm	Second Samuel	Jon	Jonah
1 K	First Kings	Mi	Micah
	[Third Kings, vulgate]	Na	Nahum
2 K	Second Kings	Hab	Habbakuk
	[Fourth Kings]	Zep	Zephaniah
1 Ch	First Chronicles	Hg	Haggai
2 Ch	Second Chronicles	Zec	Zechariah
Ezr	Ezra	Mal	Malachi
Neh	Nehemiah [2 Ezr]		
Tb	Tobit	Mt	Matthew
Jdt	Judith	Mk	Mark
1 Mc	First Maccabees	Lk	Luke
2 Mc	Second Maccabees	Jn	John
Jb	Job	Ac	Acts of the Apostles
Ps[s]	Psalm[s]	Rm	Romans
Pr	Proverbs	1 Cor	First Corinthians
Qo	Ecclesiastes, Qoheleth	2 Cor	Second Corinthians
Sg	Song of Songs	Gal	Galatians
Ws	Wisdom	Eph	Ephesians

Ph	Philippians	1 Pt	First Peter
Col	Colossians	2 Pt	Second Peter
1 Thes	First Thessalonians	1 Jn	First John
2 Thes	Second Thessalonians	2 Jn	Second John
1 Tm	First Timothy	3 Jn	Third John
2 Tm	Second Timothy	Jude	Jude
Ti	Titus	Rv	Revelation
Phlm	Philemon		
Heb	Hebrews	LXX	Septuagint
Jm	James	VL	Vetus Latina

OTHER ABBREVIATIONS

Adv V	Fifth Sermon for Advent
CCCM	Corpus Christianorum, Continuatio Medievalis series
CCSL	Corpus Christianorum, Series Latina series
Circ	Sermons for the Feast of the Circumcision
Conf.	John Cassian, *The Conferences (Conlationes)*
Epi	Sermons for the feast of the Epiphany
Nat II	Second Sermon for Christmas
PL	J.-P. Migne, *Patrologia cursus completus, series Latina*
Pl	Sermon for the feast of the Conversion of Saint Paul
RB	Rule of Saint Benedict
SBOp	Sancti Bernardi Opera, edd. Jean Leclercq, H. M. Rochais, C. H. Talbot
VNat IV	Fourth Sermon for Christmas Eve

Bernard of Clairvaux

Sermons for Advent and the Feasts of Christmas, Epiphany, and the Conversion of Saint Paul

ON THE LORD'S ADVENT

SERMON ONE

The Six Aspects of Advent

1. TODAY, brothers, we celebrate the beginning of Advent. Its name, at least—like those of the other solemn seasons—is familiar enough and known to all the world, yet the reason behind the name is perhaps not so. Adam's unhappy children, having left aside activities that are true and bring salvation, seek instead what is fleeting and ephemeral. To whom shall we liken the people of this generation, and to whom shall we compare them?* We see that they cannot be torn away and separated from what brings them earthly and bodily comfort. They are like people who have fallen into the water and are in danger of drowning. You see them clinging tenaciously to whatever first comes to hand, refusing to let it go for any reason, whatever it may be, even though it can do them no good at all*—roots of plants and such things. Even if people should come to help them, they often clutch them so closely that the rescuers can help neither them nor themselves. And so they perish in this sea great and wide;* they perish miserably while they pursue what is going to perish and leave aside things of substance, things that could extricate them and save their lives* if only they were to grasp them.

*Lk 7:31

*Is 30:5

*Ps 104 [103]:25

*Jm 1:21

3

Jn 8:32

You will know it and it will set you free, is said not of triviality but of truth. You then, my brothers, to whom—as to little children—God reveals things

*Mt 11:25

hidden from the wise and prudent,* mull over carefully what is truly salutary. Weigh well the reasoning behind this Advent—this coming. Ask who it is who comes, whence, and whither, why, when and by what means he comes. Such curiosity is undoubtedly praiseworthy and healthy, nor would the universal Church celebrate this present 'coming' with so much devotion were there not some great

*Eph 5:32

mystery* concealed within it.

2. First then, in company with the apostle [Luke], ponder with amazement and wonder how great is

*Ac 2:7, 12;
Heb 7:4
°Lk 1:32
†coaltissimus

the One* who is advancing toward us. As Gabriel testifies, he is the Son of the Most High,° and is himself therefore Also Most High.† We are not allowed to suppose that the Son of God is any less than the Father! No, we must acknowledge that he is utterly as high as the Father and of the same dignity. Does anyone not know that the sons of princes are themselves princes, and the sons of kings kings? But what does it mean that, of the three Persons in whom we believe, whom we acknowledge and adore in the sublime Trinity, the Father does not come, nor the Holy Spirit, but the Son? For myself, I do not think that this was done without cause, but *who has known*

Rm 11:34

the mind of the Lord? Or who has been his counselor?

The Son's coming was not accomplished apart from the loftiest counsels of the Trinity, and if we consider the cause of our exile, we can perhaps note—even if only in part—how appropriate it was

*Lucifer
°Is 14:12

that the Son should set us free. That Daystar* who rose at dawn, was cast down° and fell headlong because he tried to usurp the likeness of the Most High and thought equality with God—which be-

*Ph 2:6

longs to the Son—something to be grasped.* The

Father was zealous on his Son's behalf and seems
to have declared by his action that *vengeance is mine,
I will repay.* At once you will see *Satan falling from
heaven like a flash of lightning.*

How can you be proud—you who are dust and
ashes?* If God did not spare the angels in their pride,
how much less you, who are decay and worms?*
[Lucifer] did nothing; he committed no deed. He
only thought pride and, *in a moment, in the twinkling
of an eye,* he was cast irretrievably down, because, as
the Prophet says, *he did not stand in the truth.*

3. Shun pride, my brothers, I beg you. Shun it to
your utmost! Pride is the beginning of every sin.*
Pride swiftly, with an everlasting mist, darkened Lucifer, sparkling more brightly than all the stars,* and
transformed into a devil one who was not only an
angel but the chief of angels. Pride instantly caused
him to envy human beings, and the wickedness he
conceived* within himself he brought to birth in
them, persuading them* that by tasking the forbidden tree they would become like God, knowing
good and evil.*

What do you offer, what do you promise, you
wretch, when the Son of the Most High* has the key
of knowledge*—or rather, he is himself the key, the
key of David, who shuts and no one opens?[1] In him
are all the treasures of wisdom and knowledge hidden;* would you steal them wickedly to give them to
human beings yourself?

You see how [Lucifer] is truly what the Lord said,
a liar, and the father of lies. He was a liar when he said, *I
will be like the Most High,* and he was the father of lies
when he poured out the poison of his deceit upon
human beings, telling them, *You shall be like gods.* You

Rm 12:19
Lk 10:18

*Si 10:9
**Rm 11:21;
Si 19:3*

1 Cor 15:52
Jn 8:44

**Si 10:13
[10:15]*

*Jb 3:9

*Jb 15:31
*Ps 7:14 [15]

*Gen 3:5-6

*Lk 1:32
*Lk 11:52

*Col 2:3

Jn 8:22
Is 14:14

Gen 3:5

---

[1] Rv 3:7; used on 20 December as one of the 'Great O' Advent
antiphons on the *Magnificat.*

too, you human being, if you see thieves, you go
along with them.* My brothers, you noted the text
read tonight from Isaiah, in which the Lord says, *Your
leaders are faithless*—or, as another translation has it,
are disobedient—*the companions of thieves.*

4. In fact, our leaders, Adam and Eve, the leading
figures of our race, were *disobedient* and *the companions
of thieves*; at the instigation of the serpent—or rather
of the devil in the guise of a serpent—, they tried
to steal what belongs to the Son of God. The Father
did not ignore the insult to the Son*—*for the Father
loves the Son*—but immediately took vengeance° on
humanity and made his hand heavy upon us.† We
have all sinned in Adam, and in him we have all received a sentence of condemnation.*

What should the Son do when he sees the Father
zealous on his behalf and unsparing of any creature?
'See', he says, 'because of me the Father is losing his
creatures. The first angel ached for my high state, and
had a following that believed in him; but the Father's
zeal immediately and terribly took vengeance on
him, striking him and all his followers with an incurable wound, with cruel chastisement.* Humankind
wanted to steal knowledge as well, notwithstanding
it is mine, but He had no mercy on them and his eye
was unsparing.* "Is God concerned about oxen?"°
He had made only two noble creatures who were
sharers in reason and capable of blessedness: angels
and human beings. Yet on my account he has lost
many of the angels and all of the human beings.
Therefore, so that they may know that I love the
Father,* let those whom he seems somehow to have
lost on my account be restored to him through me.
If this storm has arisen on my account, says Jonah, *pick
me up and throw me into the sea!*

'They all envied me. I am coming, and I am showing myself to be such that anyone who chooses to

*Ps 50 [49]:18

[Is 1:23]

*Pr 12:16
Jn 5:20
°Dt 32:43
†Ps 32 [32]:4
*Rm 2:23;
1 Cor 15:22

*Jer 30:14;
2 Mc 9:5

*Dt 7:16;
Ezk 16:5
°1 Cor 9:9

*Jn 14:31

Jon 1:12 VL

be envious, who aches to imitate me, may do so, and
this emulation may become a good thing. Yet I know
that the rebel angels have shifted over to a partiality
for malice and evil,* and that they have not sinned
out of some ignorance or weakness. Therefore, those
unwilling to repent must perish. The Father's love
and the King's honor love judgement'.*

5. It was for this that He created human beings in
the beginning:* to fill the empty places and to repair
the ruins of Jerusalem.° He knew that no way of return is open to the angels. He recognizes the pride
of Moab—that he is exceedingly proud* and that
his pride leaves no room for the remedy of repentance and therefore none for pardon. Yet he created
no creature in place of human beings, intimating by
this that humanity is still to be redeemed. Humanity
had been overthrown by malice from without, so
love from without can benefit them.

So then, Lord, I entreat, be pleased to rescue me,
for I am weak,* for I was stolen away out of my
homeland and, being innocent, was cast here into
this pit.° No, not entirely innocent, yet innocent
enough in comparison with the one who led me
astray. I was taken in by a life, Lord. Let Truth come
so that falsehood can be exposed and that I will recognize the truth and the truth will set me free,* if
only I altogether renounce falsehood once exposed
and cling fast to truth once recognized. To do otherwise would be, not a human test,* nor a human sin,
but diabolical stubbornness. To persist in evil is diabolical, and those who linger in sin* in the devil's
likeness deserve to perish with him.

6. Now, my brothers, you have heard who it is
who comes. Now consider whence he comes and
whither he goes. He comes from the heart of God
the Father into the womb of the virgin Mother; he
comes from highest heaven to the lower parts of

*1 Cor 5:8

*Ps 99 [98]:4

*Gen 1:27-28;
Mt 19:4
°Is 61:4
*Is 1:66;
Jer 48:29

*Ex 34:9;
Ps 40:13
[39:14]; Ps 6:2
°Gen 40:15

*Jn 8:32

*1 Cor 10:13

*Rm 6:1

*Ps 19:6 [18:7];
[Si 24:45]
°Bar 3:37 [38]

Ps 73 [72]:25-26
Ps 23 [22]:4

*Ps 139 [138]:8
[Ps 87:6]
*Jn 1:5

*Ps 16 [15]:10;
Ac 2:27

*Eph 4:10

Ac 10:38

Ps 19:5-6
[18:6-7]
*Paul
Col 3:1

*Heb 2:10

1 K 19:7;
Is 30:27

the earth.* What then? Must we not also dwell on the earth?° Yes, if only he remain on it! Where will it be well without him, and where can it be ill with him? *What have I in heaven? And what besides you do I desire on earth? You are the God of my heart and God is my portion forever! Though I walk in the midst of the shadow of death, I will fear no evils, for you are with me.* Yet now, as I see, you are descending to earth, and even down into hell itself,* not as vanquished but *as one free among the dead*—like the light that shines in the darkness and the darkness did not overcome it.* Hence your soul is not abandoned to hell nor does your holy body see corruption on earth.*

The Christ who descended is the same as he who also ascended that he might fill all things.* Of him it is written that *he went about doing good and healing all who were oppressed by the devil*; and elsewhere that *he rejoiced as a giant to run his course. His rising is from highest heaven and his circuit to its farthest end.* How rightly does the Apostle* cry out: *Seek the things that are above, where Christ is, seated at God's right hand!* In vain would be he strive to lift up our hearts if he did not also teach us that the pioneer of our salvation* is now stationed in heaven.

But let us see what comes next. Although we find an abundance of material at hand—and extremely rich, too—the limitations of time do not permit a lengthy sermon.

To us who are reflecting on who is coming, an utterly great and indescribable Majesty has been made known. To us looking up to the place whence he comes, a great way has been opened to view—according to the witness of the one who, moved by the prophetic Spirit, wrote, *Behold, the name of the Lord comes from afar.* Again, to those straining to see whither he goes, an incalculable and all but unimaginable condescension has appeared in that such stateliness has deigned to descend into this dreadful prison.

7. Who can now doubt that something great was the reason that such Majesty deigned to descend from so far away to so undeserving a place? Something great, certainly—great mercy, abundant compassion and overflowing love. For what purpose, should we believe he came? This is what we must now look into, according to the plan we set out.

We should find no difficulty on this score, since clearly both his words and his deeds proclaim the reason for his coming. He hastened down from the mountains to look for the hundredth sheep which had strayed,* and so that *the Lord's mercies may confess him and his wonderful works to the children of men* more openly, he came on our behalf. Wondrous is the condescension of the God who seeks, and wonderful the dignity of the humanity thus sought! If you wish to boast of this, you will not be a fool*— not because of any worth of your own, but because the One who made you makes so much of you. All riches, all earthly glory and everything pursued on earth is tiny in comparison to this glory—indeed it is nothing in comparison with it. Lord, *what are human beings that you make so much of them,* and *why do you set your heart on them?*

8. Even so, I would like to know what he meant by coming to us, and why we did not instead go to him. We were the ones in need, and the usual custom is not for the rich to come to the poor, even when they want to help them. This is so, my brothers. That we go to him was more fitting, but there was a twofold obstacle. Our eyes were darkened,* yet he dwells in light inaccessible;* and lying paralyzed on our mats° we could not reach the divine height. That is why our most gracious Saviour and Healer of souls both descended from his lofty

*Mt 18:12
Ps 107 [106]:8, 15, 21, 31

*2 Cor 12:6

Ps 144 [143]:3
Jb 7:17

*Gen 27:1; 48:10
*1 Tm 6:16
°Mt 9:2

height and dimmed his brilliance for our weak eyes. He clothed himself in a sort of lantern—that is, with the glorious body, perfectly pure of any stain, that he took. This is that ever-swift and bright-shining cloud on which the Prophet foretold he would be taken up to go down into Egypt.*

*Is 19:1

9. Now it is time to consider the time at which the Saviour came. He came—I believe you are not unaware of this—not at the beginning of time or at its midpoint, but at its end. This is done not inappropriately; on the contrary, Wisdom wisely arranged* that help should first be brought when the need was great, though not unaware that the children of Adam are prone to ingratitude.

*Ws 8:1

Evening was drawing on and the day was nearly over;* the Sun of Righteousness° had withdrawn just so far that his great brilliance and warmth could hardly be perceived on earth. The light of divine knowledge was fairly weak, while wickedness abounded and the fervor of divine love* had grown cold.* Now no angel appeared, no prophet spoke. They desisted, as if overcome by despair at humanity's great hardness and stubbornness. 'Yet as for me', says the Son, '*then I said, Behold, I am coming!*' So it is, so it is, *when gentle silence enveloped all things and night was in the midst of its swift course, your almighty Word, O Lord, came from his royal throne.*[2]

*Lk 14:29
°Mal 4:2

*caritas
*Mt 24:12

Ps 40:7 [39:8]

Pondering this the Apostle said: *When the fullness of time came, God sent his Son.* Surely a fullness and abundance of the things temporal had brought about a loss and forgetfulness of things eternal. Eternity came opportunely, when temporality was at its strongest. To give only one example, temporal peace

Gal 4:4

[2] Ws 18:14–18, used as an antiphon on the *Benedictus* on the Sunday within the Octave of Christmas.

was then so complete that the whole world could be registered at the decree of one single person.* *Lk 2:1

10. You now grasp the person of the One coming and each place—that is, that to which and from which he comes; of the cause and of the time you are not unaware. One thing remains: the way by which he comes—and this too we must diligently* *Mt 2:7, 8 look into so we can meet him as he should be met. Just as he once came visibly in the flesh* to achieve *1 Jn 4:2 salvation in the midst of the earth,* so he comes *Ps 74 [73]:12 every day invisibly in the Spirit to save the souls of every person, as is written: *The Spirit before our face is Christ the Lord.* That you may be aware that this Lam 4:20 vL spiritual coming is a hidden one, the text continues: *Under his shadow we shall live among the nations.* Therefore it is appropriate that, if the sick lack the strength Ibid. to go any great distance to meet so great a physician, they should at least try to raise their heads and rise a little when he comes. O humankind, you need not sail across the seas* or pierce the clouds or cross the *Dt 30:13 Alps!* No grand way is being shown to you. Run *Si 35:21 to your own self to meet your God! *The Word is near you, on your lips and in your heart!* Run to compunc- Rm 10:8 tion of heart and confession of lips to escape at least the dunghill of a wretched conscience, for there the author of purity cannot appropriately enter.

These things have been said of that coming by which he deigns to illumine the mind of each person with invisible power.

11. We may also consider the way of his manifest coming, for *his ways are beautiful ways and all his paths are peaceable. Look,* says the bride, *he is coming—leap-* Pr 3:17 *ing upon the mountains, bounding across the hills!* You Sg 2:8 see him coming, fair one, but you could not see him earlier, when he was at rest. You said, *Show me, you whom my soul loves, where you feed your flock, where you rest.* While he rests he feeds the angels for all Sg 1:7

Dn 12:3

eternity,* he satisfies them with the vision of his everlastingness and changelessness. But do not be unmindful of yourself, fair one, because that vision became wonderful for you; it is high, and you can-

*Ps 139 [138]:6

not attain it.*

*Mi 1:3

But look, he has gone out from his holy place!* He, who feeds the angels when at rest, has made a

*Hos 6:2

beginning, and thus he will heal us!* He who could not be seen earlier when resting or feeding will be seen coming and food. Look, he comes, *leaping upon the mountains, bounding across the hills!* Interpret the mountains and hills as the patriarchs and prophets, and read in the book of generations how he comes leaping and bounding: *Abraham was the father of Isaac,*

Mt 1:2-16

Isaac was the father of Jacob, and so on. From these mountains—as you will discover—appeared the root of Jesse. And from this root, according to the Prophet, came forth a shoot, and from that a flower,

*Is 11:1-2

on which the sevenfold Spirit rested.*

The same prophet speaks more clearly of this in another place. *Behold*, he says, *a virgin shall conceive and shall bear a son, and his name shall be called Em-*

Is 4:14; Mt 1:23

manuel, which means, *God with us.* The flower he mentioned earlier is that very Emmanuel, and what he had called a shoot he has now more expressly

*virgam . . . virginem

called a virgin.*

But we must reserve consideration of this lofty mystery for another day. The material deserves a sermon of its own and today's sermon has already been a long one.

On the Reading from Isaiah:
The Lord said to Ahaz:
'Seek a sign for yourself concerning
the way of your adversary'

1. WE HAVE HEARD Isaiah urging King Ahaz to ask a sign from the Lord, either in the depths of hell or in the heights above.* We have also heard his reply, which has the outward form—but not the power— of loving kindness.* This is why he deserved the reproof of the One who gazes on the heart,* the One whom human thoughts praise.*

I will not ask, said [Ahaz]. *I will not put the Lord to the test.* Ahaz was raised to the height of a royal throne, and was cunning with the words of human wisdom;* Isaiah had therefore heard from the Lord, '*Go, tell that fox* to ask for himself from the Lord a sign in the depths'. The fox has a hole,* but if it should descend into hell,* the one who ensnares the wise in their cunning is there.* Again, 'Go', says the Lord, 'tell that bird to ask for himself a sign in the heights above'. The bird has a nest,* but if it should ascend to heaven,* the One who opposes the proud,° who— with a power that is his own—treads on the necks of the proud and self-important is there.*

*Is 7:10-12

*2 Tm 3:5
*1 Sm 16:7
*Ps 76:10 [75:11]

Is 7:12

*1 Cor 2:4
Lk 13:32
*Mt 8:20
*Ps 139:6 [138:8]
*Jb 5:13;
1 Cor 3:19
*Mt 8:20
*Ps 139 [138]:8
°1 Pt 5:5

*Jos 10:24;
Si 24:11

13

Ahaz forbore asking a sign of the exalted power or of the incomprehensible depth of wisdom. Therefore the Lord himself promises a sign of good will toward the house of David* so that an exhibition of love may draw to himself those in awe neither of power nor of wisdom. *In the depths of hell* may mean that love than which no one has greater, so that one might descend into hell by dying for one's friends.* In that case Ahaz is being warned either to fear the majesty of the one who reigns on high or to embrace the love of the one who descends into hell. A person who neither reflects on the majesty with reverence nor ponders the love with ardent affection is a burden not only to humans but even to God.* *Therefore,* he says, *the Lord himself will give you a sign* which will clearly manifest both his majesty and his love. *Behold a virgin shall conceive and shall bear a son, and his name shall be called Emmanuel,* which means *God with us.*

Do not run away, Adam, for God is with us! Do not be afraid, O human being, do not take fright at the sound of God's name, for God is with us! He is with us in the likeness of flesh,* with us for our welfare. He has come for our sake, as one of us, like us,* subject to suffering.*

2. Next he says, *He shall eat butter and honey*—as if to say, he will be a child and will be fed on the food of babies—*that he may know to refuse evil and choose good.* Here too you hear of good and evil, as with the forbidden tree, and with the wood of transgression,* but the second Adam makes a much better division than did the first. He chooses the good and rejects the evil, unlike the one *who loved cursing and it came on him, and would not have a blessing and it was far from him.*

In the earlier words, *He shall eat butter and honey,* you can see the choice made by this child. May his

*Is 7:13

*Jn 15:13;
Rm 5:7

*Is 7:13

Is 7:14; Mt 1:23

*Rm 8:3
*Gen 3:22
*Jm 5:17

Is 7:15

*Gen 3:22; 2:17

Ps 109:17
[108:18]

grace be with us, that he may somehow grant us worthily to experience and fittingly present to our understanding what he bestows on us! Sheep's milk gives us two products, butter and cheese. Butter is rich and moist, while cheese is dry and hard. This child of our knows how to choose well, for he eats the butter, but not the cheese.

Who is that hundredth sheep which went astray, which says in the psalm, *I have gone astray like a sheep that is lost?* Surely it is the human race, which the solicitous shepherd goes looking for while the other ninety-nine sheep are left alone in the mountains. In this sheep you will find two things, a nature sweet and good—exceedingly good—like butter, and the corruption of sin, like cheese. See then how well our child, who took our nature as his own—but without any of the corruption of sin—chooses! You read of sinners that *their heart is curdled like milk* because the yeast of malice* and the curdling agent of sin has corrupted the purity of milk.

Ps 119 [118]: 176; Mt 18:12

**Ps 119 [118]:70; 1 Cor 5:8*

3. So, too, the bee possesses sweet honey, and also possesses a sharp sting. There is a bee that feeds among the lilies* and dwells in the flower-decked homeland of the angels. From there it has flown to the town of Nazareth—which means 'blossom'—and comes to the fragrant flower of perpetual virginity. There it settled, there it clung.

**Sg 2:16*

The one who sang of mercy and judgement along with the prophet* is familiar with both the honey and the sting of this bee, yet when he came to us he brought only the honey and not the sting—that is, he brought mercy and not judgement. Once, when his disciples were urging him to have a town that would not receive him consumed by fire, he declared that the Son of Man had come, not to judge the world, but to save it.* This bee of ours had no sting. Somehow he had laid it aside when he showed

**Ps 101 [100]:1*

**Lk 9:54; Jn 3:17*

Ps 62:10 [61:11]

Jn 5:22

mercy and not justice in suffering so undeservedly. *Do not trust in wrongdoing*; do not sin with hope. Our bee can at any time get back its sting and plunge it violently into the innermost parts of sinners, *for the Father judges no one, but has given all judgement to the Son.*

Our child eats butter and honey now, when he has so united in himself the good of human nature to divine mercy that he is a true human being—having no sin—and a God of mercy—exercising no judgement.

*Virga

*Is 11:1-2

*Sg 5:10

*1 Pt 1:12

*[Sg 2:1]

4. I think it is already clear who is the shoot* coming forth from the root of Jesse, and who is the flower on which the Holy Spirit rests.* For the shoot is the virgin Mother of God; the flower her Son. Assuredly the Virgin's Son is the flower, a flower radiant and ruddy, chosen out of thousands,* a flower into which the angels long to gaze,* a flower whose fragrance brings the dead back to life, a flower of the field, as he testifies,* not of the garden. The field blossoms without any human assistance—not sown by anyone, not dug with a hoe, not fertilized with manure. Thus indeed, thus did the Virgin's womb flower, thus did Mary's inviolate, untouched, and chaste womb[1] bring forth, as from an eternally verdant pasture, a flower whose beauty would see no corruption* and whose glory would never fade.

*Ps 16 [15]:10

*Rv 4:10

*Eph 2:18

O Virgin, O lofty shoot, to what holy heights do you sublimely rise! Even all the way up to the One seated on the throne,* even to the Lord of majesty! Nor is this strange, for you send the roots of your humility down into the depths. O truly heavenly twig, more precious and more holy than all others! O truly tree of life,* which alone was worthy to bear the fruit of salvation!

---

[1] See *Inviolata*, C. U. J. Chevalier, *Repertorium hymnologium*, (1892) 9.093.

Your cunning, malign serpent, has been detected, your falsehood plainly laid bare! You imputed to your Creator two things, you charged him with lying and with resentment, but in both you are convicted of lying. Dead from the beginning is the one you told, *You shall not die*, and *the Lord's truth remains forever.* Answer now, if you can, whether [God]— who did not withhold this chosen shoot and its exalted fruit—could have begrudged humanity any tree or the fruit of any tree? He who did not spare his own Son, how has he not given us everything else with him?* *Gen 3:4*
Ps 117 [116]:2

5. If I am not mistaken, you have already noted that the Virgin is herself the royal road* by which the Saviour came, going forth from her womb like a bridegroom from his wedding chamber.* Let us keep to the way, then, which, if you remember, we began to trace in the previous sermon. Dearly beloved, let us too endeavor to mount up by it to the One who by it came down to us, and by it to come to the grace of the One who by it came into our wretched state.

Though you may have access* to your Son, O blessed finder of grace, bearer of life, and mother of salvation, so that through you he—who by you was given to us*—may accept us. May your integrity plead before him for the guilt of our corruption, and may the humility which pleases God procure pardon for our vainglory. May your abundant divine love cover the multitude of our sins,* and your glorious fruitfulness confer on us a fruitfulness of merit. Our Lady, our Mediatrix, and our Advocate, reconcile us to your Son, commend us to your Son, and represent us before your Son. O blessed Lady, through the grace which you have found,* through the favor of which you were worthy, through the mercy to which you gave birth, bring it about that

Rm 8:32

Nm 21:22

Ps 19:5 [18:6]

Eph 2:18

Is 9:6

1 Pt 4:8

Lk 1:30

he who by your mediation—deigned to share our
weakness and wretchedness may by your interces-
sion—make us sharers of his glory and blessedness,
Christ Jesus, your Son, our Lord,
who is over all and blessed forever.*

On the Seven Pillars

1. IN THE LORD'S ADVENT which we are celebrating, if I fix my gaze on the person of the One who is coming, I fail to grasp the wondrousness of his majesty. If I fix my attention on those to whom he comes, I am overwhelmed by the magnitude of his condescension. Surely the angels are astonished by the strange situation—seeing below themselves the One whom above them they ever adore, and now manifestly both ascending and descending to the Son of Man.*

Jn 1:51

If I consider why he comes, I embrace—insofar as I can—the inestimable breadth of his love. If I think about how he comes, I am struck by the exaltation of the human condition. The Lord and Creator of humanity comes indeed: he comes to human beings, he comes for human beings, he comes as a human being.

But someone may ask, 'Why is he said "to come"? He has always been everywhere'. In fact, *he was in the world and the world was made by him, but the world did not know him.* It is not that someone present came, then, but that someone hidden appeared. So it is that he who in his divine form indeed dwells in light inaccessible* put on a human form in which he could be recognized. For him to appear in his

Jn 1:10

**1 Tm 6:16*

19

*Mt 19:4

own likeness that he had made from the beginning* is not inconsistent with his majesty, nor is it unworthy of God for him to show himself in the image to those unable to recognize him in his substance, so that the One who made humanity in his own image and likeness* might become known to humanity as a human being.

*Gen 1:26

2. Once a year the universal Church celebrates a solemn remembrance of the coming of such majesty, such humility, such godly love—and indeed such a glorification of ourselves. Would that this might be done always as it is done this once! How much more fitting that would be. What madness for people to desire—or to dare—to occupy themselves with any other business after the coming of so great a King! Should they not leave all else aside and free themselves entirely for worshipping him, and in his presence be mindful of nothing else?

Yet the prophet's words, *They will belch forth the remembrance of your abundant sweetness*, do not apply to everyone, because not everyone is nourished by this remembrance. Clearly, no one can belch forth something not tasted, or barely tasted; a belch comes only from fullness and repletion. This is why those whose thoughts and lives are concerned with worldly things do not belch forth this remembrance even though they celebrate it. They observe these days out of stale routine, without devotion or emotion.

Ps 145 [144]:7

Further—and still worse—the remembrance of this condescension is turned into a pretext for the flesh.* During those days you may see them preparing splendid clothes and special foods with utmost care—as if Christ at his birth would be seeking these and other such things and would be more worthily welcomed where they are more elaborately offered!

*Gal 5:13

Listen to him as he says, *With someone who has a proud eye and a greedy heart I shall not eat.* Why do you so ambitiously prepare clothes for my birthday? Far from embracing pride, I detest it. Why do you so assiduously store up quantities of food for this season? Far from accepting pleasures of the flesh, I condemn them. Clearly you are greedy of heart when you prepare so much and over so long a time, when far less would satisfy the body—and could more easily be found. As you celebrate my coming, you honor me with your lips, but your heart is far from me.* You do not worship me, but your *god is your belly and* your *glory is in* your *shame.* Unhappy is the person who worships pleasure of the body and the emptiness of worldly glory; but *happy the people whose God is the Lord.*

3. My brothers, do not fret because of the wicked or be envious of wrongdoers.* Understand instead how their lives will end.* Pity them from the heart and pray for those who are engrossed in transgression.* These wretches act as they do because they have no knowledge of God—for if they had known, they would never by such madness have provoked the Lord of glory against themselves.*

Dearly beloved, we have no excuse* for ignorance. Clearly each of you here knows Him, and if you say, 'I do not know him', you will be like worldly people—a liar.* If you do not know him, who has led you here, or how have you come here?* How else could you have been persuaded freely to renounce the affection of loved ones, the pleasures of the body, and the vain things of world, and to set your thought on the Lord* and to cast all your concern on him,° although you have deserved no good from him but only evil, as your conscience testifies?

Who, I say, could persuade you to do this if you did not know that the Lord is good to those who

Ps 101 [100]:5

*Mt 15:8
Ph 3:19

Ps 144 [143]:15

*Ps 37 [36]:1
*Ps 73 [72]:17

*Gal 6:1

*1 Cor 15:35; 2:8
*Jn 15:22

*1 Jn 4:20
*Mt 22:12

*Ps 55:22
[54:23]
°1 Pt 5:7

Lam 3:25

Ps 86 [85]:5, 15

Jn 14:23

Pr 9:1

Pr 12:3 LXX

Ps 89:14 [88:15]

hope in him* and to the soul that seeks him, and if you too had not realized that the Lord is sweet and mild, of great mercy and true?* How did you come to know these things, if not because he has come not only to you, but even into you?

4. We know his threefold coming: *to* humankind, *into* humankind, and *against* humankind. *To* all he comes without distinction, but not so *into* all or *against* all. Yet since the first and third of these comings are well known as being manifest, listen to him speaking of the second kind, which is spiritual and hidden: *Those who love me will keep my word and my Father will love them, and we will come to them and make our home with them.* Happy the person with whom you make your home, Lord Jesus! Happy the person in whom Wisdom builds herself a house, hewing seven pillars!* Happy the soul who is the seat of Wisdom! Who is this? The soul of the righteous*—and this is as it should be, for *righteousness and judgement are the preparation of your seat.*

Who among you, my brothers, longs to prepare a seat for Christ in your hearts? See what silken hangings, what carpets , what cushions you must prepare! *Righteousness and judgement* it say, *are the preparation of your seat.* Righteousness is the virtue that renders to each his due. Render then to these three what is due to them: render to superiors, render to inferiors, and render to equals what you owe them, and you will worthily celebrate the coming of Christ, preparing for him his seat in righteousness.

Render, I say, respect and obedience to someone set over you. Of these one pertains to the heart, the other to the body. To comply outwardly with our superiors is not enough, unless we also think highly of them in the very depths of our hearts.* Even if the life of someone set over us is known to be so notoriously unworthy as to admit of no concealment

*RB 7.51

or excuse at all, still—for his sake from whom comes
all authority*—even someone we know to be such, **Rm 13:1*
we must consider worthy of honor, not for any merits of person in question but out of deference to the
divine ordaining and to the dignity of the office.

5. So too with our brothers among whom we live.
To them, by the right of brotherhood and human
society we owe advice and aid. We want these things,
that they too may supply them to us: advice to instruct our ignorance and aid to assist our weakness.
Perhaps someone among you may ask himself, 'What
advice can I give my brother when I am not allowed
to say even one word to him without permission?* **RB 6.3; 7.56;*
What aid can I supply when I cannot do the small- *42.8*
est thing except under obedience?'* To this I reply: **RB 7.55; 67.7*
There will be no lack of what you can do so long
as you do not lack brotherly love. I do not think
there is any advice better than that you undertake to
teach your brother by your example what he should
do and not do, to urge him on to better things, and
to advise him, not in word or speech, but in ac-
tion and truth.* Is any aid more useful or effective **1 Jn 3:18*
than that you pray faithfully for him, that you not
neglect to reprove his faults, and not put any kind
of obstacle in his way, but be as supportive as you
can—like an angel of peace*—to remove scandals **Is 33:7*
and the occasions of scandal* from God's kingdom. **Mt 13:41*
If you show yourself to be such an advisor and aid to
your brother, you are rendering him what you owe,* **Mt 18:28*
and he has nothing to complain of.

6. Now if you happen to be set over anyone, un-
questionably you owe more far-reaching support. He
requires from you both protection and correction:
protection that he may be able to avoid sin, and correction that what he fails to guard against may at least
not go unpunished. Even if you seem to have charge
over none of your brothers, you still have under you

one to whom you are obliged to show this protection and correction. I mean your body, which your spirit has been charged with governing. You owe it protection so that sin may not exercise dominion over it and your members may not become instruments of wickedness.* You owe it correction as well, so that it may produce fruits worthy of repentance,* and be chastised and held in subjection.*

*Rm 6:12-13
*Lk 3:8
*1 Cor 9:27

Those who will have to give an account for many souls* are bound by a far heavier and more perilous obligation. Why am I so unfortunate? Where will I turn if I am found to have protected carelessly such a treasure, the precious trust* that Christ counted more precious than his own blood? If I had collected the Lord's blood as it dripped from the cross and if it had been entrusted to me in a glass vessel which I had to carry around, in what state of mind would I be in so critical a situation? Surely I have accepted responsibility for something for which a merchant of no little wisdom—indeed, Wisdom itself—shed that blood! I hold that treasure in earthen vessels* which dangers seem to threaten far more than they do vessels of glass.

*Heb 13:17

*2 Tm 1:14

*2 Cor 4:7

A burden of concern and a weight of fear have come upon me, because although I must care for both my own conscience and my neighbor's, neither is well enough known to me. Each is an inscrutable abyss, each to me is a night, and yet I am required to protect each of them. I hear the cry, *Protector, what of the night? Protector, what of the night?* I cannot ask with Cain, *Am I my brother's protector?* Yet I can humbly confess with the prophet that *unless the Lord protects the city, the one protecting it protects in vain.*

Is 21:11

Gen 4:9

Ps 127 [126]:1

In this, however, I appear to be held excused if, as I said earlier, I show in equal measure the protection and correction I owe. If the four things mentioned above are not lacking—I mean respect and obedience to those set over us, and advice and aid for the brothers—which pertains to justice—Wisdom will not find a unprepared seat.

7. Perhaps these are six of the pillars which she has hewn in the house she has built for herself.* We must look for the seventh, too, if she will deign to make it known to us. As six belong to righteousness, what keeps us from attributing the seventh to judgement? Not righteousness alone, but *righteousness,* as it says, *and judgement are the preparation for your seat.*

Now if we render what is due them to those set over us, to equals, and to inferiors, is God to receive nothing? But clearly no one can repay him what is due, because he has heaped his mercy upon us as abundantly as we have many times offended him, and because we are as weak and worthless as he is complete and self-sufficient, having no need of our goods.* Yet I have heard someone to whom he had revealed the uncertain and hidden things of his wisdom say that *the King's honor loves judgement.*

Nothing that is in him requires fuller measure from us. We have only to mention our wickednesses and he will justify us as a gift* in order that his grace may be commended. He loves the soul which is unremittingly examining itself in his sight and candidly judging itself. This judgement he demands of us only for our own sakes, for if we judge ourselves we shall not be judged.*

The wise person therefore is wary in all his deeds. He examines, scrutinizes, and weighs everything. That person honors truth who truly acknowledges and humbly confesses oneself and one's belongings at their true worth. Listen now to a clear declaration that judgement is demanded of you after righteousness: *When you have done all that you were ordered to do, say, We are only unprofitable servants.* Clearly this is, in human terms, a worthy seat, a preparation for the

*Pr 9:1

*[Ps 15:2]

[Ps 50:8];
Ps 99 [98]:4

*Rm 3:34, gratis

*1 Cor 11:31

Lk 17:10

Lord of majesty: to strive to observe the commandments of righteousness and always to regard oneself
as unworthy and unprofitable.

On the Twofold Coming and the Wings Covered with Silver

1. THAT YOU CELEBRATE the Lord's coming with your full devotion—delighting in such consolation, amazed at such condescension, and inflamed by such love—is appropriate, brothers. Yet you must ponder not only that coming at which he came to seek and to save what was lost,* but also and no less the one at which he will come and take us to himself. If only you would constantly mull over these two comings, ruminating in your hearts how much he performed in the first and how much he promised in the second! If only you would sleep between the middle allotments![1] These are the Bridegroom's two arms; between them the bride was sleeping when she said, *His left hand is under my head, and his right hand will embrace me.*

Lk 19:10

Sg 2:6

In her left hand, as we read elsewhere, are riches and glory. And in her right hand length of days. *In her left hand*, it says, *are riches and glory.* Listen, children of Adam, you greedy and ambitious race. What have

Pr 3:16

---

[1] *Inter medios cleros* [Ps 67:14]. For a patristic exegesis of this phrase, see Augustine, *Ennarrationes in Psalmos: In Psalmum* LXVII *Enarratio*, 17–20; PL 36:822–825.

you to do with earthly riches and short-lived glory, which are neither genuine nor your own? Are gold and silver really anything other than red and white earth, which only human error makes—or rather considers—precious? If they are yours, take them with you! But a human being *when he dies, will take*

Ps 49:17
[47:17-18]

nothing away, nor will his glory go down with him.

2. Virtues, not possessions, are the true riches. These conscience carries with itself, that it may be rich forever. As for glory, the Apostle says *This is our*

2 Cor 1:12
*Jn 14:17; 15:26

glory, the testimony of our conscience. This is indeed true glory, which comes from the Spirit of truth.* *The Spirit itself bears witness to our spirit that we are chil-*

Rm 8:16

dren of God. But the glory that people receive from one another—those who do not seek the glory that comes only from God*—is vain, for the children of

*Jn 5:44
*Ps 62:9 [61:10]
*Hg 1:6

men are vain.* Silly you, to store your wages into a bag with holes,* and count your reputation with others as your treasure. Are you unaware that this strongbox is not closed and has no hasp?

Are they not much wiser who keep their treasure for themselves and do not entrust it to anyone else? But will they keep it forever? Will they secrete it away forever? He will come when the secrets of

*1 Cor 4:5;
Ps 44:21 [43:22]

the heart have been exposed,* which, once disclosed, they will not boast of. So at the Lord's coming the lamps of the foolish virgins are snuffed out; the Lord does not know those who have received

*Mt 25:6, 8, 12;
6:16

their reward.* Therefore I tell you, dearly beloved, if you have something good, keeping it secret is more profitable than flaunting it. Thus beggars when they solicit alms display, not costly garments, but their half-naked bodies—and sores, if they have them— in order to move those who see them more quickly to pity. The tax collector observed this rule far bet-

*Lk 18:14

ter than the Pharisee, and so he left justified* by it—that is, because of it.

3. *The time has come, my* brothers, *for judgement to begin with the house of God. What will be the end of those who do not obey the gospel?* What will be the judgement of those who do not rise up in this judgement?* Let those who pretend that they are not being judged in the judgement now taking place—in which the ruler of this world is being cast out*—look forward to, or rather dread, the judge who will come to cast them out along with their ruler.

As for us, if we are fully judged now, we may confidently *look forward to the Saviour, the Lord Jesus Christ, who will transform the body of our humiliation, conforming it to the body of his glory.* Then will the righteous shine* so much that the learned and the unlearned° alike will be able to see. *They will shine like the sun in the kingdom of their Father.* The light of the sun will be sevenfold, like the light of seven days.*

4. When our Saviour comes, he *will transform the body of our humiliation, conforming it to the body of his glory* only if our heart has first been transformed and conformed to the humiliation of his heart. That is why he told us, *Learn of me, for I am meek and humble of heart.* Consider well these words, for humility is twofold: one of thinking; the other of feeling—here called 'the heart'. By the former we realize that we are nothing, and this we learn from ourselves and from our weakness; by the later we spurn worldly glory, and this we learn from him who emptied himself, taking the form of a servant.* When they sought him for a kingdom, he fled,* but when they sought him for the great test and shameful suffering of the cross, he willingly offered himself.*

Therefore, if we want to *sleep between the middle allotments*—that is, between the two comings—we must let our wings be covered with silver.* Thus can we preserve the appearance of the virtues that Christ enjoined by both word and example when

1 Pt 4:17
*Ps 1:5

*Jn 12:31

Ph 3:20-21
*Ws 3:7
°1 Ch 25:8
Mt 13:43
*Is 30:26

Mt 11:29

*Ph 2:7
*Jn 6:15

*Jn 18:4;
Heb 9:14

*[Ps 67:14]

he was present in the flesh. By silver then it is not inappropriate to understand his humanity, as by gold his divinity.

5. All our virtue is as far from true virtue as it is from the appearance, and all our wings are good for nothing if they are not covered with silver. Great is the wing of poverty by which we fly so swiftly to the kingdom of heaven!* But in the case of the virtues that follow, the use of the future tense indicates a promise; poverty is not so much promised as given. So we are told in the present tense that *theirs is the kingdom of heaven*, while in the other cases, *they will inherit, they shall be comforted*, and so on.

We see other poor people who if they had true poverty would appear, not so weak-willed and sad, but instead, like kings—and kings of heaven at that! Others want to be poor, on condition that they lack nothing, and they love poverty in such a way as to suffer no want. Others still are meek* but only so long as nothing is said or done without their approval. Their distance from true meekness will become obvious at the slightest provocation. How will their meekness inherit anything if it is gone before the inheritance arrives. Others I see mourning,* but if those tears came from the heart they would not so easily change into laughter. Yet now, when idle and jesting words* flow more freely than tears did before, I think that tears of this kind are not those to which divine comfort was promised, especially when a cheap comfort so readily succeeds them. Others show such furious zeal against the faults of others that they may seem to hunger and thirst for righteousness* if they were to pass the same judgement on their own sins. But now it is one weight here and another weight there, something God detests.* They rage against others with as much impudence as intensity, but flatter themselves with as much foolishness as futility.

Mt 5:3

Ibid.

Mt 5:4

RB 6.8

Mt 5:6

Pr 20:23

6. Some are merciful* over things which are no
concern of theirs, and are shocked that not everyone receives the same abundant gifts—but only so
long as they themselves are not in the least bur-
dened. Were they really merciful, they ought to do
acts of mercy out of what is their own. If they cannot give out of their earthly possessions, they should
give forgiveness out of their good will to those
who may appear to have sinned against them. They
should give a gracious gesture or a good word—
which surpasses the best gift*—to move them to
repentance. In short, they should bestow compassion and prayer on them and on all whom they see
to be in sin. Otherwise their mercy is nothing, and
it receives no mercy.

Still others so confess their sins that they can seem
to be doing it from a desire to purify their hearts*—
everything is washed clean in confession—but what
they say freely to others, they are incapable of hearing
patiently from others. If they truly wanted to be purified, as they seem to do, they would not be annoyed,
but would be grateful to those who point their stains
out to them. There are others who are very anxious
to restore peace to anyone whom they see offended,
however slightly. They would appear to be peace-
makers,* if only their own agitation—should anything seem to be done or said against them—could
be quieted with less delay and difficulty than everyone else's. Obviously, if they truly loved peace, beyond doubt they would seek it for themselves.

7. Let us cover our wings with silver, then, in our
way of life in Christ, just as the holy martyrs washed
their robes in his passion.* As much as we can, let us
imitate him who so loved poverty that, although the
ends of the earth were in his hand, he had yet no
place to lay his head.* As we cling to him as disciples,
let us read how the disciples were driven by hunger

*Mt 5:7

*Si 18:17;
*RB 31.14

*Mt 5:8

*Mt 5:9

*Rv 7:14

*Ps 95 [94]:4;
Lk 9:58

*Lk 6:1

Is 53:7; Ac 8:32

*Jn 11:35

*Lk 19:41

°Lk 6:12

*1 Cor 15:3;
Gal 1:4

*Mt 5:6

*Lk 23:34

°1 Pt 2:22

to rub heads of grain in their hands as they were going through the fields.* Let us imitate the one who *was led like a sheep to the slaughter and like a lamb before the shearers was dumb and did not open his mouth.* We read that he wept over Lazarus* and over the city* and spent the whole night in prayer,° but never that he laughed and jested. He so hungered for righteousness that he demanded great satisfaction from himself for our sins,* although he had none of his own. On the cross he thirsted for nothing else than righteousness,* he who did not hesitate to die for his enemies and who prayed for those who crucified him;* who committed no sin° and who listened patiently to what was laid on him by others; who endured so much to reconcile sinners to himself.

On the Intermediate Coming and the Threefold Renewal

1. RECENTLY WE SAID to those who have covered their wings with silver that they must sleep between the middle allotments*—representing the two comings—but we did not say where they are to sleep. In fact, midway between those two is the third coming, in which those who know Him sleep with delight. Those comings are obvious, but not this one. In the earlier he was seen on earth and lived among human beings;* then—as he himself testifies, people saw him and hated him.* In the last, *all flesh will see the salvation of our God* and *they will look on him whom they have pierced.* The intermediate coming is hidden. Only his chosen see him in themselves, and they shall heal their souls.*

In the first [coming] he came in flesh and in weakness; in this middle one he comes in spirit and in power;* in the final he will come in glory° and in majesty. Through power he comes to glory, for *the Lord of power, he is the King of glory.* Again the same prophet asks elsewhere *that I may see your power and your glory.*[j]

The intermediate coming is a kind of path by which we travel from the first to the final. In the

*[Ps 67:14]

*Bar 3:37 [38]
*Jn 15:24
Is 40:5
Zec 12:10;
Jn 19:37
*1 Pt 3:20

*Lk 1:17
°Mk 8:38;
Lk 9:26
Ps 24 [23]:10

Ps 63:2 [62:3]

33

*1 Cor 1:30

*Col 3:4

*2 Cor 1:5

Jn 14:23

Si 15:1

Ps 119 [118]:11

1 Cor 8:1

*Jn 6:51

Lk 11:28

*Is 55:2

*Pss 102:4
[101:5]; 63:5
[62:6]

first Christ was our redemption.* In the final he shall appear as our life.* In this one, that we may sleep between the middle allotments, he is our rest and consolation.*

2. So that no one may think that I am making up what I am saying about this intermediate coming, listen to him: *Anyone who loves me will keep my words, and my Father will love him, and we shall come to him.* What does *someone who loves me will keep my words* mean? I have read elsewhere that *whoever fears God will do good,* but I think that something more has been said about the person who loves: because that person will keep God's words. Where then are they to be kept? Doubtless, in the heart, as the prophet says: *I have hidden your words in my heart that I may not sin against you.* But how are they to be kept in the heart? Is it enough to keep them in the memory alone? The Apostle will tell anyone who keeps them in this way that *knowledge puffs up.* Then, too, forgetfulness easily wipes out memory.

So keep the Word of God in the same way you best keep food for your body. He is the living bread* and food for the mind. Earthly bread in the cupboard can be snatched by a thief, it can be nibbled at by a mouse, it can grow stale with age. Once you have eaten it, do you worry about any of these things? In this way, keep God's word: *Blessed are those who [hear the word of God and] keep it.* Let it enter into the bowels of your soul. Let it pass into your feelings and into your routines. Eat what is good, and you will delight in its richness.* Do not forget to eat your bread or else your heart will wither; let your soul be filled with tallow and fatness.*

3. If you keep God's word like this you will surely be kept by him. The Son shall come to you with the Father, the great Prophet who will restore Je-

rusalem shall come,[1] and he makes all things new.* The effect of this coming will be that *as we have borne the image of the earthly one, so let us also bear the image of the heavenly One.* As the old Adam spread through the whole of humanity and took possession of the whole, so may Christ—who created the whole, who redeemed the whole, and will glorify the whole, he who healed a whole man on the sabbath*—in this way secure the whole.

At one time the old human being* was within us; the deceiver himself was within us—in the hand as in the mouth and heart.* He was in the hand on two accounts: through degeneracy; and through debauchery. He was also in our hearts, through the desires of the flesh* and the desires of transient glory.

Now, however, if there is a new creation in Christ, the old has passed away.* In the hand, in place of degeneracy is innocence, and in place of debauchery is chastity. In the mouth, in place of arrogance is confession, and in place of slander is edification—so that the old depart from our mouth.* In the heart, in place of the desires of the flesh is godly love, and humility in place of transient glory.

See whether or not in these three ways every one of the chosen will receive Christ, the Word of God, for to them it is said: *Set me as a seal upon your arm, as a seal upon your heart,* and elsewhere, *the word is near, on your lips and in your heart.*

*Rv 21:5

1 Cor 15:49

*Jn 7:23

*Rm 6:6

*Rm 10:8

*Gal 5:16

*2 Cor 5:17

*1 Sm 2:3

Sg 8:6

Rm 10:8;
Dt 30:14

---

[1] Lk 7:16, Vespers antiphon for the First Sunday of Advent.

On the Threefold Coming and the Resurrection of the Flesh

1. I DO NOT WANT YOU to be ignorant, my brothers, of the time of your visitation,* or of the reason why it is visited on you at this time. This time was ordained for souls, not for bodies, and as the soul is far worthier than the body, its natural worth justifies our making it our primary concern. Then too, what we agree was corrupted first must be first restored. The soul, corrupted in guilt, caused the body too to be corrupted in punishment. Furthermore, if we want to be found members of Christ,* beyond any doubt we must follow our head. So the first thing to be restored in us is concern for the souls for whose sake he has already come, and whose corruption he first set himself to heal.

Let us keep care of the body for another time and put it off to that day on which he shall come to transform the body. The Apostle reminds us of this when he says that *we expect a Saviour, our Lord Jesus Christ, who will re-form the body of our humiliation that it may be re-configured to the body of his radiance.* At the first coming John the Baptist cries out like a herald—or rather, as *his* herald—*Behold the Lamb of God, behold him who takes away the sins of the world!* He does not say 'diseases of the body' or 'vexations

*Lk 19:44

*1 Cor 6:15

Ph 3:20-21

Jn 1:29

of the flesh', but 'sin', which is a disease of the soul and a corruption of the mind. *Behold him who takes away the sins of the world.* [Take away] from where? From the hand, from the eye, from the neck—in short, from the very flesh on which it has been so deeply impressed.

2. He takes sin away from the hands when he wipes out the sins they have committed. He takes it away from the eye when he purifies the purpose of the heart. He takes it from the neck when he sets aside abusive domination, as is written: *You have vanquished the rod of their oppressor as on the day of Midian,* and again, *The yoke will putrefy at the presence of the oil.*

Is 9:4

Is 10:27

The Apostle too asks *that sin may not reign in your mortal body.* Furthermore, in another place the same Apostle says, *I know that nothing there is no good in me, that is, in my flesh,* and elsewhere, *Unhappy man that I am! Who will free me from this body of death?* He was well aware that he would not be delivered from that worst of all roots which had been impressed in his flesh, or from the law of sin that dwells in our members, until he was released from the body itself. This is why he longed to be loose and to be with Christ.* He knew that the sin that comes between us and God cannot be completely removed until we are delivered from the body.

Rm 6:12

Rm 7:18

Rm 7:24

*Ph 1:23

You have heard of the person whom the Lord healed of a demon—how, battering and convulsing him, the demon went out of him.* In the same way, I tell you, the kind of sin that so often disturbs us—I am referring to lusts and evil desires—ought and by the grace of God can be held in check, so that sin does not reign in us and we do not present our members as instruments of wickedness. Thus there is no condemnation for those who are in Christ Jesus.* But it is cast out only in death, when we are so battered that the soul is separated from the body.

*Mk 1:26

*Rm 6:12-13; 8:1

3. You grasp why Christ came and what a Christian's purpose should be. For this reason, O body, do not anticipate the time! You can hinder the soul's salvation, you cannot bring about your own. *All things have their season.* Let the soul work now for itself—or rather, you work with it—because if you suffer with it you will also reign with it. To the degree you hinder its restoration, you hinder your own, because you cannot be restored at all until God sees his image re-formed in your soul. You have a noble guest, O flesh, noble indeed, and your welfare depends entirely on its welfare. Honor so great a guest! You are dwelling in your own land, but the soul is a pilgrim, an exile, lodging with you.

I ask you, if someone noble and powerful should want to lodge with them, would any peasant not willingly sleep in some corner of the house—or under the stairs or even in the ashes—giving up the best place to the guest, as is appropriate? *And you, therefore, do likewise.* Take no notice of your own slights or inconvenience so long as your guest can stay with you with honor. The honor is yours if for his sake you meanwhile present yourself as being without honor.

4. And in case you look down on or undervalue your guest because it seems to you to be a pilgrim and a stranger,* think carefully about what you gain from the presence of this guest. This is who grants sight to the eyes and hearing to the ears; who supplies sound to the tongue, taste to the palate, movement to all your limbs. If you possess any life, or any senses, or anything attractive, acknowledge this endowment of your guest! Indeed, its departure confirms what its presence confers. Just as soon as the soul departs the tongue will fall silent, the eyes will see nothing, the ears will go deaf, the whole body will stiffen, and the face will lose its color. In a short

Margin notes:
Qo 3:1
Rm 8:17;
2 Tm 2:12
Lk 10:37
*1 Ch 29:15;
Ps 39:12 [38:13]

time the whole corpse will decay and become putrid; all its attractiveness will turn to corruption.

Why then do you distress and wound this guest for the sake of some transient pleasure which you could not even experience except through it? Besides, if it confers so much on you when it is an exile, estranged from its master's face because of hostilities, what all will it give you when it has been reconciled? Do not, O body, do not impede this reconciliation; abundant glory is prepared for you from it. Patiently—or rather, gladly—surrender yourself to everything. Omit nothing that seems capable of furthering this reconciliation. Say to your guest: *Your Lord will remember you and restore you to your former position. Just remember me!*

Gen 40:13-14

5.Your guest will remember you entirely for nothing but good if you give it good service, and when it reaches its master it will mention you to him and speak well of its good host. It will say, 'When your servant went into exile to expiate his fault, I lodged with a poor thing that did me a kindness.* If only my master would repay it on my behalf!° First it put at my disposal all its possessions, and then even its very self. For my sake it did not spare itself, often going without food, frequently working hard, spending untold sleepless nights, putting up with hunger and thirst and even cold and nakedness'.*

*Ac 21:15;
Gen 40:14
°[Ps 137:8]

*2 Cor 11:23, 27

What then? Certainly Scripture does not lie when it says that *he will do the will of those who fear him and he will hear their prayer.* O, if only you could taste this sweetness, if only you could appreciate the glory! I am about to speak wonders, and yet for those who believe they are true and altogether beyond doubt. The Lord of hosts, the Lord of powers and the King of glory* will himself come down to re-form our bodies and to reconfigure them to the body of his splendor. How great will be the glory,

Ps 145 [144]:19

*Ps 24 [23]:10

how indescribable the rejoicing, when the Creator
of all things—who for the justification of souls had
earlier come, humble and hidden—shall come, sublime and manifest—for your glorification, O miserable flesh, no longer in weakness, but in his own
majesty and glory! Who can conceive of the day of
his coming,* when he will come down in a blaze of
light with angels going before him and the sound
of trumpets, to raise the needy body out of the dust
and catching it up to meet Christ in the air?*

6. How long will miserable flesh—foolish, blind,
and downright demented flesh—look for transient
and perishing consolations—indeed desolations,
if they should cause it to be rejected and judged
unworthy of this glory and instead be tormented
forever with indescribable punishment? Not so, I
beg you, my brothers, not so!* Instead, may our soul
take delight in reflections of this kind: may even our
flesh rest in hope.* We are expecting a Saviour, our
Lord Jesus Christ, who will re-form [the soul] and
conform it to the body of his splendor. So says the
Prophet: *My soul has thirsted for you; for you in many
ways my flesh!* The prophet's soul was longing for
the first coming, by which it knew it would be redeemed; much more did his flesh long for the later
coming and its own glorification. Then all our long-
ings are going to be fulfilled and the whole earth
shall be filled with the majesty of the Lord.* To this
glory, to this happiness, to this peace which surpasses all understanding* may he in his mercy lead
us. May he not disappoint us in our expectation,*
he who is the Saviour we expect
Jesus Christ our Lord,
who is over all, God blessed forever.*

*[Mal 3:2]

*1 Thes 4:16-17

*Ps 1:4

*Ps 16 [15]:9

Ps 63:1 [62:2]

*Ps 72 [71]:19

*Phil 4:7

*Ps 119 [118]:
116

*Rm 9:5

On the Threefold Benefit

1. IF WE CELEBRATE the Lord's coming with
   devotion, we are doing what we ought to do.
   What is more, the One who has no need of
our goods not only comes to us, but comes for our
sake. Indeed, the very magnitude of his condescension shows the extent of our neediness. Not only
does the cost of the medicine indicate the danger in
the illness, but the multitude* of remedies shows the   *[Ps 15:2]
number of diseases. Why are there varieties of gifts*   *1 Cor 12:4
if we see no diversity of needs? To run through in
one sermon all the needs we experience is difficult,
but three of them occur to me at present as common
to everyone, and in some way the most important.

No one is found among us who does not seem in
this meantime to need counsel, help, and protection.
In fact, a threefold misery is common to the human
race, and as long as we continue in the region of
the shadow of death*—in weakness of body and in   *Is 9:2
a place of temptation, we toil miserably—if we pay
close attention—under this threefold disadvantage:
we are easily led astray; we are enfeebled at work;
and our resistance is easily broken down. If we want
to discern between good and evil,* we are deceived;   *1 K 3:9
if we try to do good, we fail;* if we struggle to resist   *Gal 6:9
evil,* we are thrown down and overcome.   *Eph 6:13

2. Indispensable then is the Saviour's coming; indispensable is Christ's presence for people thus overwhelmed.* If only he will so come that by his supremely abounding condescension as he dwells in us by faith* he may illumine our blindness, help our weakness* as he stays with us,° and as he stands alongside us to protect and defend our frailty.

For if he is in us, who can now deceive us? If he is with us, what can we not do in him who strengthens us.* If he is alongside us, who can be against us?° He is a faithful counselor who can neither be deceived nor deceive. He is a strong helper* who does not weary. He is a powerful protector who speedily crushes Satan himself beneath our feet,* and destroys all his stratagems. He is God's wisdom,* always ready to instruct the ignorant. He is God's power,* who easily revives those who are flagging and rescues those in peril.

My brothers, let us hasten to this great teacher in every decision. Let us call on this vigorous helper in every task. Let us entrust our lives to this faithful defender in every struggle. This is why he came into the world:* that by dwelling in us,° with us, and alongside us, he might illumine our darkness,† lighten our labors, and ward off all dangers.

*Gal 6:1

*Eph 3:17
*Rm 8:26
°Lk 24:29

*Rm 8:31
°Lk 24:29
*1 Mc 3:15

*Rm 16:20
*1 Cor 1:21, 24
*Rm 1:16;
1 Cor 1:18

*Jn 18:37; 3:19
°Ps 78 [77]:60
†Ps 18 [17]:29

On the Proclamation of the Lord's Birth: *Jesus Christ, the Son of God, is born in Bethlehem of Judea*[1]

1. **A** VOICE OF GLADNESS has run out in our land, a voice of rejoicing and of salvation in the tents of sinners!* A good word, a word of consolation, a saying full of joy, worthy of full acceptance,° has been heard! You mountains, give praise with jubilation,† and all you trees of the forest, clap your hands before the face of the Lord, for he is coming!* *Hear, O heavens, and give ear, O earth, be amazed and give praise, all creation*—but chiefly you, O human being: *Jesus Christ, the Son of God, is born in Bethlehem of Judea.*

Who is so stony–hearted whose soul has not melted at these words?* What message could be

*Ps 118 [117]: 15; Sg 2:12; Jer 33:11
°1 Tm 1:15
†Is 49:13

*Is 55:12; Ps 96 [95]:12-13
Is 1:2

*Ezk 11:19; 36:26; Sg 5:6

---

[1] These words were sung in Chapter on Christmas Eve in cistercian monasteries. See *Ecclesiastica officia*, 3.4, *Ecclesiastica Officia. Gebräuchebuch der Zisterzienser aus dem 12. Jahrhundert*, edd. Hermann M. Herzog and Johannes Müller, Quellen und Studien zur Zisterzienserliteratur, 7 (Grevenbroich: Bernardus-Verlag Langwaden, 2003) 52/53; and *Ecclesiastica officia Cisterciensis ordinis*, ed. Bruno Griesser, *Analecta S.O.C.* 12 (1956) 184.

sweeter? What could bring more delight? Has such a thing ever been heard, or has the world ever received anything like it? *Jesus Christ, the Son of God, is born in Bethlehem of Judea.* O brief word about the abbreviated Word[2]—brief, but bursting with heavenly sweetness! Our emotions struggle, longing to pour out more widely their great store of honey-sweetness, and finding no words. This sentence contains so much grace that if I were to alter even one iota* it would immediately begin to lose its savor. *Jesus Christ, the Son of God, is born in Bethlehem of Judea.*

Mt 5:18

O birth of unimpaired holiness: to the world, honorable; to humankind, lovable—for the great benefit it confers, even to angels inscrutable—for the depth of its holy mystery, among all of them estimable—for the excellence of its unparalleled novelty // honored by the world, beloved by humanity for the great gift it brings, inscrutable even to angels because of the depth of its holy mystery! In all of these admirable in the wonderful preeminence of its unparalleled novelty, inasmuch as never before has its like been seen, nor shall there be another.[3]
O childbirth, uniquely painless,* uniquely without shame, unacquainted with corruption, not breaching but consecrating the temple of a virginal womb! O birth beyond nature and yet for nature's sake, overpowering in the preeminence of the miracle, yet restorative in the power of the mystery!

Gen 3:16

Brothers, who will declare this generation?* An angel announces, power overshadows, the Spirit startles;* the Virgin believes, by faith the Virgin con-

[Is 53:8]

Lk 1:35

---

[2] *Verbum abbreviatum* [Rm 9:28]. See Sermon One for Christmas, fn. 1, below.

[3] From the antiphon *Genuit puerpera* sung at Lauds on Christmas Day: *The child-bearer brought forth a king whose name is eternal; she has the joy of a mother and the honor of virginity; never before has its like been seen, nor shall there be another, alleluia.*

ceives, the Virgin gives birth, the Virgin remains a virgin: who would not marvel? Then is the Son of the Most High born,* God, begotten of God before all ages. The Word is born as a baby: who can marvel enough?

*Lk 1:32

2. Nor is this birth without purpose or Majesty's condescension fruitless. *Jesus Christ, the Son of God, is born in Bethlehem of Judea.* You who are in the dust, awake and sing praise!* See the Lord with salvation: he comes with salvation, he comes with ointments, he comes with glory. Jesus does not come without salvation, nor Christ without anointing, nor the Son of God without glory. Indeed, he is salvation, he is anointing, he is glory, as is written: *The Glory of a father is a wise child.* Happy the soul that, once it has tasted the fruit of salvation, is drawn and runs in the aroma of the ointment* so as to behold his glory, the glory as of the Father's Only-begotten.*

*Is 26:19

Pr 13:

*[Sg 1:3]
*Jn 1:14

Take breath, you who are lost: Jesus comes to seek and to save what was lost.* Return to health, you who are sick: Christ comes, who heals the broken-hearted* with the anointing of her mercy. Exult, whoever you are who yearn for great things: the Son of God comes down to you to make you joint heirs* of his kingdom. Therefore, I pray: '*Heal me, Lord, and I shall be healed; save me and I shall be saved;* glorify me, and I shall be glorious'. Thus surely will my soul bless the Lord and all that is within me bless his holy name, for you overlook all my iniquities, you will heal all my infirmities, you satisfy my desire with good things!*

*Lk 19:10

*[Lk 4:18];
Is 61:1

*Rm 8:17
Jer 17:14

*Ps 103 [102]:
1, 3, 5

These three things, dearly beloved, I savor when I hear that Jesus Christ, the Son of God, is born. For why do we call his name Jesus, if not because he will save his people from their sins?* And why did he choose to be called Christ, if not because he will make the yoke putrefy at the presence of the oil?*

*Mt 1:21

*[Is 10:27]

Why did the son of God become a human being, if not to make human beings children of God? *Yet who can resist his will?* It is Jesus who justifies; who will condemn?* Christ who heals; who will wound? The Son of God exalts; who will humble?

3. Jesus is born: let them rejoice, all those whose consciousness of sins used to judge them liable to perpetual damnation! The loving-kindness of Jesus far outweighs the extent and number of offenses. Christ is born! Let them be glad, those assailed by long-ingrained vices! In the presence of Christ's anointing not one single disease of the soul, however deep-seated, can hold its ground. The Son of God is born! Let them exult, those wont to desire great things, because a great benefactor has come.

Brothers, this is the heir:* let us receive him with devotion, for then the inheritance will be ours as well. He who has given his own Son, how has he not bestowed on us everything else along with him?* No one should disbelieve, no one should hang back. We have thoroughly reliable testimony:* *the Word became flesh and dwelt among us.* The Only-begotten of God wanted to have brothers and sisters so as to be the firstborn among many children.* That timorous human frailty may have no excuse to hold back: before he became a brother of human beings he became the child of a human being, he became a human being. If humanity thinks this beyond belief, our eyes support our faith.

4. *Jesus Christ, the Son of God, is born in Bethlehem of Judea.* Look at his condescension: not in Jerusalem, the royal city, but *in Bethlehem*, which is the least among the territories of Judah.* O little Bethlehem, now made great by the Lord! He who put off his greatness and became little in you has made you great.

Be glad, Bethlehem, and in all your streets today let festive *Alleluia* be sung!* What city would not, if it

Rm 9:19
*Rm 8:33-34

*Mt 21:38

*Rm 8:32

*Ps 93 [92]:5
Jn 1:14

*Rm 8:29

*Mi 5:2

*[Tb 13:22]

dared, envy you that priceless stable and the glory of that manger? Your name is now renowned throughout the world* and all generations call you blessed.° Everywhere glorious things are spoken of you, O city of God;* everywhere is being sung that a man has been born in it* and that the Most High himself has laid its foundation. Everywhere, I say, is being preached, everywhere is being shouted that *Jesus Christ, the Son of God, is born in Bethlehem of Judea.*

Not idly is added, *of Judea*; that reminds us of his promise made to our ancestors.* *The scepter*, Scripture says, *shall not be taken from Judah and a ruler from his thigh, until he comes who is to be sent, and he will be the expectation of the nations.*[ak] Salvation is indeed from the Jews,* but salvation reaching to the ends of the earth.* *Judah*, it says, *your brothers shall praise you, your hands shall be on the necks of your enemies*, and so on; this we never read about the historical Judah, but we see it fulfilled in Christ. He is the Lion of the tribe of Judah,* about whom Scripture also adds, *Judah is a lion's whelp; to the prey, my son*, it says, *have you gone up.* Christ is the great spoiler who carried off the spoils of Samaria before he knew how to call 'father' or 'mother'.* He is the great spoiler who ascending on high had led captivity captive* and yet has taken nothing away, but instead given gifts to human beings.

The words *Bethlehem of Judea* recall to our minds these and other similar prophecies which have been fulfilled in Christ—and also, in fact, were foretold of him. No one should ever ask whether any good can come from Bethlehem!*

5. As for ourselves, we also learn from this how the One who chose to be born in Bethlehem would choose to be received. Perhaps someone then thought that a lofty palace was to be sought for him, so that the King of glory*might be received

*1 Sm 18:30
°Lk 1:48
*Ps 87 [86]:3
*Ps 87 [86]:5

*Ac 13:32; 26:6

Gen 49:10
*Jn 4:22
*Is 49:6;
Ac 13:47
Gen 49:8f

*Rv 5:5

Gen 49:9

*Is 8:4
*Eph 4:8;
Ps 68 [67]:19

*Jn 1:46

*Ps 24 [23]:7ff.

Ws 18:15

with glory, but not for this did he come from his royal throne.*

Pr 3:16; Bar 3:14

In his left hand are riches and honor; in his right hand length of life. An eternal profusion of all these was stored up in heaven, but poverty was not found among them. Yet on earth this sort of thing was common and more than common, and no human being knew its value.* Longing for poverty then, the Son of God came down to choose it for himself and to make it valuable to us by his assessment of it. *Adorn your bridal chamber, O Zion*[4]—but with humility, with poverty. He is content with these swaddling clothes* (as Mary bears witness); these are the silks he delights to be wrapped in. Sacrifice to your God the abominations of the Egyptians!*

Rm 5:20; Jb 28:13

Mt 2:7

Ex 8:26

6. Consider, finally, that *he is born in Bethlehem of Judea* and be careful how you may be found to be at Bethlehem of Judea, and now, so that he may not refuse to be received in you. Bethlehem means 'house of bread'[5] and Judah means 'confession'.[6] You, then, if you fill your soul with the food of the divine word and faithfully receive—even if not with the devotion it deserves, then with as much as you can muster—the bread that comes down from heaven and gives life to the world[7]—that is, the body of the Lord Jesus—then the new flesh of the resurrection may renew and preserve the old wineskin* of your

Mt 9:17

---

[4] Antiphon sung at the blessing of candles on 2 February, the Feast of the Purification of Mary and Presentation of Christ in the Temple, also known as 'Candlemas'.

[5] Jerome, *Liber nominum*; PL 23:1214; and Gregory the Great, *Homilia in Evangelium 8.1* (PL 76:1104), read during the third Nocturn of Matins on Christmas Day.

[6] *Confessio*, meaning 'confession' is its several senses. See Jerome, *De interpretatione hebraicorum nominum*; CCSL 72:67, 19; *Liber nominum*; PL 23:1228.

[7] Jn 6:51.

body. Thus mended by this bonding it will be capable of containing the new wine that is in it. Then, if you live from faith and have no reason to groan because you have forgotten to eat your bread,* then you become a Bethlehem, worthy indeed to receive the Lord, if only that affirmation is not lacking.

Rm 1:17;
Ps 102 [101]:4

Let Judah then be your sanctuary;* put on confession and comeliness,* the robe Christ specially accepts on his servants. The Apostle commends both things to you briefly when he says that *belief in the heart leads to righteousness, confession in the mouth leads to salvation.* Righteousness in the heart is bread in the house; righteousness is bread, and *blessed are those who hunger for righteousness, for they will be satisfied.* Therefore let righteousness be in your heart, the righteousness that comes from faith,* for this alone is glorious in God's sight.* Let the confession that leads to salvation be in your mouth, and then confidently receive him

Ps 114 [113]:2
Ps 104 [103]:1

Rm 10:10

Mt 5:6

Rm 9:30
Rm 4:2

who is born in Bethlehem of Judea,
Jesus Christ
the Son of God.

SERMON TWO

On the Chant:
O Judah and Jerusalem

1. *O JUDAH and Jerusalem, fear not.*[1] We are addressing true Jews, Jews not in the letter but in the spirit, Abraham's offspring, whose promised increase we see realized.* Not the children of the flesh, but the children of the promise are counted as offspring. We are not talking to the Jerusalem that kills the prophets.* How can I bring her comfort, that Jerusalem over which the Lord wept,* and which was given over to ruin? We are speaking to the new Jerusalem that comes down out of heaven.* *Fear not, O Judah and Jerusalem.*

*Rm 2:28-29;
Gal 3:29;
Gen 22:17

*Mt 23:37

*Lk 19:41

*Rv 21:2

Fear not, true confessors, you who confess the Lord not only with your mouths, but just as much with all and every part of you! You have clothed yourselves with confession[2] as with a garment*—or rather, all that is within you confesses the Lord* and all your bones say, *O Lord, who is like you?* You are

*Ps 109 [108]:18
*Ps 103 [102]:1
Ps 35 [34]:10

---

[1] 2 Ch 20:17. Used as a responsory on the Vigil of Christmas; *Ecclesiastica officia*, 3.39; Herzog and Müller (Christmas Eve, sermon one, fn. 1), 55. The full text is *O Judah and Jerusalem, fear not. Tomorrow you shall go forth and the Lord will be with you.*

[2] 'Judah' means either 'confession' or 'praise' according to Jerome, *Liber Nominum* (PL 23:1228): *Juda laudatio sive confessio.*

not like those who confess that they know God, but
deny him by their actions.* *Ti 1:16*

True confession, my brothers, is when all your
works are God's works and confess him. Let them
however, confess with a twofold confession, so
that you are clothed with double garments*—that *[Pr 31:21]*
is, with confession of your sins and confession of
divine praise. Then will you be true Jews, if your
whole life confesses that you are sinners deserving of
far greater punishments, but that God is supremely
good and exchanges the eternal punishments you
have deserved for these light and transitory ones.
Anyone who does not fervently long for repentance
appears by his actions to say that he has no need
of repentance, and thus does not confess faults and
cannot be helped by repentance—and thus does
not confess divine goodness.

As for you, be true Jews; be the true Jerusalem
so that you may no longer fear anything. Jerusalem is 'the vision of peace'³—vision, not possession—to whose borders—not to its beginning or its
middle—the Lord has brought peace.* If, therefore, *Ps 147:14*
you do not have peace—or indeed because in this
world you cannot have perfect peace—at least look
at it, ponder it, consider it, and long for it. Let the
eyes of your heart* be turned toward it, and your *Eph 1:18*
intention directed toward peace, so that everything
you do, you do out of longing for this peace which
surpasses all understanding.* In everything have this *Ph 4:7*
as your intention: that being reconciled, you may
have peace with God.* *Rm 5:1*

---

³ *Urbs Jerusalem beata, dicta pacis visio* (Jerusalem, blessed city,
vision of peace) was the hymn for feasts of the dedication of
a church. The nineteenth-century translation is 'Light abode,
celestial Salem, vision whence true peace doth spring'.

2. To these people we say, *Fear not!* These people we console, not those who have not known the way of peace.* For these latter to be told *tomorrow you shall go forth* would be a caveat, not a consolation. Only those who long to be let loose* and yearn to go forth,* who see peace and who know that, if the earthly homes they live in are lost, they have a building from God, but not those who have gone mad and relish their chains. People like this should not be said to have 'gone forth' by dying, so much as to have 'gone into', because they go neither into light nor into liberty, but into prison, into darkness, into hell.

But you are told, *Fear not, tomorrow you shall go forth*, and no longer will there be fear within your borders. You have indeed many enemies: the flesh—no enemy can be nearer than that; the present evil age—which surrounds you on every side; the rulers of darkness—who, gathered in the air, block your path.* Yet *fear not, tomorrow you shall go forth*—that is, very soon. Tomorrow is very soon. This is why holy Jacob said: *My righteousness will answer for me tomorrow.*

Three days there are we read about: *after two days he will revive us; on the third day he will raise us up.* One day is under Adam, the second is in Christ, the third is with Christ. This is why it adds there, *Let us know, let us press on to know the Lord*, while here it says, *Tomorrow you shall go forth, and the Lord will be with you.* This is said to those who have cut their days in half,* for whom the day of their birth has perished*—the day of Adam, the day of sin, which Jeremiah also cursed, saying *Cursed be the day on which I was born!* We are all born on that day. If only for all of us that day would perish, the day of clouds and obscurity, the day of darkness and whirlwinds* which Adam made for us, which the enemy made—the enemy who said that *your eyes will be opened.*

*[Ps 13:3]

*2 Cor 5:1
*Ph 1:23

*Gal 1:4;
Eph 6:12

Gen 30:33

Hos 6:2 [3]

Hos 6:2

*Ps 55:23 [54:24]
*Jb 3:3

Jer 20:14

*Zep 1:15

Gen 3:5

3. But look, *the new day of redemption has dawned on us, the day of reparation of the past, of everlasting felicity.*[4] *This is the day which the Lord has made; let us rejoice and be glad in it* because tomorrow we will go forth. From what—if not from the confines of this present age, from the prison of this body, from the chains of necessity, curiosity, vanity, and pleasure, which shackle the feet of our emotions even against our wills?

Ps 118 [117]:24

What has our spirit to do with earthly things? Why does it not long for spiritual things, seek spiritual things, savor spiritual things? O spirit, you who are from above, what have you to do with things below? *Seek the things that are above, where Christ is, seated at the right hand of God. Savor the things that are above, not those on the earth.* But *the corruptible body weighs down the soul and the earthly habitation presses down on the mind that ponders many things.* The many necessities of this wretched body hold us back. The snare of base desire and earthly pleasure prevent the spirit from soaring and swiftly drags it back down , if it ever should happen to rise.

Col 3:1-2

Ws 9:15

But *fear not; tomorrow you shall go forth* from the pit of misery and the bog of dregs. In order to lead you out of there he too was stuck fast in the mire of the deep.* *Fear not; tomorrow you shall go forth* from the body of death* and all the corruption of sin. Live this day in Christ, that you may walk as he walked; for *whoever says 'I abide in Christ' ought to walk just as he walked. Fear not,* because *tomorrow you shall go forth,* and so you will be with the Lord forever.*

*Ps 40:2 [39:3]

*Ps 69:2 [68:3]
*Rm 7:24

1 Jn 2:6
*1 Thes 4:17

Yet because *and the Lord will be with you* is expressly said, we are to understand that, while we are in the body, we can be with the Lord—that is, cleave to his

---

[4] Verse from the responsory *Hodie nobis* for the Night Office of Christmas, also used as an antiphon at Christmas Vespers.

will—but he is not with us so that he assents to our
wills. We would choose to be freed now; we yearn to
Ph 1:23   depart,* we long to go forth—but he still puts us off
for a specific reason. *Tomorrow you shall go forth, and
the Lord will be with you,* so that whatever we will, he
shall will, shall disagree in nothing with our will.

4. And so *Judah and Jerusalem, fear not* if you can-
Jm 4:2   not yet attain* the perfection you are longing for.
Let your humbleness of your confession supply what
the imperfection of your way of life lacks. God's eyes
Ps 139 [138]:16   have beheld your imperfect being.* On that account
has he commanded his commandments to be kept
Ps 119 [118]:4   absolutely,* so that when we see our imperfect being
failing and unable to fulfill its obligations, we may flee
toward mercy and say, *Because your mercy is better than
Ps 63:3 [62:4]   life.* Then we, who cannot appear in the garments of
innocence or righteousness, can appear garbed in
confession. Confession and beauty are in the Lord's
Ps 96 [95]:6   sight,* provided that—as we have said—they come
not from the mouth alone but from the whole per-
Ps 35 [34]:10   son, so that all our bones may ask,* *Lord, who is like
Ps 96 [95]:6   you* and ask it with a gaze fixed on peace along and
with a longing for reconciliation with God.

To such persons is said *O Judah and Jerusalem, fear
not; tomorrow you shall go forth.* As soon as the soul leaves
the body, all the affections and all the desires which
meanwhile held it bound and scattered throughout
the entire world will go forth from this snare, *and the
Lord will be with you.* If you fix your eyes on yourself,
and not on what is awaiting you, this can seem too
much to you. Does not the entire world look forward
Rm 8:20   to this? Creation was subjected to futility* and, at the
fall of the human being whom the Lord had made
Ps 105 [104]:21   lord of his house and ruler of all his possessions,* the
whole inheritance was simultaneously corrupted. By
this was the air disturbed, the earth cursed in the deeds
Gen 3:17   of Adam,* and everything subjected to futility.

5. Obviously the inheritance will not be re-stored until the heirs are restored. This is why, as the Apostle testifies, it *groans and is in labor until now.* We have become a spectacle not just to this world, but to angels and to mortals.* *The righteous wait for me,* Scripture says, *until you reward me.*

The martyrs, too, though they called for a day of judgement—not as if eager for vengeance, but as longing for the perfection of blessedness which they were then on the point of enjoying—the mar-tyrs *received a divine reply: Bear up a little while, until the number of your brothers and sisters is complete.*[5] They have already received a single raiment, but they will not be clothed in double garments* until we too are clothed. We hold their bodies as pledges and as surety, and without their bodies they cannot be made per-fect, nor will they receive them without us. Hence the Apostle says of the patriarchs and prophets, *God provided something better for us, that they would not be made perfect apart from us.* Oh if only we too could realize how they look forward to our coming, how much they long for it, how eagerly they seek it, how gladly they listen to good things about us!

6. Why do I speak of those who have learned compassion from what they suffered, when the holy angels too long for us?* Are not the walls of the heavenly Jerusalem to be rebuilt* from these worms and from this dust? Do you think about how much the citizens of heaven long for the ruins of their city to be rebuilt? How anxious they are to have the living stones* that are to be built up along with them come to them? How they hurry as interme-diaries between us and God, very faithfully bearing our groans to him and very dutifully bearing his

Rm 8:22

*1 Cor 4:9

Ps 142:7 [141:8]

Rv 6:11

*[Pr 31:21]

Heb 11:40

*1 Pt 2:5
*Ps 51:18
[50:20]

*1 Pt 2:5

---

[5] Rv 6:11, used in the responsory *Sub altare Dei* on the feast of the Holy Innocents, 28 December.

grace back to us? Plainly, those who have now become our servants will not think it beneath them to have us as their companions. *Are they not ministering spirits, sent to serve for the sake of those who receive the inheritance of salvation?* Let us hurry, I beg you, dearly beloved, let us hurry! The whole multitude of the heavenly court is waiting for us. We made the angels rejoice when we were redirected toward repentance;* let us go on, and let us hurry to fill up the joy they take in us.

Woe to you, whoever you are, who decide to return to the mud, to turn back to the vomit!* Do you think that those whom you want to deprive of the great joy they have so hoped for will be on your side at the judgement? They rejoiced when we came to repentance as if over people whom they saw recalled from the very gates of hell.* What will they feel now, if they see those who already have one foot in paradise turning away from the gates of paradise and going backwards?* Even if our bodies are below, our hearts can be above.

7. Run, brothers, run! Not only the angels, but the very Creator of the angels himself is waiting for you! The wedding is ready,* but the house is not yet full; they are still waiting for those who will complete the wedding. The Father is waiting and longing for you, not only out of the great divine love with which he has loved you*—the love that led the Only-begotten who is in the Father's bosom,* to declare that *the Father loves you*—but for his own sake, as he says through the prophet: *It is for my sake that I am about to act, not for yours.*

Who can doubt that what he promised the Son— saying, *Ask of me and I will give you the nations for your inheritance,* and in another place, *Sit at my right hand until I make your enemies a footstool for your feet*—must be fulfilled? His enemies will not all be destroyed

Margin references:

Heb 1:14

*Jb 42:10

*2 Pt 2:22

*Is 38:10

*Jn 18:6

*Mt 22:8;
Lk 14:22

*Eph 2:4
*Jn 1:18
Jn 16:27

Ezk 36:22

Ps 2:8
Ps 110 [109]:1

as long as some of them are still fighting against us, who are his members.* This promise will not be fulfilled until death, the final enemy, is destroyed.*

As for the Son, is anyone ignorant of how much he longs for the fruit of his birth,* and of the whole life he led in the flesh—and of course the fruit of his cross and death, the fruit for which he paid with his precious blood?* Will he not hand over to God the Father the kingdom he has obtained?* Will he not restore to him his own creatures, for whom the Father sent him to earth?

The Holy Spirit too is waiting for us. The Spirit is the godly love and graciousness* to which we have been predestined from eternity, and most surely he wants to have accomplished what he has predestined.

8. So then, since the wedding is ready and the whole throng of the heavenly court is longing and waiting for us, let us not run aimlessly;* let us run with desires and with progress in the virtues. To get under way is to progress. Let each one of us say, *Look on me and have mercy according to the judgment of those who love your name.* Have mercy, not as I deserve, but as they have decided. Let us also say, *As his will is in heaven, so may it be done,* and again, *May your will be done.* We know that Scripture says, *If God is for us, who is against us? Who will bring a charge against God's elect? Am I not allowed to do what I choose?*

In the meantime, let this be our consolation, dearly beloved, until we go forth: that the Lord may be with us. May he by his great mercy bring us to that happy going forth and to that shining tomorrow! May he condescend to visit us on this nearest tomorrow and to be with us. Then, should anyone perchance be held back in some temptation, by the mercy of the One who came to proclaim release to

*1 Cor 6:15
*1 Cor 15:26

*[Ps 106:37]

*Mt 27:6
*1 Cor 15:24;
Ac 20:28

*Gal 5:22

*1 Cor 9:26

Ps 119 [118]:132

1 Mc 3:60
Mt 6:10
Rm 8:31
Rm 8:33
Mt 10:15

*Is 61:1

captives,* tomorrow he may go forth! Let us accept
with wholesome joy the crown of our child King,
given by the One who lives and reigns
    with the Father and the Holy Spirit,
      God, throughout all ages.
        Amen.

On the Chant:
Today you shall know that the Lord will come[1]

1. **Y**OU WHO ARE EARTHBORN *and you who are mortal, hear this!* You who are in the dust, awake and sing praise!* A physician is coming to the sick, a redeemer to those who have been sold, a path to wanderers, and life to the dead. Yes, One is coming who will cast all our sins into the depths of the sea,* who will heal all our diseases,* who will carry us on his own shoulders° back to the source of our original worth. Great is the might, but more wonderful is the mercy in that the One who could help us willed to come to our assistance! *Today,* Scripture says, *you shall know that the Lord will come.*

These words occur in Scripture, of course, in their own place and time. Mother Church, however, has not inappropriately adopted them for the eve of the Lord's birth. The Church, I say, who possesses the counsel and the spirit of her Bridegroom and God,

*Ps 49:1-2
[48:2-3]
Is 26:19

*Mi 7:19
*Ps 103 [102]:3
°Nm 7:9;
Lk 15:5*

---

[1] Ex 16:6-7, used as the Invitatory in the Mass and as a responsory in the Night Office on Christmas Eve. The text continues: *and in the morning you shall see his glory* (below, par. 7).

*Sg 1:12

*Sg 4:9

whose beloved lies between her breasts,* having and holding princely possession of the throne of her heart. She is the one who has wounded his heart,* and who pierces with the eye of contemplation the abyss of the hidden things of God and makes an everlasting dwelling for him in her heart, and for herself in his heart.

When, then, the Church either alters or exchanges words in the divine Scriptures, this arrangement of the words is more forceful than the original—perhaps as much more forceful as that which separates reality from symbol, or light from shadow, or mistress from handmaid.

2. *Today you shall know that the Lord will come.* By my reading, there are two days which are expressly commended to us in these words. The first—which runs from the fall of the first human being to the end of the world,—was a day that we know the saints

*Jb 3:1; Jer 20:14

often cursed.* On that most radiant day on which he was created, Adam was cast out; and thrust forcibly into the difficulties of things, he encountered a day of darkness, almost totally deprived of the light of truth. On this day we all of us are born—if day we must call it rather than night—were it not that the indomitable mercy has left us the light of reason, like a tiny spark.

The second day will exist in the splendor of the

*[Ps 109:3];
Dan 12:3

*1 Cor 15:54

saints for all eternity.* Then will break that utterly serene morning to which mercy was promised; then will night be swallowed up in victory;* then, shadow and darkness having been dispersed, will the splendor of the true light stream out equally over everything, above and below, inside and outside. *Let me hear of your mercy in the morning,* says the saint; and *We have been filled with your mercy in the morning.*

Ps 90 [89]:4

But let us return to our own day, which is called *a watch in the night* because of its brevity, and de-

scribed as *nothingness and emptiness* by that familiar   *Is 40:17*
mouthpiece of the Holy Spirit who says that *all our*
days have passed away, and *my days have passed away*   *Ps 90 [89]:9*
like smoke,* *my days have faded like a shadow.*° *Few and*   **Ps 102:3 [101:4]*
evil are all the days of my life,† says the holy patriarch*   *°Ps 102:11*
who saw the Lord face to face.°   *[101:12]*
    †Gen 47:9 VL

Indeed on this very day God bestows reason on   **Jacob*
human beings and endows us with understanding.   *°Gen 32:30*
Yet as we leave this world he must enlighten us with
the light of his own knowledge, for if we should
leave the prison house and the shadow of death[2] with
our light quenched, we will be incapable of being
enlightened for all eternity. This is why the Only-
begotten of God, the Sun of justice,* like a huge   **Mal 4:2*
and brilliant candle has enkindled and enlightened
the prison of this world—so that everyone willing
to be enlightened can come near him and be united
to him so that nothing may come between them
and him. *Our sins are barriers between us and God.*   *Is 59:2 VL*
When these have been taken down we are indeed
joined to him to be enlightened by and, as it were,
incorporated into, the true light. The quenched
light is so immediately united to the shining and
burning light* that it is enlightened—insofar as we   **Jn 5:35*
can identify the effect of what is invisible by an example from what is visible.*   **Rm 1:20*

3. At this great and brilliant star let us then, as the
prophet says, light for ourselves the light of knowl-
edge* before we leave the darkness of this world. If   **Hos 10:12 VL*
we do otherwise we will pass from darkness into
darkness—and everlasting darkness at that. But what
is this knowledge? Surely it is to know *that the Lord*
will come, even if we cannot know when he will
come. This is all that is asked of us.

---

[2] Jer 52:31; Jb 3:5. Cf. Advent antiphon *O Clavis David.*

But, you say, everyone knows this. Even those who
are only nominal believers know *that the Lord will
come*, that *he will come to judge the living and the dead*
and to repay everyone for what each has done.* Not
everyone knows this, my brothers, nor even many;
few know it, for in truth few are saved.* Do you
think that those who rejoice and delight in the wickedness of their deed* while they are doing wrong
either know or stop to think *that the Lord will come?*
If they say they do, do not believe them.* Anyone
who says he knows God and does not keep his commandments is a liar.* The Apostle says, *They profess
that they know God, but they deny him by their actions,*
for *faith apart from works is dead.* They would not so
defile themselves with every kind of impurity if they
knew or were worried that the Lord is going to
come. They would instead stay awake and not allow
their consciences to be so violently broken into.*

4. The first degree of knowledge brings about repentance—that is, sorrow—changing laughter into
lamentation, singing into wailing, joy into sorrow.
What formerly gave you intense pleasure begins to
dissatisfy you, and you particularly recoil from what
you particularly used to want. Scripture says that
those who increase knowledge also increase sorrow, so that
the proof of true and holy knowledge is the sorrow
that ensues.

In its second degree knowledge brings about
amendment, and as a result you no longer present
your members to sin as instruments of wickedness,
but you curb gluttony, throttle lust, put down pride,
and make the body that formerly served sin into
a servant of holiness. Repentance without amendment gains nothing. As the Sage says, *When one builds
and another tears down, what do they gain but hard work?*
Those who wash after touching a corpse and then
touch it again, gain nothing by the washing;* but in

Nicene Creed
*Mt 16:27

*Lk 13:23

*Pr 2:14

*Mt 24:23

*1 Jn 2:4
Ti 1:16
Jm 2:20

*Mt 24:43

Qo 1:18

Si 34:28
*Si 34:30

the Saviour's words, they must take care that nothing worse happens to them.* Yet because these people cannot hold on to [repentance and amendment] very long without remaining tirelessly alert and attentive to themselves, [knowledge] in the third degree brings about attentiveness.* Now people begin to walk attentively with their God,* thoroughly examining everything so as not to offend the eyes of his awesome Majesty even in the most trivial thing. They are enkindled by repentance, they catch fire in amendment, they give light in attentiveness—and so they are renewed within and without.

5. At this point they already begin to breathe again after the affliction of evils and sorrow.* They moderate their fear with spiritual joy so as not to be overwhelmed by excessive sadness* at the enormity of their misdeeds. Consequently, though they fear the Judge, they trust the Saviour, for their fear and their joy together now ride out to and converge in him. Fear frequently overcomes joy, but more often joy drives out fear and confines it beneath the secret places of its happiness. Fortunate is the conscience in which a struggle of this kind is carried on uninterruptedly, until what is mortal is swallowed up by life,* until the fear that is partial is done away with and the joy that is complete takes its place.* For fear is not everlasting, but everlasting joy will be theirs*

They are already burning and shining,* but they should not yet presume that they are in a house where they can bear the lighted torch around without any fear of draughts. They must remember that they are out in the open, and take care to shield what they are bearing with both their hands, not trusting the air even if it seems calm. Abruptly, at an unexpected hour,* it will change, and if they remove their hands even a little the light will be extinguished. Even if the heat should scorch the hand

*Jn 5:14

*sollicitudo
*Mi 6:8

*Ps 107 [106]:39

*2 Cor 2:7

*2 Cor 5:4
1 Cor 13:10
*Is 61:7
*Jn 5:35

*Lk 12:40

of the bearer—as sometimes happens—they should choose to suffer rather than withdraw their hands, because in a moment, in the blink of an eye,* it can be snuffed out.

*1 Cor 15:52

If we were in that house not made with hands, eternal in the heavens,* where no foe enters and no friend exits, we would have nothing to fear. As it is, we are exposed to three exceedingly malign and powerful winds: the flesh, the devil, and the world. These attempt to extinguish the enlightened conscience by blowing evil desires and illicit impulses into our hearts, spinning you around so suddenly that you scarcely know where you are coming from or where you are going.* Although two of these [winds] quite often die down off for a time, no one has ever wrested a respite from the blowing from the third. Therefore the soul must be sheltered by both pairs of hands—of the heart and of the body—for fear that what has already been lighted may be extinguished. We must not give way, even if the grave heat of temptations should violently afflict us in both [heart and body], but we must say with the saint, *My soul is always in my hands.* Let us choose rather to burn than to give way. And as we do not easily forget what we are holding in our hands, so we must never forget the interests of our souls and we should make this the chief occupation of our hearts.

*Mk 14:58; Heb 9:11-12

*Jn 3:8

Ps 119 [118]: 109

6. So then, once our loins are thus girded and our lamps are burning, we must keep watch by night over the flock* of our thoughts and actions. Then whether the Lord comes in the first watch, or in the second, or in the third, he will find us prepared.* The first watch is uprightness of action—trying to bring your whole life into line with the Rule you have vowed, not passing beyond the bounds that your forebears set* to all the exercises of this way of life, not turning aside either to the right or to the left.*

*Lk 2:8

*Lk 12:35, 38-40

*Pr 22:28
*Nm 20:17

The second is purity of intention, so that an artless eye will make the whole body light;* whatever **Mt 6:22*
you do, you should do for God's sake, and graces
may return to the place from which they come to
flow out again.* **Qo 1:7*

The third is the safeguarding of unity, so that, situ-
ated as you are in a community, you put what others
want before what you want—so that you will stay
among your brothers not only without quarrels but
with grace, supporting them all, praying for them all.
Then may be said of you, too: *Here is some one who loves
his brothers and the people of Israel; here is someone who
prays hard for the people and for the holy city of Jerusalem.* *2 Mc 15:14*

On this day, then, the coming of the Only-begotten
enkindles in us true knowledge—the knowledge, I
say, that teaches us *that the Lord will come*—and this
[knowledge] shall be an everlasting and stable foundation for our way of life.

7. *And in the morning*, the text says, *you will see his
glory.*[3] O morning! O day which in the courts of the
Lord is better than thousands!* In you month will **Ps 84:10 [83:11]*
succeed month and sabbath succeed sabbath, and the
splendor of light and the fervor of divine love will
shine on the dwellers on earth even to the most exalted phenomena! Who dares to think, let alone speak,
of you? In the meantime, my brothers, we are building up our faith so that if we cannot see the wonders
that are reserved for us, we can at least contemplate
something of the wonders that have been done for
us on earth. In taking our flesh, the almighty Majesty
did three things, brought about three interminglings,
so wonderfully unique and uniquely wonderful that
nothing like them has ever been done or ever again
shall be done on earth. Joined one to the other are
God and humanity, mother and virgin, faith and the

---

[3] See above, par. 1, fn. 1.

human heart! These interminglings are astonishing, more wonderful than any other wonder; how things so different and so divided from one another could be joined together!

8. First, consider the creation, the position and the disposition of things—how much power there was in their creation, how much wisdom in their positioning, how much graciousness into their composition. In their creation, see how many and how great are the things powerfully created; in their position, how wisely everything was set in place; in their goodness, how graciously the highest and the lowest things were joined together by a godly love as admirable as it is amiable. He united life-giving energy to this earthly dust*—as in trees, for example, so that loveliness arises in the leaves, beauty in the flowers, flavor and medicine in the fruit. Not content with this, he added to our dust the power of sensation—as in beasts, so that they not only have life but may also be sentient, having a fivefold capacity for sensation. He added still more to ennoble our dust, introducing into it the energy of reason—as in human beings, who not only live and sense, but also distinguish between helpful and harmful, between good and evil, between true and false.

*Gen 2:7

[God] also wanted to elevate our weakness to a yet more ample honor. Majesty compressed himself to join to our dust the best thing he had, which is himself. God and dust, majesty and weakness, utter lowliness and utter sublimity were united in a single person. Nothing is more sublime than God, nothing is lower than dust—and yet God descended into dust with great condescension and dust ascended into God with great honor, so that whatever God did in it, the dust is believed to have done, and whatever the dust bore, God is said to have borne in it by a mystery as ineffable as it is incomprehensible.

And notice that, as in the one Divinity there is a Trinity of persons but a unity of substance, so in this unique intermingling there is a trinity of substance but a unity of person; and just as there the persons do not rend the unity and the unity does not diminish the Trinity, so here the person does not confound the substances and the substances do not break up the unity of the person. The supreme Trinity has revealed this trinity to us—a wondrous work, a work unique among all and above all its work! Word and soul and flesh have come together in one person, and these three are one and this one is three, *not by confusion of substance but by unity of person*. This is the first and surpassing mingling, and it is the first among three. Remember, O man, that you are dust and be not proud; remember that you are joined to God and be not ungrateful!

Athanasian Creed

9. The second union is 'virgin' and 'mother'; astounding and unique. Never since the world began has it been heard* that there was a virgin who gave birth, that a mother remained a virgin. Never, in the ordinary course of events, can virginity be predicated of fecundity or fecundity of virginity. [Mary] is the only person in whom virginity and fecundity have met together.* Here, just once, something has been done that had not happened before and never will again, for nothing like it has been seen before and nothing like it will follow. [4]

*Jn 9:32

*Ps 84:10 [84:11]

The third union is 'faith' and 'the human heart'. This one is inferior to the first and the second, but perhaps no less formidable. The wonder is that the human heart has accommodated faith in these two matters—how it was able to believe that God is a human being, and that a virgin exists who bore a

---

[4] From the Lauds antiphon *Genuit puerpera*. See Sermon One for Christmas Eve, fn. 2.

Dan 2:43 child. As iron and clay cannot be joined* so these two cannot be united unless the Spirit of God bonds them together.

Are we to believe then that the one who is laid in the manger, who cries in his cradle, who suffers all the indignities children have to suffer, who is scourged, who is spat upon, who is crucified, who is laid in the sepulcher and shut away between two stones *Bar 3:25* is the high and immeasurable* God? Is she really a virgin, who nurses her child, whose husband—her constant companion at bed and board—takes her to Egypt and brings her back, accomplishing so long and secret a journey alone with her? How could the human race, the whole earth, be persuaded of this? And yet it was so easily and so powerfully persuaded that the multitude of believers makes it credible to me. Young men and maidens, old and young to- *Ps 148:12* gether* have chosen to die a thousand deaths rather than forsake this faith even for a moment.

10. And this is indeed an excellent mingling, but more excellent still is the second, and the third the most excellent of all. Ear has heard the first, but eye *1 Cor 2:9* has not seen it,* for the great mystery of our reli- *1 Tm 3:16* gion* has been heard and believed even to the ends *Is 64:4* of the earth, and yet *eye has not seen, apart from you* how, within the confines of the virginal womb, you joined to yourself a human body. Eye has seen the second, because this unique Queen, who *treasured all* *Lk 2:19* *these words, pondering them in her heart,* regarded herself as both fecund and virgin. Joseph, who was no less witness to than guardian of her virginity, recognized it too. The third ascends into the human heart when what happened is believed, even though we believe more by seer than by sight, when we hold with utter firmness what was said and done, doubting nothing.

See in the first what God gives you; in the second, by what [he gives it]; and in the third, for what. He gave you Christ, through Mary, for our healing. In the first is a remedy, a poultice fashioned from God and man to heal all our infirmities.* These two spe- *Ps 103 [102]:3* cies were compounded and mingled together in the Virgin's womb as in a mortar, being mixed smoothly with the Holy Spirit as by a pestle. Because you were not worthy to be given this gift, it was given to Mary, so that through her you might receive what- ever you were to have. Because she was a virgin, she has been heard because of her reverence* on *Heb 5:7* your behalf and on that of the whole human race. If she were simply a mother, that would have been enough for her to have been saved through child- bearing; if she were simply a virgin, that would have been enough for her—but no blessed fruit of her womb* would ransom the world. *Lk 1:42*

While the first union is a remedy, then, the second is a help, because God wanted us to have nothing that does not pass through Mary's hands. In the third, however, is merit, because when we firmly believe these things we gain merit, and in faith is salvation, because the one who believes will be saved.* *Mk 16:16*

On the Medicine of the Spouse's Left Hand and the Delights of His Right Hand

1. THE USAGES OF OUR ORDER does not require a sermon today, but tomorrow will be so much taken up with the celebration of Masses that the short time left over will not allow a long sermon. Therefore I think it not inappropriate to prepare your hearts* for such great solemnity today, especially since the depth of this mystery is extremely profound and unsearchable.* It is like a spring of life°—and the more we take from it the more abundantly it gushes forth, without ever being drained.

*1 Sm [1 K 7:3]

*Rm 11:33
°Ps 36:9 [35:10]

Well then, I know how great is the tribulation you endure for Christ. If only your consolation through him may be as great.* To offer you worldly consolation I neither wish, nor am I allowed. Consolation of that kind is cheap and does no good, and we must fear even more that it is a hindrance to true and salutary consolation. So then, the One who is the delight and glory of the angels has himself become the salvation and consolation of the wretched; the One who—great and sublime in his own city—be-

*2 Cor 1:5-6

70

stows enormous blessings on its citizens, is the one who—now small and lowly in exile—gives enormous joy to exiles. The One who is the glory of the Father in highest heaven has become on earth peace to persons of good will.* *Lk 2:14*

A child has been given* to children so that a great one may be given to the great, and that the great and glorious one may afterwards make great and glorious those whom the child justifies.* Surely this is why the *Vessel of election*, because he had received from the fullness of this child—who, even though small, is full, full of grace and truth,* and in him dwells the whole fullness of divinity bodily*—this is why Paul uttered that good word you have so frequently heard during these days: *Rejoice in the Lord always; again I say, Rejoice!* *Is 9:6*

Rm 8:30
Ac 9:15

Jn 1:14
Col 2:9

Ph 4:4

Rejoice! he says, in the disclosure: rejoice again in the promise, for both hope and reality are full of joy! Rejoice, because you have already received the gifts of the left hand; rejoice, because you are awaiting the rewards of the right. *His left hand*, Scripture says, *is under my head, and his right hand will embrace me.* Yes, the left hand raises and the right enfolds; the left heals and justifies, the right embraces and blesses; the left holds merits, the right, rewards. In the right hand, I say, are delights; in the left, medicines. *Sg 2:6*

2. But observe this kind physician, observe this wise physician. Consider carefully how novel are the medicines he bears. See how he has brought medicines that are not only precious, but beautiful, not only health-giving, but also delightful to the eyes and sweet to the taste. Then look at his first medicine, the first thing he carries in his left hand, and you find it was conceived without seed. Take note, I beg you, what kind of thing it is, how novel, how admirable, how lovable, how pleasant! What is fairer than a chaste birth?* What is more glorious *[Ws 4:1]*

than a holy and pure conception, in which nothing is shameful, nothing sordid, nothing corrupt?

But because our wonder at its novelty—agreeable though it is—would perhaps hold us less enthralled did our minds not find delight in reflecting on the effect and the benefit of salvation, this conception is not only glorious in itself—in its outward appearance—but it is also precious in its inward power. Thus, as it is written, in the Lord's left hand are *Pr 3:16*   found riches together with glory;* the riches of salvation, I say, together with the glory of novelty.

Who *can make clean something conceived of unclean* *[Jb 14:4]*   *seed* if not you, who alone were conceived without any unlawful and unclean pleasure? In my very root and origin I have been infected and tainted; my conception was unclean—but here is One by whom this shame can be taken away. He takes it away; on him alone it has not fallen.

3. I possess the riches of salvation by which to redeem the uncleanness of my own conception: Christ's supremely pure conception. Add to this, *Si 36:6*   Lord Jesus, *renew the signs, perform fresh wonders*, because familiarity has made the former ones lose their value. Sunrise and sunset, the earth's fertility, the changing seasons—all are wonders, great wonders, but we have seen them so often that no one notices them now. *Renew the signs, perform fresh wonders. Behold*, he says, *I make all things new.* Who is saying this? The Lamb who was seated on the *Rv 21:5*   throne,* the Lamb wholly gracious, wholly delightful, wholly anointed—for this is the meaning of his name—Christ. Who could view as harsh or hard the One who brought his mother no harshness, no injury at his birth? O truly new wonder! He was conceived without shame, born without pain! Eve's *Gen 3:16*   curse* was transformed in our Virgin, for she bore a child without pain. Yes, the curse was transformed

into a blessing, as was foretold by the angel Gabriel: *Blessed are you among women.*

Lk 1:28

O fortunate lady, alone among women in being blessed and not cursed, the only one free from the universal curse and a stranger to the pain of child-bearing! Do not be surprised, brothers, if the one who bore the pains of the whole world brought no pain to Mary. As Isaiah said, *Surely he has borne our infirmities.*

Is 53:4

Human frailty fears two things: shame and pain. He came to take away both and hence he accepted both, when—to pass over the rest—the wicked condemned him to death, and to an hideously shameful death.* To give us confidence that he would take these things away from us, he first kept his mother immune from both, so that his conception was without shame, and his birth was without pain.

*Ws 2:20

4. Riches are still accumulating, glory is increasing, signs are being renewed, fresh wonders being done!* Not only was he conceived without shame and born without pain, but his mother too is without corruption. This is truly new and unheard of! A virgin gave birth and remained inviolate after the birth; she possessed the fecundity of offspring with the integrity of her flesh, and had the joy of being a mother with the honor of being a virgin.[1] Now I await with confidence the glory promised me, incorruption in my own flesh, in view of his having preserved incorruption in his mother. How easily can he, who kept his mother from forfeiting incorruption by giving birth, clothe this corruptible body in incorruption* in rising from the dead.

*Si 36:6

*1 Cor 15:53

5. Yet you have still greater wealth, more ample glory. The mother is without corruption of her

---

[1] From the antiphon *Genuit puerpera.* See Sermon One for Christmas Eve, fn. 2.

virginity, the Son is without any spot of sin. Eve's curse does not befall the mother, nor on her child has fallen that universal condition of which the prophet said, *No one is clean from filth, not even a child who has

Jb 14:4 vl   lived one day on earth.* Here is a child without filth, he alone among human beings is true—or rather, he is truth itself! Behold the lamb without blemish, the

Jn 1:29   Lamb of God who takes away the sins of the world. Who can better take sins away than the One whom sin does not befall? Surely he is able to wash me clean, he whom all know to be unstained. May this

Jn 9:6   hand wipe my eye clean with mud, the only hand without dirt on it. May he take the speck out of my

Lk 6:42   eye, he who has no log in his own eye—or rather, may he take the log out of my eye, who has not the slightest bit of dust in his own.

6. We have seen the riches of salvation and life. We have seen his glory, as of the Only-begotten of the

Jn 1:14   Father. Do you ask, 'From what Father?' *He will be
Lk 1:32   called the Son of the Most High.* Who the Most High is, is obvious, but in order to leave no ground for misunderstanding, the angel Gabriel said to Mary, *The Holy One to be born of you will be called Son of

Lk 1:35   God.* O truly holy! Lord, *you will not let your Holy
Ac 13:35;   One see corruption* because you did not take incor-
Ps 16:10   ruption away from his mother. Wonders increase, riches multiply, the treasury is opened. She who gives birth is both mother and virgin; he who is born is God and man.

But shall the Holy be given to dogs, or pearls

*Mt 7:6   to swine? Let our treasure be hidden in a field,°
°Mt 13:44   our money put in a sack. Let his conception without seed be concealed by his mother's betrothal, his painless birth by the child's crying and suffering. Let the incorruption of the child-bearer be concealed by purification according to the Law, the baby's innocence by the customary circumcision.

Conceal, I say, Mary, conceal the brightness of the new Sun. Lay the baby in a manger, wrap him in swaddling clothes,* for those clothes are our riches. *Lk 2:7 More precious than any purple cloth are the Saviour's swaddling clothes, and this manger is more glorious than the gilded thrones of kings. Richer than all wealth and treasure is the poverty of Christ. What is richer, what is more precious, than the humility with which we purchase the kingdom of heaven and acquire divine grace. As Scripture says, *Happy are the poor in spirit, for theirs is the kingdom of heaven,* and according to Solomon, *God resists the* *Mt 5:3* *proud, but gives grace to the humble.* You have humility *1 Pt 5:5; Jm 4:6;* commended to you in the nativity: in it he emptied *Pr 3:34* himself, taking the form of a servant, and was found with the characteristics of a man.* *Ph 2:7

7. Do you want to find riches still more precious and glory still more surpassing? You possess love in his passion. *Greater love than this has no one, that one lay down one's life for one's friends.* These are the riches *Jn 15:13* of salvation and glory: the precious blood by which we were redeemed, and the Lord's cross in which we—with the Apostle—glory: *May I never glory in anything,* he says, *save in the cross of our Lord Jesus Christ.* And, he said: *I decided to know nothing among* *Gal 6:14* *you except Christ Jesus and him crucified.* The left hand *1 Cor 2:2* is Christ Jesus and him crucified, while the right hand is Christ Jesus and him glorified.

Christ, he said, *and him crucified.* Perhaps we are that cross on which we remember Christ having been fastened. A human being has the shape of a cross, and if we extend our hands we show this quite clearly. Yet Christ said in the psalm, *I am stuck fast in the mire of the deep.* That we are mire is obvi- *Ps 69:2 [68:3]* ous, because we were formed out of mire.* Yet then *Gen 2:7 VL* we were the mire of paradise while now we are the mire of the deep. *I am stuck fast,* he says, not 'I have passed through', not 'I have gone back'. *I am with*

Mt 28:20

you to the consummation of the world. Just so, long ago, while Tamar was giving birth, Zerah first put out only his hand, and this was bound with a crimson

*Gen 38:27-30

thread* in token of the Lord's passion.

8. We are now holding his left hand, but still we must cry out, *'Stretch out your right hand to the work*

[Jb 15:15]
*Jn 14:8
*Ps 112 [111]:3

of your hands!' Lord, extend your right hand to us and we shall be satisfied.* *Glory and riches,* Scripture says, *are in their house,* the house of those who fear the Lord. But what is in your house, Lord? Surely,

Is 51:3

thanksgiving and the voice of praise. Happy are those who live in your house, O Lord. They will be praising you for

Ps 84:4 [83:5]

ever and ever.

Eye has not seen, ear has not heard, nor has it risen into the human heart, what God has prepared for those

1 Cor 2:9
*1 Tm 6:16
°Ph 4:7

who love him. This is light inaccessible,* the peace that surpasses all understanding,° the spring is incapable of going upwards but can only go downwards. No eye has seen the inaccessible light, no ear has heard the inconceivable peace. Beautiful were the feet of

*Rm 10:15;
Is 52:7

*Ps 19:4 [18:5]

those who spread the good news of peace,* but even though their sound may have gone out to all the earth,* they were unable to grasp in its full extent that peace which surpasses all understanding, much less convey it to the ears of others.

Yet even Paul himself says, *Brothers, I do not suppose*

Ph 3:13

Rm 10:17
*2 Cor 5:7

that I have grasped it. True, *faith comes by hearing,* and *hearing through the word of God*—faith, not sight*— and the promise—not the disclosure—of peace. And indeed peace is even now present on earth to persons of good will,* but what is *this* peace in com-

*Lk 2:14

parison with the fullness and surpassing greatness of *that* peace? Hence the Lord himself said, *'My peace*

Jn 14:27

I give to you, my peace I leave with you. Of my peace, which surpasses all understanding and is peace upon peace, you are not yet capable. Therefore I give you

a homeland of peace, and in the meantime I leave
the way of peace'.*

Lk 1:79

9. But what does it mean when we say *it has not
risen into the human heart?* Surely that it is a spring
which cannot go upwards. We know that it is the
nature of springs to follow the course of valleys and
to turn aside from the crags of the hills. As Scripture
says, *You make a spring gush forth in the valleys; the waters will pass through the midst of the hills.* That is why

Ps 104 [103]:10

I try so often to remind you, whom I love, that *God
opposes the proud, but gives grace to the humble.* A spring

*Pr 3:34; Jm 4:16;
1 Pt 5:5*

does not reach ground higher than the place proper
to it, but from there it flows downward or forward.

You may discern from this rule of thumb that the
ways of grace are not blocked by pride, especially
as we read that the first proud being who, according to Scripture, is *king over all the progeny of pride*

Jb 41:34 [25]

said, not, 'I will be *higher* than', but 'I will be *like* the
Most High.* Nevertheless, the Apostle does not lie,

Is 14:14

for [Lucifer] exalts himself above everything that is
believed to be a god or is worshipped as a god.*

2 Thes 2:4

Human hearing is horrified at such a statement; if
only we were equally horrified at wicked thoughts
and feelings! I tell you, not only [Lucifer], but every
proud person exalts himself above God. God wants
his will to be done, and the proud want their wills
to be done.

So far there is an appearance of equality. But
notice the disproportion. God wants his will done
only in things that reason approves, but the proud
want their wills done both with reason and against
reason. You see how this is a high place and that
the streams of grace do not reach it. *Unless you are
converted,* [Jesus] says, *and become like this child*—he
is speaking of himself, the spring of life* in whom

Ps 36:9 [35:10]

the fullness of all graces dwells* and from whom it

Col 2:9

flows—*you shall not enter the kingdom of heaven.* Well,

Mt 18:3

then, make channels. Scatter the mounds of earthly and high-flown thoughts, be conformed to the Son of Man—not to the first man, because the spring of grace does not ascend into the hearts of persons who are carnal and earthly. Cleanse your eyes as well, that you may be able to see sheer unadulterated light, and incline your ear* to obedience, that you may at some time attain to everlasting ease and peace upon peace.

Ps 45:10[44:11]; RB Prol. 1

Light exists for serenity, peace for tranquility, the spring for abundance and eternity. Take the spring as being the Father, from whom the Son is born and the Holy Spirit proceeds; the light as being the Son, who is the brightness of eternal life* and the true light that enlightens everyone coming into this world;* and peace as being the Holy Spirit, who rests especially on the quiet and the humble.* Nor do I say this as if these are exclusive properties of each person, for the Father too is light—so that the Son is light from light.* And the Son too is peace— *our peace, who has made both into one.* And the Holy Spirit too is a spring of water gushing forth to eternal life.*

Ws 7:26

Jn 1:9
Is 11:2

Nicene Creed
Eph 2:14

Jn 4:14

10. But when shall we attain these things? When, Lord, will you fill me with gladness, with your presence?* We rejoice in you,° for you, the Dayspring from on high, have visited us.† Again we rejoice as we wait for the blessed hope* at your second coming. But when will the fullness of gladness come— not from the remembrance of you but from your presence, from your appearance, not from our expectance? *Let your moderation be known to everyone,* says the Apostle. *The Lord is near.* It is right then that our moderation be known just as the moderation of our Lord God has become known to everyone. What would be more incongruous than that a human being, aware of his own weakness, should

Ps 16 [15]:11
°*Ph 4:4*
†*Lk 1:78*
Ti 2:13

Ph 4:5

act immoderately, seeing that the Lord of majesty
has appeared moderate among humankind? *Learn
of me,* he says, *for I am meek and humble in heart,* so   Mt 11:29
that your moderation too may become known to
others.[2]

Now the words that follow—*the Lord is near*—
should be understood of his right hand. He says of
his left hand: *Behold, I am with you all days, even to
the consummation of the world.* The Lord is near, my   Mt 28:20
brothers! *Have no anxieties at all,* he is at hand and   Ph 4:6
he will appear swiftly. Do not lose heart,* do not   *2 Thes 3:13
grow weary. *Seek him while he can be found, call upon
him while he is near.* The Lord is near to the broken-   Is 55:6
hearted,* near to those who wait for him, who wait   *Ps 34:18 [33:19]
for him in truth.*   *Ps 145 [144]:18

Do you want to know then how near he is? Listen to the bride as she sings of the bridegroom that
Behold, he is standing behind the wall! Take this wall   Sg 2:9
to mean your body, an obstacle which intervenes
so that you cannot yet contemplate the one who is
near. This is why Paul desired to depart and be with
Christ and cried out in his wretchedness, *Unhappy   Ph 1:23
man that I am, who will deliver me from the body of this
death?* So too the Prophet says in the psalm: *Bring my   Rm 7:24
soul out of prison that I may confess your name!*   Ps 142:7 [141:8]

---

[2] Moderation, moderate translate *modestia, modestus*: unassum-
ing, modest, unassertive.

SERMON FIVE

On the Chant:
*Make yourselves holy today and
be prepared; tomorrow you shall see
within you the majesty of God*[1]

1.　**A**S WE ARE ABOUT to celebrate the ineffable mystery of the Lord's birth, my
brothers, we are rightly bidden to be prepared in all holiness. The Holy of holies is present;
present is the One who said, *Be holy, for I the Lord
your God am holy.** How else can what is holy be
given to dogs, and pearls to swine,* unless the former be first purified from wrongdoing and the latter from lawless pleasures, and in addition the dogs
take every precaution to avoid their vomit* and the
swine their wallowing in the mud?

　Long ago, when about to receive the divine commandments, the carnal Israel was made holy by regulations for the body, by various washings, by offerings
and sacrifices—things that could not perfect the
consciences of those performing them.* But all these
have passed away; they were imposed until the time
came to set things right. This time has now arrived.

*Lv 19:2
*Mt 7:6

*Pr 26:11;
2 Pt 2:22

*Heb 9:10

[1] Responsory at Vigils on Christmas morning, based on Lev
20:7.

This is the right time then for perfect holiness to be
pointed out to you—an inner washing is enjoined on
us, a spiritual purifying is required. As the Lord says,
Blessed are the pure in heart, for they shall see God. For   Mt 5:8
this we live, brothers. To this have we been called, for
this day has today dawned upon us. Once it was night
when no one could work.* It was night throughout   **Jn 9:4*
the whole world before the rising of the true light,
before the birth of Christ. It was night for every single
one of us before our conversion and inner rebirth.

2. Were not the deepest night and the thickest
darkness upon the whole face of the earth* when   **Gen 1:2; 7:3*
long ago our ancestors worshipped counterfeit gods
and with utterly insane sacrilege adored sticks and
stones? Was it not also a murky night for each of
us when we were living in this world as if we were
without God,* when we were strutting after our   **Eph 2:12*
cravings,* when we were pursuing the allurements   **2 Pt 3:3*
of the flesh, when we were giving in to our worldly
desires,* when we were parading our members to   **Ti 2:12*
sin as instruments of evil, and when we were serving
one evil after another*—things of which we are now   **Rm 6:19-21*
deservedly ashamed, as works of darkness? *Those who
sleep, sleep at night,* says the Apostle, *and those who are
drunk, are drunk at night.* And this is how you once   1 Thes 5:7
were, but you have been awakened and you have
been made holy*—if indeed you are *children of light*   **1 Cor 6:11*
and children of the day, not of the night or of darkness.   1 Thes 5:5

'The herald of the day'[2] then is also the one who
cries out, *Be sober, be vigilant.* To the Jews at Pen-   1 Pt 5:8
tecost he said of his fellow disciples, How *are these
people drunk when it is only nine in the morning?* This is   Ac 2:5: 'the third
what his fellow apostle says: *The night is far gone, the*   hour'
day is near. Let us then cast off the world of darkness and

---

[2] From verse two of the hymn *Aeterne rerum Conditor,* sung at
Sunday Lauds in winter; 'the herald' here is applied to Peter.

put on the armor of light. Let us walk decently, as in the
day. Let us cast off the works of darkness, he says—he
means drowsiness and drunkenness, because—as we
recalled above—*Those who sleep, sleep at night and*
those who are drunk, are drunk at night. Being in day-
time then, let us not sleep, but let us walk, and walk
decently, not drunkenly.

Do you see anyone whose *soul sleeps through dreari-*
ness to all that is good? Such a person is still in the
darkness. Do you see someone drunk on absinthe,*
wiser than is fitting* but not to the point of sobri-
ety, someone whose eye is not filled with seeing nor
ear with hearing,* who loves money or something
similar and never has enough, and who drinks like
someone with dropsy? This is a child of the night
and of darkness.* These two are not easily separated,
according to Scripture, because *the idle are filled with*
desires—that is, the drowsy are filled with drunkenness. Let us therefore make ourselves holy today.
And let us be prepared—prepared yet today—by
shaking off the deep sleep of night; and made holy as
in the day from the drunkenness of night by reining
in the impetuosity of harmful cravings. *On these two*
commandments hang all the Law and the Prophets—and
these are to turn away from evil and to do good.*

3. But these things are for today. We will spend
tomorrow, neither in making ourselves holy nor in
preparation, but in the contemplation of Majesty.
Tomorrow, [the Church] sings, *you shall see within you*
the majesty of God. This is what the patriarch Jacob
said: *Tomorrow shall my honesty answer for me.* Today
righteousness is being cultivated; tomorrow it shall
deliver its promise. Today we practice it; tomorrow
it will bear fruit. In other words, what we have not
sown we shall not reap.* Those who disparage holiness now shall not see Majesty then, and the Sun
of glory shall not rise for those on whom the Sun

Marginal references:
Rm 13:12-13

Ps 119 [118]:28
*Lam 3:15
*Rm 12:3

*Qo 1:8

*1 Thes 5:5

Pr 13:4 vl

Mt 22:40
*Ps 37 [36]:27

→ fn. 1
Gen 30:33

*Gal 6:8

of righteousness* has not risen. Nor shall tomorrow   *Mal 4:2
dawn on those who have not lived in the light today.
The One who today became for us *righteousness from*
God the Father will appear tomorrow as our life, so   1 Cor 1:30
that we too may appear with him in glory.*   *Col 3:4

Today a child is born to us,* so that human be-   *Is 9:6
ings may not contrive to glorify themselves,* but   *[Ps 9:39]
may instead be changed to become like children.*   *Mt 18:3
Tomorrow the Lord will be presented as *great and*
greatly to be praised so that we too may be glorified in   Ps 48:1 [47:2]
praise* when everyone will have praise from God.°   *Ps 69:30 [68:31]
Surely those he justifies today he will glorify to-   °1 Cor 4:5
morrow, and the vision of majesty will succeed the
attainment of holiness.

This vision, which consists in nothing other than
likeness, is not empty. *We will be like him, for we will*
see him as he is. Hence here too [Scripture] says, not   1 Jn 3:2
simply *you will see the majesty of God,* but *in you* is expressly added. Today, as in a mirror,* we see ourselves   *1 Cor 13:12
in him, when he takes on what is ours; tomorrow
we shall see him in ourselves, when he will already
be giving us what is his, while showing himself to
us and taking us into himself. This is what he promised: that he would pass by and wait for us, while in
the meantime we receive from his fullness, clearly
not glory upon glory, but grace upon grace.* As it is   *Jn 1:16
written: *The Lord will give grace and glory.* So do not   Ps 84:11 [83:12]
slight the early gifts if you yearn for those that follow.
Do not turn up your nose at the first course if you
want to receive what follows, or refuse to take what
is on the platter because of the platter it is on. The
Peacemaker made an incorruptible litter[3] for himself, providing for his use an imperishable body in

---

[3] Sg 3:9. Bernard replaces *rex Salomon* with *Pacificus.* 'Platter'
and 'litter' both translate *feraculum,* a conveyance, a thing on
which something is carried.

which to serve the banquet of salvation. *You will not let your Holy One see corruption,* he says. This is what Gabriel was speaking of to Mary: *The Holy One to be born of you will be called Son of God.*

4. Let us then be made holy by this Holy One so that we may see his majesty when the day begins to dawn. *A holy day has dawned for us,*[4] a day of salvation, not of glory or of happiness. Until there is proclaimed the passion of the Holy of holies—of him who suffered on *parasceve,* the Day of Preparation— we all are rightly told, *Make yourselves holy today, and be prepared.* Make yourselves more and more holy by going from strength to strength,* and be prepared by persevering. But in what are we to make ourselves holy? I have read of a certain person* in Scripture that *in his faith and gentleness* God *made him holy.* We cannot please people without gentleness any more than we can please God without faith.* Rightly are we advised to be prepared in what brings us into accord with God, whose majesty we are about to see, and with one another, so that we may see [that majesty] equally in ourselves. This is why we must provide good things not only in God's sight but also in the sight of other persons,* so that we may be acceptable, not only to our King but to our fellow citizens and comrades in arms as well.

5. Above everything else, we must seek faith, of which we read: *purifying their hearts by faith. Blessed are the pure in heart, for they shall see God.* Entrust yourself, therefore, to God. Commit yourself to him. Cast your thought on him, and he shall sustain you so that you may say with confidence and faith that *the Lord takes thought for me.* Persons who love themselves* do not appreciate this—people who pretend

Ac 13:34 [35];
Ps 16:10

Lk 1:35

→ *fn 1*
**Ps 84:7 [83:8]*

**Moses*
Si 45:4

**Heb 11:6*

**2 Cor 8:21*

Ac 15:9
Mt 5:8

Ps 40:17 [39:18]
**2 Tm 3:2*

---

[4] Neh 8:9, in the responsory *Beata viscera* at the Night Office, and the *Alleluia* at the day Mass of Christmas.

to knowledge, who are absorbed in their own affairs, who take good care of the flesh in its desires* and are deaf to the voice that says, *Cast all your care upon him, because he cares for you.*

*Rm 13:14

1 Pt 5:7

Now, to trust in oneself is not faith but faithlessness. To place confidence in oneself is not trust but mistrust. The genuinely faithful are those who do not trust in themselves or hope in themselves; they become to themselves like broken vessels* and so lose their lives as to preserve them for eternal life.* Yet only humility of heart prevents the faithful soul from leaning on itself for support. Forsaking themselves, they come up out of the desert, leaning on their beloved, and thereby overflowing with delights.*

*Ps 31:12
[30:13]
*Jn 12:25

*[Sg 8:5]

6. Surely if we are to be made perfectly holy we must also learn from the Holy of holies gentleness and the grace of living with others. As he himself says, *Learn from me, for I am gentle and humble in heart.* What is to prevent us from describing persons of this sort as 'overflowing with delights'? They are kind and gentle, and abounding in mercy.* They have become all things to all people.* And they have poured over everyone a sort of oil of gentleness and calmness. This has been so poured into them, so poured over and poured upon them that it seems to have been distilled in every direction.

Mt 11:29

*Ps 86:5 [85:5]
*1 Cor 9:22

Happy are those who have been prepared by this twofold holiness, those who can say, *My heart is prepared, O God, my heart is prepared.* Today they possess the fruit of holiness;* tomorrow they will possess its goal, eternal life. They shall see the majesty of God, because eternal life is truly this—as Truth tells us: *This is eternal life, that they may know you, the true God, and Jesus Christ whom you have sent.* On that day, which no other will follow, the righteous Judge will bestow on them the crown of righteousness.* Then

Ps 57:7 [56:8]
*Rm 6:22

Jn 17:3

2 Tm 4:8

Is 60:5

shall they see and overflow, and their hearts will wonder and expand.* How far will they expand? To the point of seeing within themselves God's majesty. Do not think, my brothers, that I can explain this promise to you in words.

7. *Make yourselves holy today, and be prepared;* tomorrow you shall see and rejoice, and *your joy shall be full.* What can this majesty not fill? It will overfill

Jn 15:11

and overflow when they put into your laps a good measure, pressed down, shaken together, and overflowing.* Indeed, it will overflow to the point that

Lk 6:38

it will immeasurably exceed in sublimity not only what we deserve but even what we desire. [God] has the power to do more than we are able to understand or to hope for.

Our desires seem to consist mainly in three things: what is appropriate; what is useful; and what is pleasing. These are what we crave. All of us crave all of them, but one person craves this more and another that. One is so given over to pleasure as not to give enough thought to decency and usefulness. One broods over profit, neglecting integrity and enjoyment. One is equally careless of both pleasure and usefulness and pursues only, or chiefly, honor. The desire for these things is not reprehensible, provided that we seek them where we can truly find them. Where these things truly exist they are one, and this one is the supreme good, supreme glory, supreme usefulness, supreme pleasure. This indeed, insofar as we can grasp it here below, is the object of our hope, the vision of Majesty in us that has been promised to us, *so that God may be all in all,* all that is enjoyable,

1 Cor 15:28

all that is useful, all that is honorable.

On the Proclamation of His Birth

1. WE HAVE HEARD an announcement full of grace, worthy of acceptance: *Jesus Christ, the Son of God, is
born in Bethlehem of Judah.*[1] My soul has melted at
these words.*Yes, and my spirit burns within me° as
it hastens with its usual desire to communicate this
joy and exultation to you. Jesus, Saviour: what is so
necessary to the lost, so desirable to the wretched,
so useful to the hopeless? Where else would we
find salvation? Where else would we find even a
frail hope of salvation[c] under the law of sin, in the
body of death,* in the evil of the day° and place of
affliction,† if not in the birth for us of this new and
unhoped for salvation?

As for you, perhaps you hope for salvation, but
you recoil from the severity of the healing process,
aware of your own frailty and illness. Do not be
afraid.* Christ is entirely forbearing, and gentle,°
and abounding in mercy. He is anointed with the
oil of gladness beyond his companions,* especially
for those who receive, though not the fullness itself,°
at least from the fullness of this anointing. To keep

*Sg 5:6
°Is 26:9

*1 Thes 5:8
*Rm 7:23-24
°Mt 6:34
†[Ps 43:20]

*Lk 1:30
°Ps 86[85]:5

*Ps 45:7 [44:8];
Heb 1:9
°Jn 1:16

[1] In cistercian monasteries, these words were sung out in
Chapter on Christmas Eve. See Sermon One, fn. 1.

you from thinking, when you hear that the Saviour is forbearing, that he might be ineffectual, *the Son of God* is added. As is the Father, so is the Son, who is able to act whenever he chooses.*

*Ws 12:18

Or perhaps, having heard about the usefulness of salvation and the joyfulness of anointing you may mutter something or other, anxious, I suppose, about his good character. You are thankful that the Saviour is near you as you lie paralyzed upon a mat* or rather half dead on the road between Jerusalem and Jericho.* You rejoice still more that the physician is not harsh, nor does he use unpleasant medicines; otherwise the short course of healing might strike you as harder to bear than your protracted illness. In this way many people, even to this day, perish as they flee from the physician because they do indeed know Jesus, but do not know Christ. In a human way they reckon the irksomeness of the remedy prepared for them on the basis of the multitude and malignity of their maladies.

*Mk 2:4

*Lk 10:30

2. But now that you are sure of the Saviour and recognize that he is no less the Christ, who uses not a cautery but ointment, who heals not by searing but by soothing, I think that one thing can still affect a freeborn creature. This is the supposition— God forbid!—that the person of this Saviour may seem not sufficiently worthy. I suppose, however, that you are not so ambitious and greedy for glory, not such a fanatic for acclaim, that you would decline to receive this gift from your fellow servants if any of them were able to grant it. If this were an angel or archangel, or came from one of the higher ranks of the blessed spirits, your animosity would have much less reason to cavil. As it is, you must receive this Saviour with still greater devotion in that he has inherited a name more excellent* than all others, Jesus Christ, the Son of God. See if the angel

*Heb 1:4

did not quite clearly commend these three things[2] in speaking to the shepherds, explaining the good news of great joy. He said: *For to you is born this day a Saviour who is Christ the Lord.*   *Lk 2:10-11*

Let us exult, then, brothers, in this birth, and give thanks for it many times over. The utility of salvation, the delicacy of anointing, and the majesty of the Son of God so gracefully elucidate it that nothing of all we desire is missing—not the suitable, not the pleasant, not the decent. Let us exult, I say, ruminating within ourselves and belching to one another the good word, the lovely sentence: *Jesus Christ, the Son of God, is born in Bethlehem of Judah.*

3. Let no irreligious, ungrateful, and irreverent person answer me, 'This is nothing new. It was heard in the past. It was done in the past. Christ was born in the past'. Yes, 'in the past', and 'before'. No one will be surprised at this 'in the past' and 'before' who has come across this prophetic phrase: *forever and beyond.*   *Ex 15:18*
Christ was born not only before our time then but before all time. That birth made darkness its hiding-place*—or, to be more exact, it dwells in light   **Ps 18:11 [17:12]*
unapproachable.* It lies hidden in the Father's heart,   **1 Tm 6:16*
on a mountain shady and well-wooded.[3] He was born that he might to some extent be made known. In time he was born of flesh; born in flesh the Word was made flesh.*   **Jn 1:14*

We should not be surprised if even today we say in the Church that *Christ, the Son of God, is born,* when so long ago, surely of the same person, it was said *unto us a child is born.* In the past this message began   *Is 9:6*
to be heard, and none of the saints ever wearied of it. Christ Jesus is the Son of God yesterday and today and forever.* Hence the first man, the father   **Heb 13:8*

---

[2] See Christmas Eve Sermon 6.7, above.
[3] Hb 3:3 LXX, as in the Advent responsory *Alieni.*

*1 Cor 15:45;
Gen 3:29
°Eph 5:32

Eph 5:31

*Jn 8:56

*Gen 24:2-3

Ps 132 [131]:11

Lk 2:4

Rm 15:8

*Heb 1:1

*Rm 8:28

Is 64:1

*1 Jn 1:1
*Lk 10:23

Jn 20:19

Rm 1:17; Gal
3:11; Hab 2:4

of all the living,* uttered a great mystery,° which the Apostle afterward applied more clearly to Christ and to the Church: *A man will leave father and mother and will cleave to his wife, and they shall be two in one flesh.*

4. Hence Abraham, the father of all who believe, rejoiced to see this day; he saw it and was glad.* Would he have ordered his servant, who was swearing to him by the God of heaven, to place his hand under his thigh* if he had not seen in advance that this same God of heaven would be born from that same thigh? God also revealed the plan of his heart to the man after his own heart, to whom he swore the truth—and he will not disappoint him—that *I shall set the fruit of your womb upon your throne.* This is also why he is born in Bethlehem of Judah—as the angel says, *In the city of David*—on behalf of the truth of God, to confirm the promises made to the patriarchs. In many and various ways this was revealed to the other patriarchs and prophets as well.*

God forbid that those who love God* ever heard this with indifference—unless the one who said, *I entreat you, Lord, send the one you will send,*[4] may seem indifferent, or unless the one who cried out, *O that you would rend the heavens and come down* and other similar things, was holding back. It was he the holy apostles saw and heard, and their hands touched, the Word of life.* To them in particular was said, *Blessed are the eyes that see what you see!*

Last of all, this has been preserved for us believers too, and entrusted to the treasuries of the faith. As he himself said, *Blessed are those who have not seen and have believed.* This is our share in the Word of life. What gives life, what overcomes the world, is surely not to be held lightly! For *the righteous live by faith,* and *this is*

---

[4] Ex 4:13, as in the responsory *Obsecro* on the First Sunday of Advent.

the victory that overcomes the world, our faith. It is a kind   *1 Jn 5:4*
of paradigm of eternity, encompassing within its vast
embrace at one and the same time all things past,
present, and future, so that nothing is passed over,
nothing passes away, nothing precedes it.

5. Rightly then, in testimony to your faith,* when   **Heb 11:39*
the sound of this greeting came to your ears you
leapt for joy,* you gave thanks, you bowed down to   **Lk 1:44*
the ground and adored,[5] coming together as under
the shadow of his wings and trusting beneath his
pinions.* At hearing of the Saviour's birth has not   **Pss 17 [16]:8;*
every single one of you cried out in your heart, *It is*   *91 [90]:4*
good for me to cleave to God—or more likely, what the   *Ps 73 [72]:28*
same prophet says, *O my soul, be subject to God.*   *Ps 62:5 [61:6]*

Unhappy are those who only make a pretense of
prostrating, who humble their bodies while their
hearts are unbending. *There are those who humble*
themselves wickedly, but inwardly are full of deceit. Those   *Si 19:26 [23]*
who take scant thought for their need, who scarcely
feel their discomforts, who are little alarmed by dangers, who resort with skimpy devotion to the remedies of the salvation that has dawned, who are less
than serious in their surrender to God and less than
faithful in singing *Lord, you have become our refuge*—   *Ps 90 [89]:1*
the adoration of these people is barely acceptable,
their prostrations scarcely genuine, their humility of
scant value, and even their faith hardly victorious
and barely alive. What does he say, *Blessed are those*
who have not seen and have believed? As if to believe   *Jn 20:29*
him does not seem in some sense already to see. But
notice carefully to whom this was said, and when:
to someone who was rebuked for believing what
he had seen. To have seen, and therefore to believe

---

[5] Cistercians prostrated themselves in prayer when the birth
of Christ was proclaimed in Chapter on Christmas Eve. *Ecclesi-*
astica Officia 3.4; Herzog-Müller, 52.

Jn 8:39f

in, him is not the same as to have seen by believing. How else are we to believe that Abraham, *your ancestor, saw this day of the Lord,* except by believing? And how are we to take what has been sung to us tonight: *Make yourselves holy today and be prepared: tomorrow you will see within you the majesty of God,*[6] if not that to see with the mind is to make present with earnest devotion and to recall with unfeigned faith the great *mystery of loving-kindness which was revealed in the flesh, justified in the spirit, appeared to angels, was preached among the Gentiles, was believed in the world, was taken up into glory*?

1 Tm 3:16

6. Always new then is what is always renewing minds; never old is what never ceases to bear fruit and never decays. This is the Holy which is not allowed to see corruption.* This is the new human being, who is incapable ever of becoming old. He brings to genuine newness of life even those whose bones all grew old.* This is why, if you notice, that even in this present utterly joyful proclamation we quite appropriately say, not 'he was born', but 'he is born': *Jesus Christ, the Son of God, is born in Bethlehem of Judea.* As he is still in a sense still being immolated every day so long as we proclaim his death,* so too does he seem to be being born so long as we faithfully commemorate his birth.

*Ac 13:35;
Ps 16 [15]:10

*[Ps 31:3]

*1 Cor 11:26

Tomorrow therefore we shall see the majesty of God, not in itself but 'in us': majesty in humility, power in weakness, God in a human being. He is *Emmanuel, which means, God with us.* Listen to something clearer still: *The Word became flesh and dwelt among us.* From then on and henceforward, *we have seen his glory, but the glory as of the Only-begotten of the Father;* we have seen him *full of grace and truth.* We

Mt 1:23

Jn 1:14

---

[6] Lv 20:7, used in the responsory *Sanctificamini* in the Night Office of Christmas.

have seen, not the glory of power and of splendor, but the glory of fatherly loving-kindness, the glory of grace, of which the Apostle says, *In the praise of the glory of his grace.*

Eph 1:6

7. So that is how he is born. But *where* do you think? *In Bethlehem of Judah.* It would not become us to pass by Bethlehem. *Let us go even to Bethlehem*, the shepherds say, not 'Let us go by Bethlehem'. What if it is a poor little village? What if it seems the least in Judea?* This is no unbefitting the One who, though he was rich, for our sake became poor,* and though he was a great Lord and greatly to be praised,* was born a little child for us,* and said, *Blessed are the poor in spirit, for theirs is the kingdom of heaven*; and again, *Unless you change and become like this child, you shall not enter the kingdom of heaven.* This is also why he chose a stable and a manger, a house of clay* and a lodging place for beasts: so that you might know that he is the One who raises the poor from the dunghill* and saves both men and beasts.

Lk 2:15

*Mt 2:6; Mi 5:2
*Col 8:9
*Ps 48:1 [47:2]
*Is 9:6
Mt 5:3

Mt 18:3
*Jb 4:19

*Ps 112 [113]:7;
36:6 [35:7]

8. If only we too may be found a Bethlehem of Judah, that he may deign to be born within us too, and that we may be worthy to hear, 'For you who fear God, the Sun of righteousness will arise!'* This may be what we recalled above, the need for making ourselves holy, and for preparing, to see within us the Lord's majesty. According to the prophet, *Judea became his holiness*, which means that everything is washed clean in confession;[7] and 'the house of bread'—which 'Bethlehem' means[8]—will perhaps seem particularly to suggest preparation. How does a person who says that *in my house is no bread* prepare

*Mal 4:2

Ps 113 [114]:2

Is 3:7

---

[7] Jerome *Interpretatio nominum hebraicorum*; PL 23:825; CCSL 72:67, 19. See also, PL 23:781, 1148, 1227.

[8] Isidore, *Etymologiarum libri XX*, 1.23; PL 82:530. Jerome, *Interpretatio nominum hebraicorum*; PL 23:1147.

so as to be able to receive so great a guest? Because
this person was unprepared he had to knock on his
friend's closed gate at midnight and say that *a friend
of mine has come to me from his journey, and I have nothing to set before him.*

Lk 11:5-6

Their hearts are prepared to hope in the Lord, says the
prophet—surely referring to the righteous—*their
hearts are strengthened; they shall not be moved.* A heart
not strengthened is not prepared. We know—on the
testimony of the same prophet—that *bread strengthens
the human heart.* The heart of someone who forgets to
eat his bread is not prepared, but dry and bloodless.
Someone who, forgetful of what lies behind, strains
forward to what lies ahead*—that person is prepared
and not troubled* at keeping the commandments
of life.

Ps 112 [111]:7-8

Ps 102 [103]:15

*Ph 3:13

*Ps 119 [118]:60

You see how we must avoid one kind of forgetfulness and long for another. The whole tribe of
Manasseh[9] does not cross the Jordan, but neither
does the whole tribe choose a home for itself on
the near side.* Some forget the Lord° their Creator
and others keep him always in their sight,† forgetful
of their own people and their father's house.* The
one forgets the things of heaven, but the other the
things that are on earth;° the one things present;
the other things future; the one what is seen, the
other what is not seen;* and lastly, the one what
is his own, and the other what belongs to Jesus
Christ.* Both are Manasseh and both are forgetful,
but the one is forgetful of Jerusalem, the other of
Babylon.* One [is forgetful] of what hinders and
is prepared; the other is forgetful of what helps and

**Nm 32:33;
Josh 22:4, 7.
°Is 51:13
†Ex 25:30;
Ps 16:8; Ac 2:25
*Ps 45:10 [44:11]
°Col 3:2*

*2 Cor 4:18

*Ph 2:21

*Ps 137 [136]

[9] Manasseh means 'forgetful' or 'what is forgotten', according
to Jerome (*Interpretatio nominum hebraicorum*; PL 23:1170; CCSL
72:82, 6 and 137,15) and Augustine, *Enarrationes in Psalmo, In
psalmum* 59.9 (PL 36:719; CCSL 39:761, 19-20).

of what it is not helpful to forget; and he is utterly unprepared to see within himself the Lord's majesty. He is not a 'house of bread' in which the Saviour can be born, not a Manasseh to whom will appear the One who rules Israel and is enthroned upon the cherubim. *Appear before Ephraim, Benjamin, and Manasseh*, Scripture says.* I am of the opinion that these are three who are saved, whom another prophet names Noah, Daniel, and Job;* they are also represented by the three shepherds to whom the angel brought the good news of great joy* at the birth of the Angel of Great Council.*

9. See whether they are not perhaps the three Magi* as well, coming—now no longer only from the East, but even from the West*—to sit at table with Abraham, Isaac, and Jacob. Perhaps connecting the offering of frankincense to Ephraim*—a name that means 'to be fruitful'[10]—will not seem inappropriate, because the offering of suitable incense as 'a pleasing odor'* is characteristic of those whom the Lord has appointed to go and bear fruit°—that is, of those holding authority in the Church.

As for Benjamin, the *son of the right hand*, he must offer gold—that is, this world's goods—so that the faithful people who have been placed on his right may be worthy to hear from the Judge that *I was hungry and you gave me food*, and so forth. Furthermore, if Manasseh wants to be a person to whom God appears, let him offer the myrrh of mortification, which in my opinion is particularly demanded of our profession. All this has been said to keep us from belonging to that part of the tribe of Manasseh which stayed on the near side of the Jordan; instead,

*Ps 80:1-2
[79:2-3]*

Ezk 14:20

Lk 2:10
Is 9:6

Mt 2:1
Mt 8:11

Gen 41:52

*Ezk 16:19;
20:28*
°Jn 15:16*

Gen 35:18

Mt 25:31-36

---

[10] Philo Josephus (Ps-Jerome), *Libri nominum hebraicorum pars quaedam ex operibus philonis judaei collecta*; PL 23:1285. Cf. Jerome, *De nominibus hebraicis*; PL 23:845.

may we forget what lies behind and strain forward
and inward to what is before us.*

Ph 3:13

10. Let us go now to Bethlehem and see this word
which the Lord has brought to pass* and revealed to
us. It is *the house of bread*, as we have already said. It
is good for us to be there.* Where the Lord's word
is, the bread that strengthens the heart* cannot be
lacking. As the Prophet says, *Strengthen me by your
words!* Human beings live by the word that comes
forth from the mouth of God.* They live in Christ;
Christ lives in them. There he arises; there he appears. Nor has he any love at all for faltering and
wavering hearts; he loves hearts steady and strong.
Someone who complains, who is indecisive, who
hesitates, who considers wallowing in the mud and
turning back to his vomit,* forsaking his vows, shift-
ing his intention, is not Bethlehem, is not a house of
bread. Only famine—and severe famine—compels
him to go down to Egypt,* to feed pigs, to eat husks,
for he is living far from the house of bread, from the
house of the Father, where even the hired hands are
known to have bread enough and to spare.*

Christ is not therefore born in hearts like these
which lack the courage of faith, indeed lack the
bread of life.* On the testimony of Scripture, *the
righteous live by faith.* The soul's true life—which is
Christ—can dwell in our hearts only through faith.*
How else is Jesus born in them, how else does salvation dawn for them, seeing that the statement that
only those who persevere to the end will be saved is
absolutely true and certain?*

Because Christ is scarcely to be found in such persons, and they are not among those who are told *you
have been anointed by the Holy One*, the unanimous
opinion about them is that their hearts have surely
withered since the time they forgot to eat their bread.*
Much less do people of this kind belong to God's

Lk 2:15

Mt 17:4
Ps 104 [103]:15

Ps 119 [118]:28
Mt 4:4

2 Pt 2:22

Gen 12:10

Lk 15:14-17

Jn 6:35
Gal 3:11
Eph 3:17

Mt 10:27

1 Jn 2:20

Ps 102:4 [101:5]

Son, because his Spirit can rest only on those who are peaceful and humble and tremble at his words.* No partnership* can exist between eternity and such mutability, between the One who is and someone who never perseveres in the same state.* Nevertheless, however firm we may be, however steadfast, however well prepared, however much we have enough bread to eat and to spare* through the gift of the One we daily address in our prayers, *Give us today our daily bread*, we still have to add the words that follow: *Forgive us our debts*. Otherwise, *if we say that we have no sin, we deceive ourselves and the truth is not in us*. Indeed, he himself is the Truth, who is born not simply in Bethlehem, but *in Bethlehem of Judah, Jesus Christ, the Son of God*.

11. Let us then come into his presence with confession,* that, both holy and prepared, we too may be found a Bethlehem of Judah, and we may be worthy to see the Lord born within us. Moreover, if any soul* has advanced to the point—a great thing for us!—that it is a fruitful virgin, a star of the sea,[11] full of grace and having the Holy Spirit coming upon it,* then I think he will deign not only to be born in her, but also of her. None surely would presume to claim this for themselves, save only those whom he himself specially indicated, as if to point them out, when he said, *Here are my mother and my brothers*.

In fact, listen to one of these persons: *My little children, for whom I am again in labor until Christ is formed in you*. If Christ appeared to be born in them while he was being formed in them, can we not

*Is 66:2 VL
*1 Pt 5:9

*Jb 14:2

*Lk 15:17

Lk 11:3
Mt 6:12

1 Jn 1:8

*Ps 95 [94]:2

*Anima, fem.

*Lk 1:28, 35

Mt 12:49

Gal 4:19

---

[11] From the hymn *Ave Maris Stella*, sung at Vespers on feasts of the Blessed Virgin Mary. See Jerome *In Evangelium secumdum Matthæum* (PL 30:535) and *De nominibus hebraicorum Novi Testamenti, Ex Matthaeo* (PL 23:1160); Isidore, *Etymologiae* 7.10.1 (PL 82:289); and Bede, *In Lucam* 1 (CCCM 120:31).

also presume to say that Christ was likewise born of Paul, who was in some sense giving birth to Christ in them?

And you, ungodly Synagogue, you bore this Son for us, acting like a mother but not loving like a mother. You thrust him from your lap, casting him out of the city* and lifting him up above the earth,° as if saying to the Church of the nations†—as well as to the Church of the first fruits which is in heaven, *Let him be neither mine nor yours, but divide him.* Yes, divide him, I say, not between both but from both. When he was driven out and lifted up—not very far, but far enough that he was neither within your walls nor on the earth—you closed him in on every side with a sword to prevent his going too far one way or the other, with the result that, once separated from you, he would reach neither. Cruel mother indeed! You wanted to make him untimely born when no one could receive him whom you thrust away. Realize, then, what you have accomplished—or rather, that you have accomplished nothing. The daughters of Zion* are everywhere coming out to see King Solomon wearing the diadem with which you have crowned him.* Leaving his mother, he will cleave to his wife, that they may be two in one flesh.* Driven from the city and lifted above the earth, he is drawing all things to himself,*

he who is over all
God blessed forever.
Amen.

*Lv 14:40
°Jn 12:32
†Rm 16:4

1 [3] K 3:26

1 Cor 15:8

*Sg 3:11

*Sg 3:11
*Eph 5:31

*Jn 12:32

On the Five Springs

1. **G**REAT IS THIS DAY'S solemn feast of the Lord's birth, dearly beloved; but the short day requires me to shorten my sermon. What wonder if we make our word short when God the Father has made his Word abbreviated![1] Do you want to know how long [his Word was] and how short he made it? *I fill heaven and earth*, says this Word; now, made flesh,* he has been laid in a narrow manger.° *From everlasting and to everlasting*,[2] says the Prophet, *you are God*, and see, he has become an infant one day old.*

Jer 23:24 VL
*Jn 1:14
°Lk 2:7
Ps 90 [89]:2
*Jb 14:4 VL

Why was it, brothers, why was it necessary that the Lord of majesty so empty himself, so humble himself,* so abbreviate himself? Was it not that you might do likewise?*Already he is crying out by his example what later he will proclaim by his words: *Learn of me, for I am meek and humble in heart,* so that the one who tells us *what Jesus began to do and to teach* may be found truthful.

*Ph 2:7-8
*Jn 13:15

Mt 11:29
Ac 1:1

---

[1] *Verbum abbreviatum*, the Word truncated, curtailed, or shortened; taken from the Vulgate phrase *Verbum breviatum* in Rm 9:28.

[2] The psalm verse *A sæculo et in sæculo* . . . was used as the graduale on the twenty-first Sunday after Pentecost.

Consequently, my brothers, I beg and earnestly entreat you not to allow so precious a model to be shown you in vain, but to be conformed to it, and *Eph 4:23*   renewed in the spirit of your minds.* Be zealous for humility, which is the foundation and guardian of the virtues. Pursue it, for it alone can save your *Jm 1:21*   souls.* What is more unworthy, what is more hateful, what is more deserving of punishment than for persons who see the God of heaven become a child *[Ps 9:39]*   to presume to glorify themselves on earth?* Where majesty has emptied itself, for a worm to be inflated and to swell up is intolerable insolence.

2. This then is the reason why the one who in the form of God was equal to the Father emptied him-*Ph 2:6-7*   self, taking the form of a servant.* He emptied himself, however, of majesty and power, not of goodness and mercy. What does the Apostle say? *The gracious-*
Ti 3:4   *ness and humaneness of God our Saviour have appeared!*

His power had appeared before in the creation of things, his wisdom appeared in their governance; but the goodness of his mercy has now appeared, especially in his humaneness. His power had been made *Dt 26:8*   known to the Jews in signs and wonders,* which is why you find over and over again in their law, *I am*
Lv 18:5, 6, 21;   *the Lord, I am the Lord.* His majesty was made known
19:12   to philosophers, who are fully convinced in their
Rm 14:5   own minds,* that—in the Apostle's words—*what is*
Rm 1:19   *known about God is plain to them.* Nonetheless the Jews were oppressed by the power, and the philosophers, searchers of majesty, were overwhelmed by the *[Pr 25:27]*   glory.* Power required subjection, majesty required admiration—neither required imitation.

Lord, let your goodness appear, to which human-*Gen 1:27*   kind, created in your image,* can be conformed! Majesty, power, and wisdom we are unable to imitate, and emulating them does us no good. How long is your mercy restricted solely to the angels;

how long does your judgement fall on the rest—
along with the whole human race? *Lord, your mercy
reaches to the heavens, and your truth to the clouds,* con-
demning the whole earth and the powers of the air.*
Let your mercy widen its boundaries,* let it stretch
out its cords,* let it expand its lap, let it reach mightily from one end to the other and order all things
well!* Your lap has been restricted by judgement,
Lord; loosen your belt, and come, flowing with
mercies, overflowing with love!

3. What are you afraid of, human beings? Why
do you tremble *before the face of the Lord, because he
comes?* He comes not to judge the earth but to save
it.* Once you were persuaded by some faithless servant to take the royal diadem by theft and to set it
on your own head.* You were caught in the theft—
why would you not be afraid? Why would you not
flee from his presence?* Perhaps he was brandishing
a flaming sword.* Now, in exile, *you eat your bread in
the sweat of your brow.*

But look, a voice is heard on earth,* because the
Sovereign is coming!*Where will you go from his
spirit, or where will you flee from his presence?* Do
not flee, do not fear. He is not coming with weap-
ons, he is seeking not to punish but to save. And in
case you are even now saying, *I heard your voice, and I
hid myself,* look, he is a baby, and he has no voice. The
sound of his crying inspires compassion more than
trembling; if it strikes terror in anyone, it is not you.

He became a little child. The virgin mother wraps
his tender limbs in swaddling clothes*—and do you
still tremble with fear?* Or will you realize from
this that he has not come to destroy but to save
you,* not to bind but to set you free? It is as though
the power and wisdom of God* is already fighting against your enemies, already trampling on the
necks of the proud and haughty.

Ps 36:5 [35:6]
*Eph 2:2
*Ex 34:24
*Ps 140:5 [139:6]

*Ws 8:1

Ps 96:13 [95:12]
*Jn 3:17

*1 Mc 11:13

*Ps 139 [138]:7
*Ps 7:13
Gen 3:24, 19
*Sg 2:12
*Is 3:1; etc.
*Ps 139 [138]:7

Gen 3:10

*Lk 2:7
*Ps 14 [13]:5

*Lk 9:56
*1 Cor 1:24

4. Your enemies are two, sin and death—that is, death of the body and of the soul. He comes ready to battle against both to the end, and he will save you from both. Do not be afraid! Indeed he already overcame sin in his own person when he took a human nature free from all contagion. Great was the violence done to sin, and that it was truly defeated we know when the nature, which sin boasted it had totally infected and seized, was found to be, in Christ, completely unscathed by it. Henceforward [Christ] pursues your enemies and overtakes them; he does not turn back until they give way.* *Ps 18:37 [17:38] He struggles against sin in his whole way of life. In his words as well as by his example he attacks it, but in his passion he binds it, binds the strong one, and seizes his belongings.* *Mt 12:29

Now, in the same order, he first overcomes death in himself when he rises, the first fruits of those who have fallen asleep* and the firstborn from the dead.° *1 Cor 15:20 °Col 1:18 Afterward he will battle against it to the end in all of us as well, when he raises up our mortal bodies,* *Rm 8:11 and the final enemy, death, is destroyed.* *1 Cor 15:26 On this account he, when risen, was clothed in beauty*— *[Ps 92:1] not, as earlier, when newborn, wrapped in swaddling clothes. On this account the one whose lap first overflowed with mercy, the one who judged no one, girded himself when he arose; he seems somehow to have gathered them into his lap, overflowing with mercy, with the girdle of righteousness.* *Is 11:5 Henceforth he is prepared for the judgment that will take place at our resurrection. On this account, too, he came earlier as a child to dispense mercy and, anticipating the final judgement to come, to temper it with mercy.

5. Although he came to us as a little child, what he brought is not little, what he conferred on us is not little. If you ask what he brought: first of all he

brought mercy, according to which, as the Apostle
testifies, he saved us.* Nor does this benefit only   *Ti 3:5*
those he found when he came; it is a spring which
can never be exhausted. Christ the Lord is for us a
spring in which we are washed—as it is written, *he*
has loved us and washed us from our sins. Of course this   *Rm 1:5*
is not water's only use. Not only does it wash away
filth but it also quenches thirst. *Happy will they be,*
says the Sage, *who will linger in wisdom and will medi-*
tate on righteousness, and a little later, *She will give him*   *[Si 14:22]*
the water of saving wisdom to drink. Yes, *saving wisdom,*   *Si 15:3*
because the wisdom of the flesh is death,* and the   **Rm 8:6-7*
wisdom of the world is even hostile to God.*   **1 Cor 3:19*

Only the wisdom that comes from God is saving,
according to the definition of Saint James—it is first
modest, then peaceable.* The wisdom of the flesh is   **Jm 3:17*
sensual, not modest; the wisdom of the world is tur-
bulent, not peaceable. The wisdom that comes from
God is indeed first modest, seeking not its own inter-
ests but those of Jesus Christ,* so that people do not   **1 Cor 13:5;*
carry out their own wills but ponder what is the will   *Ph 2:21*
of God. Then it is peaceable, not full of itself, but yield-
ing instead to another's counsel and judgement.*   **Rm 12:2; 14:5*

6. The third use of water is irrigation, which is
necessary especially for young plants.* Without it   **[Ps 143:12]*
they will either progress poorly or die completely
from dryness. Those who have sown the seeds of
good works must then seek out the waters of devotion. If irrigated by the spring of grace, the garden
of a good way of life will not dry out but will flour-
ish in perpetual greenness. The Prophet prays for
people of this kind: *And may your whole burnt offering*
be fat. So too you read in praise of Aaron that fire   *Ps 19:4 [20:3]*
consumed his sacrifice every day.* All this seems to   **Si 45:14 [17]*
suggest nothing other than that good works should
be seasoned with the fervor of devotion and the
sweetness of spiritual grace.

Do you think we can find a fourth spring, so that we may recover a paradise made extremely pleasant by the waters of four springs? If we do not hope that the earthly paradise* will be restored to us, how will we hope for the kingdom of heaven? *If I have told you about earthly things and you do not believe me, how will you believe me if I tell you about heavenly things?* But now we must let our expectation of what is to come be strengthened by the disclosure of what is before us. We have a paradise much better and far more delightful than our first parents had, and our paradise is Christ the Lord.

*Gen 2:10

Jn 3:12

In him we have already found three springs; let us look for a fourth. We have the waters of forgiveness from the spring of mercy to wash away sins. We have the waters of discernment from the spring of wisdom to quench our thirst. We have the waters of devotion from the spring of grace to water the plants of good works. Let us look for boiling water, the waters of zeal, to cook our food. These waters soften and cook our affections, and they come bubbling up from the spring of love. This is why the Prophet says, *My heart became hot within me, and as I mused a fire burned.* In another place too, *Zeal for your house,* he says, *has consumed me.* Loving righteousness from the sweetness of devotion, of course he has a hatred for wickedness* from the fervor of zeal.

Ps 39:3[38:4]
Ps 69:9 [68:10]

*Ps 45:7 [44:8]

See whether it was not of these springs that Isaiah foretold that *with joy you will draw water from the Saviour's springs.* And so you may know that this promise refers to the present life and not the life to come, notice what follows: *You will say on that day, Praise the Lord and call upon his name!* Calling refers to the present, as in *Call upon me in the day of distress.*

Is 12:3

Is 12:4
Ps 50 [49]:15

7. Furthermore, of these four springs, three seem to correspond to the three orders in the Church, one to each of them, while the first is common to

all. In many ways we all offend* and need the spring
of mercy in which we can wash away the filth of
our offenses. We all have sinned, I say, and fallen
short of the glory of God.* Prelates, celibates, and
couples all—if we say we have no sin, we deceive
ourselves.* Therefore because no one is clean from
filth* we all need the spring of mercy, and Noah,
Daniel, and Job³ must hasten to this spring with the
same longing.

As for the other springs, Job must seek especially
the spring of wisdom. Because he walks so much in
the midst of snares, for him to turn away from evil*
seems a great thing. Daniel must run to the spring of
grace for he needs to lard his deeds of penance and
the hardships of abstinence with the grace of devotion. It is fitting that we do everything with cheer-
fulness because *God loves a cheerful giver.* Our earth is
not at all receptive to this kind of seed—that is, to a
good way of life. It will easily perish, easily wither,
unless it is helped by frequent irrigation. That is why
we rightly ask for this kind of grace in the Lord's
Prayer under the term *daily bread.* We must fear that
the terrible curse of the prophetic imprecation may
perhaps fall upon us: *Let them be like the grass on the
housetops that withers before it is plucked.* The spring of
zeal is especially appropriate for Noah because this
zeal should especially adorn prelates.

8. So then Christ reveals these four springs to
us in himself while we are still living in the flesh.*
The fifth, which is the spring of life,* he promises
us after this age. The Prophet was thirsting for this
spring when he said, *My soul has thirsted for God,
the living spring.* Perhaps it was because of the four

*Jm 3:2

*Rm 3:23

*1 Jn 1:8
*Jb 14:4 VL

*Ps 37 [36]:27

2 Cor 9:7

Lk 11:3

Ps 129 [128]:6

*Gal 2:20
*Ps 36:9 [35:10]

Ps 42:2 [41:3]

---

³ See Ezk 14:14. Noah represents *praelati,* those who hold
office in the Church, Daniel represents the celibate, *continentes,*
and Job the married, *conjugi.*

*Jn 19:34
springs that he was wounded in four places* while he was still alive on the cross, and because of the fifth that he was pierced in the side when he had already *Jn 19:30 given up his spirit.* He was still living when they *[Ps 21:17] dug into his hands and his feet* so that he might offer us four springs from himself while we are still living. The fifth wound he received when he had already breathed his last so that he might open to us a fifth spring within himself after death.

While talking about the mysteries of the Lord's birth we have come unexpectedly to ponder the mysteries of his passion. But it is no wonder if we seek in his passion what Christ brought in his *Gen 42:27; birth: it was then that the sack was cut open* and [Ps 29:12] he poured out as the price of our redemption° the °[Ps 48:9] money concealed in it.

On the Three Comminglings of Divine Power

1.   G**REAT ARE THE WORKS** *of the Lord,*   *Ps 111 [110]:2* says the Prophet. Great are all his works, brothers—indeed, great is he!—but we must especially look at those that seem greatest among them. This is why the same Prophet sings, *The Lord has done great things for us!*   *Ps 126 [125]:3*

Three of his works particularly proclaim his wonderful dealings with us: our primal creation, our present redemption, and our future glorification. How each of these proclaims the greatness of your works, O Lord!* To you it belongs to show your   **Ps 92:5 [91:6]* people the power of your works;* as for us, let us at   **Ps 111[110]:6* least not be silent about these same works.

In these three works, my brothers, we must reflect on a threefold commingling of heavenly work and divine power. In the first work, our creation, God formed human beings from the dust of the earth and breathed into our face the breath of life.* What   **Gen 2:7* a craftsman, what a joiner of things! At his nod the dust of the earth and the breath of life are cemented together. The dust, of course, had already been created earlier, when in the beginning God created heaven and earth,* but the breath has not a general   **Gen 1:1*

107

but a particular constitution; it is not created in the mass, but is breathed exquisitely into each being.

*Leo the Great,
Sermo 21.3*

Recognize your dignity, O human being,* recognize the glory of human constitution! Along with the world, you have a body, for it is fitting that the being set over the whole aggregate of this physical creation resemble it at least in part. But you have something more sublime as well, and are not in any way to be matched with other creatures. Bound together and united within you are flesh and soul, one of them 'formed' and the other 'breathed in'.

2. But to whose advantage is this commingling? Whom does this union benefit? According to the wisdom of the children of this age, when lower things are joined to higher, those who have power prevail and use the humbler at their whim. The stronger grind the less strong under foot, the learned mock the ignorant, the clever manipulate the artless, and the powerful despise the weaklings.

Not so in your work, God, not so in your commingling! Nor for this did you join breath to dust, the sublime to the humble, a worthy and excellent creature to an abject and useless mass! Who cannot see, brothers, how much soul benefits body? Would unbesoulled flesh not be an insensate trunk? From the soul comes beauty, from the soul growth, from the soul clarity of vision and the sound of the voice—in brief, every sense is from the soul. Divine love is what this union commends to me, divine love is what I see written on the very page of my own creation, divine love is what the utterly gracious hand of the Creator not only proclaims to, but bestows upon, me.

3. Great would this union have been, dearly beloved, if only it had continued constant. As it is, although protected by a divine seal—for God created humanity in his own image and likeness*—the seal has alas been broken and the unity dissipated. While

Gen 1:26-27

the seal was still new, the worst of thieves approached and broke it, and so, with the divine likeness altered, wretched humankind has been compared to senseless beasts, and has become like them.* *Ps 49:12, 20 [48:13, 21]*

God made human beings upright. This is his likeness, of which it is written that *upright is the Lord our God, and no iniquity is in him.* He made humanity *Ps 92:15 [91:16]* true and just as well, as he himself is truth and justice. Nor could that union be disunited while the integrity of the seal endured. Then came the forger, promising the ignorant a better seal, and alas, alas! he broke what had been impressed by the divine hand. *You will be like gods,* he said, *knowing good and evil.* *Gen 3:5*

O spiteful one! O wicked one! What good is the likeness of this knowledge to them? Let them be like gods, indeed, upright and just; let them be true, like God, whom no sin touches. While this seal endures the unity will endure. Now we wretches experience what the cunning of diabolical deceit talked us into. Once the seal is broken, a bitter divorce, a melancholy dissolution ensues. Where is what you said, evil one: *You will never die?* Look! We all die; no *Gen 3:4* human being lives and does not see death.* *Ps 89:48 [88:49]*

4. But what is to be, Lord God? Is your work never to be restored, and is the one who has fallen never going to rise?* No one can remake us save the *Ps 41:8 [40:9]* One who made us. Therefore, *because of the misery of the needy and the groans of the poor, I will now rise up, says the Lord. I will place them in safety; I will deal loyally for them.* Then *the enemy will have no advantage over* *Ps 12:5 [11:6]* *them, nor the child of iniquity have power to harm them.* *Ps 89:22 [88:23]* I am making a new commingling, he says, where I am setting my seal more distinctly and unassailably; not one made in my image,* but the very image *Gen 1:26* itself,* the brightness of my glory and the figure of *2 Cor 4:4; Col 1:15* my substance;° one not made, but begotten before °*Heb 1:3* the ages. And, lest you fear that it may be broken, he

Ps 21:16 [22:15] has said, *My strength is dried up like a potsherd,* such a potsherd that not even 'the hammer of the whole earth'[1] can in any way damage it.

So while the first union was made out of two, the second is now a conjoining of three, so that from this you may learn to approach the mystery of the Trinity. The Word that was in the beginning with *Jn 1:1-2* God, and that was God;* the soul that was created from nothing and did not exist before; the flesh, taken from the mass of corruption, yet by divine craft kept free from any corruption as no flesh ever yet had been—these [three] are combined by an indissoluble bond in the unity of a person. You have in them a threefold genus of power: what did not exist was created; what had perished was restored; what was above all things was made a little lower *Ps 8:5;* than the angels.*
Heb 2:7, 9

Mt 13:33 These are the measures of flour in the gospel that are evenly leavened* to be the bread of angels which *Ps 78 [77]:25* humans eat,* the bread that strengthens the human *Ps 104 [103]:15* heart.* Happy the woman, blessed among women,° *Lk 1:42* in whose chaste womb this bread was baked when the fire of the Holy Spirit overshadowed her!* Happy, *Lk 1:35* I tell you, the woman who stirred the leaven of her faith into these three measures. Indeed, she conceived in faith, she gave birth in faith, and, as Elizabeth said, *Blessed is she who believed, because what was* *Lk 1:45* *spoken to her by the Lord has come to pass.*

Do not be surprised that I say that the Word was united to flesh by means of her faith, when he received his very flesh from her flesh. Surely, that this *Mt 13:33* is said in a parable of the kingdom of heaven* can be no obstacle to this present interpretation. Nor does it seem inappropriate for the kingdom of heaven to be compared to Mary's faith, by which it is restored.

[1] Jer 50:23, a reference to the king of Babylon.

5. No creature whatever, therefore, can undo the bond of this union. Not even the prince of this world* has any power over him, nor was John [the Baptist] himself worthy to untie the thong of his sandal.* What then? Surely it has to be undone to some extent, or else what has been undone is not done up again. Unbroken bread, hidden treasure, concealed wisdom—what use are all of these?* John was right to weep when no one was found to open the book and undo its seals;* as long as it stayed closed no one of us could gain access to that divine wisdom.

Open the book, thou Lamb of God, true meekness! Offer to Jewry your hands and feet for piercing* so that the treasure of salvation and plentiful redemption* concealed in them may come forth. Then *break your bread for the hungry.* Only you can break it, you who alone are able to stand in order to repair what is breached. In that breach only you* have the power of laying down your life, to take it up again* when you choose.

By your mercy, then, let this temple be somewhat undone,* but not utterly undone. Let the flesh be separated from the soul, but let the Word preserve the incorruption of the flesh while bestowing full liberty on the soul—so that, alone among the dead, the soul may act in liberty,* leading out of the dungeon the prisoners who sit in darkness and the shadow of death.[2] Let the holy soul lay down the spotless flesh, but to be taken up again on the third day, so that in dying he may destroy death,* and that human life may rise with him as he rises.

So it was done, dearly beloved, and let us rejoice that it was so done. By that death, death died, and

*Jn 14:30

*Lk 3:16

*Mt 13:44;
Si 20:30, 31

*Rv 5:4-5

*Ps 22:16 [21:17]
*Ps 130 [129]:7
Is 58:7

*Ps 106 [105]:23

*Jn 10:17-18

*Jn 2:19

*[Ps 87:6]

*Col 3:3-4

---

[2] Is 9:2, 42:7, used in the Advent Magnificat antiphon *O Clavis David* on December 20.

we have been born anew into a hope of life through
the resurrection of Jesus Christ from the dead.*

   6. Now who will tell what will take place in the
third union? *Eye has not seen, nor ear heard, nor has
it entered into the human heart, what God has prepared
for those who love him.* The consummation will come
about when Christ hands the kingdom over to the
God and Father,* and the two will be no longer in
one flesh but in one spirit.* If the Word, in cleaving
to flesh, became flesh,* much more will one who
cleaves to God be one spirit with him.

   In this intermediate moderate union humility is
shown, and extremely great humility,[3] but in this
union the perfect glorification we are waiting for
and longing for is laid up for us*—if it is for us. If
we remember that in the first conjoining—in which
a human being is made by joining soul and flesh—
love is commended, then rightly is humility preeminent in the second, because only the virtue of
humility is a restorative for wounded love. Moreover,
that a creature of rational soul is united to an earthly
body is not wholly to be attributed to humility. It is
not mingled with flesh by its own choice, but is infused by being created, and created by being infused.
Clearly this is not so for the supreme Spirit. Being
more completely good, he came to an undefiled
body of his own free choice and pleasure. Rightly,
then, does glorification follow love and humility, because without love nothing can profit us,* and no
one, unless he humbles himself, will be exalted.*

*1 Pt 1:3

1 Cor 2:9

*1 Cor 15:24
*1 Cor 6:16-17
*Jn 1:14

*2 Tm 4:8

*1 Cor 13:3
*Lk 14:11

---

[3] SBOp 4:256, 9, has *Et in hac quidem unione, media humilitas
. . .* We have read *media* as modifying *unione.*

On Christ's Birth and Passion, On Mary's Virginity and Fruitfulness

1. **B**ROTHERS, I am pondering two kinds of things in this birth of the Lord. They are not only distinct, but also very unlike. The Child who is born is God; and the mother of whom he is born is a virgin; and the birth itself is painless. A novel light shines out of heaven in the darkness;* the angel brings good news of great joy; a multitude of the heavenly host gives praise; glory is given to God, and peace to people of good will. The shepherds go with haste, they find what was described to them, they tell it to others; everyone who hears is filled with wonder.*

Is 9:2

Lk 2:10-18

These, and things like them, dearly beloved, pertain to divine power, not to human frailty. They are vessels of gold and silver by which we minister at the Lord's table even to the needy today, on account of the great solemnity. We are not to take them away; it is not the gold platter and goblet that are given to us, but the food and drink that are on them. *Observe carefully*, says the Sage, *what is set before you.*

Pr 23:1 VL

As for me, I recognize as mine the time and place of this birth, the tenderness of the infant body, the

113

crying and tears of the baby, and also the poverty and night watches of the shepherds to whom the Saviour's birth is first announced. These things are mine, they are done for me, they are set before me, they are set out for me to imitate.

In winter Christ was born, he was born at night: are we to believe that chance determined that he to whom winter and summer, day and night, belong was born in such intemperate weather and in darkness? Other babies do not choose when they are born—those who have hardly yet begun to live possess no use of reason, no freedom to choose, no ability to deliberate. Christ, my brothers, although he was not a human being, still he was in the beginning with God, and he was God;* and inasmuch as he is the power of God and the wisdom of God,* the same wisdom and power as now was his. So, when the Son of God was about to be born—with the choice to select whatever time he wanted—he chose fairly distressing circumstances, especially for a baby, the son of a poor mother who scarcely had swaddling clothes with which to wrap him and a manger in which to lay him. Although the need was so great, I hear no mention being made of pelts. The first Adam was clothed in garments of pelts;* the second was wrapped in swaddling clothes.*

Jn 1:1
1 Cor 1:24

Gen 3:21
Lk 2:7
Jn 12:31

This is not the world's judgement*—either he is mistaken or the world is wrong. Divine wisdom, however, cannot be mistaken. Rightly then is the shrewdness of the flesh—and this is death—hostile to God, and the shrewdness of the world called foolishness.* What then? Christ, who does not make mistakes, chooses what is quite distressing to the flesh. So then, it is better, it is more advantageous, it is more suitable it should be chosen. If anybody should teach or advise something different they are to be avoided as seducers.

Rm 8:7;
1 Cor 3:19

2. Now, moreover, he also chose to be born at night. Where are those who take action to display themselves so brashly? Christ chooses what he judges most salutary; you choose what he rejects! Which of the two of you is the wiser? Whose judgement is more just? Whose opinion is more balanced?

Then let Christ be silent—he does not vaunt himself, he does not claim greatness, he does not declare himself—and look, an angel announces him, and a multitude of the heavenly host praises him!* You, then, you who follow Christ, hide the treasure you have found.* Love to be unknown. Let a stranger's mouth praise you; let your own be silent.*

Lk 2:13

Mt 13:44

Pr 27:2

In addition, Christ is born in a stable and laid in a manger. Is he not the one who says, *Mine is the earth and its fullness?* Why then does he choose a stable? Obviously, to reject the glory of the world and to condemn worldly vanity. His tongue does not yet speak, and everything about him cries aloud, preaches, declares the good news. Not even his infant limbs are silent.

Ps 50 [49]:12

In everything is the world's judgment censured, turned upside down, and confuted. What human being, if given the choice, would not choose a strong body and the age of understanding rather than of babyhood? O Wisdom, drawn out of secret places!* O Wisdom, truly incarnate and veiled! And yet, brothers, he is the child promised long ago by Isaiah, knowing how to reject evil and choose good.* The body's self-indulgence, then is evil, but hardship is good; in fact, the wise Child, the infant Word, chooses the latter and rejects the former. The Word became flesh,* weak flesh, infant flesh, tender flesh, powerless flesh, flesh incapable of any work, of any effort.

[Jb 28:18]

Is 7:14-15

Jn 1:14

3. And truly, brothers, the Word became flesh and dwelt among us. While he was in the beginning with God,* he lived in light unapproachable° and no one

Jn 1:14
°1 Tm 6:16

could grasp it. *For who has searched into the mind of the Lord, or who has been his counselor?* A fleshly person will not perceive what belongs to the Spirit of God,* but now even the fleshly can grasp what has become flesh. If they know how to hear nothing except flesh, look, the Word has become flesh; let everyone hear it, even in the flesh.

O human being, Wisdom is presented to you in flesh: the Wisdom that was once concealed. Look how it now presses on the very senses of your flesh! It preaches to you, if I may say so, in a fleshly way: Flee pleasure, *because death is stationed near the gateway of delight*; repent, because this is how the kingdom comes near.* The stable preaches this to you, the manger proclaims it, the infant's limbs clearly speak it, the tears and crying proclaim the good news.

Christ cries, yes, but not like other babies, or at least not for the same reason others do. In others the senses prevail, in Christ unwavering affection.[1] Other babies are passive, not active, inasmuch as they do not as yet have the use of the wills. They whimper from suffering, Christ from co-suffering.[2] They bewail the heavy yoke laid on all Adam's children;* Christ the sins of Adam's offspring. For these sins he now sheds; later he will shed blood as well.

O hardness of my heart! O Lord, if only, as your Word became flesh, so my heart too might become fleshly! In fact, you promised this through the Prophet: *I will take away from you the heart of stone and give you a heart of flesh.*

4. Brothers, Christ's tears cause in me both shame and sorrow. I was playing outside in the streets, and in the seclusion of the king's bedroom a judgement of death was delivered against me. His Only-begotten

Rm 11:34
*1 Cor 2:14

RB 7.24
*Mt 3:2

*Si 40:1

Ezk 36:26

---

[1] *affectus*, a steadfast, rather than transitory, affection (*affectio*).
[2] *ex passione . . . ex compassione.*

heard it; he went out, having laid aside his diadem, clothed in sackcloth with ashes sprinkled on his head, his feet bare, weeping and wailing* because his poor servant had been condemned to death. Suddenly I observe him coming. I am amazed at the novelty. I inquire as to the cause, and I hear it. What am I to do? Shall I go on playing, and play his tears false? Obviously if I am insane and mentally unbalanced, I shall not follow him, nor shall I mourn with him as he mourns. You see where my shame comes from? And my sorrow and fear, where do they come from? I reckon the amount of my danger from consideration of the remedy. I was unaware; I seemed healthy to myself—and look, the Virgin's Son, the son of the Most High God,* is sent and ordered to be killed, to heal my wounds with the balm of his precious blood.

*2 Sm 15:30

*Mk 5:7

Recognize, O human being, how grievous are the wounds for which Christ the Lord had to be wounded! If they had not been death-dealing,* and eternally death, never would the Son of God have died to heal them. Therefore I am ashamed, dearly beloved, carelessly to ignore my own suffering, for which I see so much co-suffering shown by such great majesty. The Son of God suffers with us and weeps; a human being is suffering—and who is laughing? In this way the sheer appraisal of the remedy heightens both my sorrow and my fear.

*Jn 11:4

5. But if I diligently observe the instructions of the physician, there will be an opportunity for consolation. Just as I recognize the seriousness of the disease for which so great a remedy is prescribed, so too, from this very fact, I conclude that it is not incurable. A wise doctor—or indeed, Wisdom himself—would not uselessly apply the most precious drugs. Moreover, everyone agrees that their application would be useless, not only if the cure would be

easy without them, but much more if it would be impossible even with them. Once conceived, then, hope moves us to repentance and quite powerfully enkindles our desire.

Clearly another ground for consolation is what was shown to the shepherds as they kept watch*—a visitation and an address from the angels. *Woe to you who are rich, you who have your consolation*, so you no longer deserve to have a heavenly one! How many who were noble according to the flesh, now many powerful, now many of the wise of this world,* were resting on soft coverlets at that hour, and not one of them was held worthy to see that new light, to know that great joy, and to hear the angels singing *Glory to God in the highest!*[3]

Therefore let human beings realize that those who do not know human toil* do not deserve to be visited by angels. Let them realize how pleasing to the citizens above is toil whose purpose is spiritual, seeing that they mark out by their announcement— such a happy announcement—those who toil for their physical livelihood, spurred on by physical necessity. In them they recognize the human pattern by which God established that Adam should eat his bread in the sweat of his brow.*

6. I beseech you, dearly beloved, to consider quite carefully how much God does for your encouragement and salvation.* His words must not be found in you unfruitful, words so living and active,* words sure and worthy of full acceptance,* words not so much on the lips as in the labor. Do you think, my brothers, that it would be only a small disappointment to me if I knew that the very word I am speaking to you now was to wither away in your hearts empty and without profit? And who am I,

*Lk 2:8

Lk 6:24

*1 Cor 1:26

*Ps 73 [72]:5

*Gen 3:19

*2 Cor 1:6
*Heb 4:12
*1 Tm 1:15, 4:9

---

[3] Lk 2:14, as in the *Gloria* used in the Mass.

and what are my words? If an insignificant person would be grieved because so paltry a labor of his voice is useless, in fact nothing, much more justly will the Lord of majesty feel displeasure if our rigor or carelessness should render meaningless his, such great, work. Do not let this happen to your servants, you who deigned to put on the form of a servant for their salvation,*

>the Only-begotten of God the Father,
>who is over all,
>God blessed forever.*

*Ph 2:7

*Rm 9:5

ON THE LORD'S BIRTHDAY

SERMON FOUR

On the Lowliness and Humility of Christ's Birth

1. **A**CKNOWLEDGE, dearly beloved brothers, the greatness of today's solemnity[1]—the day for it is short, and the expanse of earth is narrow. It is extended both in place and in time. It first takes possession of the night, and it fills heaven before it fills earth. The night was made as bright as the day when a new light from heaven shone round[2] the shepherds at an *untimely hour of the night*.[3] And that you may know in what place the joys of this solemnity began to be celebrated, the joy that already belongs to the angels is going to be preached to all people. Yet immediately a multitude of the heavenly host was present, resounding with *Lk 2:9-13* divine praises.* This is why this solemn night—more

---

[1] Chrysogonus Waddell, 'The Liturgical Dimension of Twelfth-century Cistercian Preaching', in Carolyn Muessig, *Medieval Monastic* Preaching (Leiden: Brill, 1998) 335–349, here 344–345, points out that in two sentences Bernard alludes to liturgical texts from the offices of Christmas Vigils, Easter Vigils, Saint Benedict, and the Preface of the Christmas Mass. See the following notes for his illustrations.

[2] From the preface of the Mass for Christmas.

[3] [3 K 3:20] used as the seventh responsory for the Office of Saint Benedict.

than others—is spent in psalms, hymns, and spiritual canticles,* and why we must unhesitatingly believe that, above all in these vigils, the heavenly princes are going ahead of us, joined with those singing psalms,* in the midst of young women playing on timbrels.

How many altars are gleaming today with gems and gold! How many walls are everywhere decorated with tapestries? Do you think the angels turn aside to these, and turn away from ragged human beings? If this is so, why did they appear to the shepherds of the sheep rather than to the kings of the earth or the priests of the temple? And why does the Saviour himself, to whom both gold and silver belong,* consecrate holy poverty in his own body? Then surely, why is that poverty spoken of by angels in such detail? Not without some mystical reason is the Saviour wrapped in swaddling clothes and laid in a manger, and this is plainly declared to us by the angel as a sign: *This*, he says, *will be a sign for you: you will find a child wrapped in swaddling clothes.* Your swaddling clothes were set as a sign, Lord Jesus, yet a sign which even to this day many oppose.* Many indeed are called, but not many are chosen, and so not many are signed.*

I recognize, truly I recognize Jesus, the great high priest, clothed in filthy garments while he argues with the devil.* I am speaking to those who know the Scriptures and to whom the prophetic vision of Zechariah is not unfamiliar. When indeed our Head had been lifted up above our enemies,* from this time clearly he has changed his garment, he has clothed himself in beauty, he has been wrapped in light as with a robe.* He gave us an example so that we too may do the same.* In fact, in a fight an iron breastplate* is more useful than a linen robe, even though the one is a burden and the other an honor. A day will come when the members too will follow

Eph 5:19;
Col 3:16

[Ps 67:26]

Hg 2:8

Lk 2:12

Lk 2:34

Lk 2:12, 34;
cf. Rv 7:4-8

Zec 3:1-3;
Jude 9

Ps 27 [26]:6

Ps 104 [103]:1-2
Jn 13:15
Rv 9:9

the Head, so that the body, now whole, will sing
praise with one spirit,* and say, *You have removed my*
sackcloth and girdled me with joy!

2. *You shall find a child,* the Evangelist says, *wrapped*
in swaddling clothes and lying in a manger. And a little
later, *They came,* he says, *with haste, and found Mary*
and Joseph, and the child lying in the manger.

Why is it that humility alone seems to be commended by the angel, yet it is not the only thing
the shepherds found? Perhaps the angel particularly
commends humility because, when the others fell
through pride, he himself had stood firm in humility. Or perhaps humility is proclaimed from heaven
because it is to be presented as the virtue proper to
divine majesty.

Yet alone it could not be found, for grace is always given to the humble.* *They found,* then, *Mary*
and Joseph, and the child lying in the manger. Just as the
Saviour's infancy demonstrates manifest humility,
so continence is suitably represented by the Virgin,
and justice by Joseph, a just man,* whose praise is
in the gospel.* Does anyone not know that continence is owing to the flesh? Justice, however, is
the virtue that assigns everyone what is due them,[4]
and this is necessary with regard to our neighbors.
Furthermore, humility reconciles us to God, makes
us subject to God, and in us pleases God. As the
blessed Virgin says, *God has looked on the humility of*
his handmaiden.

Consequently those who fornicate sin against
their own bodies;* those who are unjust sin against
their neighbors; those who are overbearing and

Marginal references:
*1 Cor 14:15
Ps 30:11 [29:12]
Lk 2:12, 16
*Jas 4:6; Pr 3:34
*Mt 1:19
*2 Cor 8:18
Lk 1:48
*1 Cor 6:18

---

[4] The definition given by M. Tullius Cicero (106–43 BC), *De*
finibus bonorum et malorum 5.23.65; and in *The* Institutes *of Jus-*
tinian, B. Moyle, trans. (third edition: Oxford: Oxford University Press, 1896) 3–5.

puffed up sin against God. The fornicators disgrace themselves, the unjust trouble their neighbors, and the proud, so far as is in their power, dishonor God. *My glory I give to no other*, says the Lord.* And the proud say, 'I will take it for my own, even if you do not give it'. Nor does the angelic distribution, giving glory to God and peace to people,* please them. Therefore they do not worship God, but exalt themselves against God, which is clearly irreligious and faithless. What is religion if not worship of God?* And who worships God if not someone who is willingly subject to him, and, as the eyes of servants are on the hands of their master, have the eyes of their hearts on their Lord?*

*Is 42:8

*Lk 2:14

*Augustine, De civitate Dei 10.1; Jb 28:28 VL

*Ps 123 [122]:2

3. So that Mary and Joseph, and the child lying in the manger, may always be found in us, *let us live soberly, justly, and religiously in this present age, while we wait for the blessed hope and coming of the glory of the great God*. To this end the grace of God appeared, instructing us; through this, too, his glory is going to appear. You have it thus: *The grace of God has appeared to all people, instructing us to renounce impiety and worldly desires, and to live soberly, justly, and religiously in this present age, while we wait for the blessed hope and coming of the glory of the great God*. Grace appeared in a little child to instruct us; 'he will be great', however, as Gabriel said of him, and those whom the little child instructs in humility of heart and meekness* he will afterward magnify and glorify, he, the great and glorious one who is coming,

Jesus Christ, our Lord.

Ti 2:12

Ti 2:11-12

*Ti 2:11-13; Lk 1:32; Mt 11:29

On the Father of Mercies, Who Has Mercy on Our Many Miseries

1. *B**LESSED BE THE GOD** and Father of our Lord Jesus Christ, the Father of mercies and God of all consolation, who consoles us in all our affliction.* Blessed be he, who out of the boundless love with which he loved us,* sent us his beloved Son* in whom he was well pleased;° through him we have been reconciled and have peace with him.† This Son is to be for us both the mediator of this reconciliation and the pledge. We have nothing to fear, my brothers, under so constant a mediator, nothing to doubt concerning so sure a pledge. But what kind of mediator is this, you ask, who is born in a stable, laid in a manger, wrapped like other infants in swaddling clothes,* who cries like the others—a baby who lies there just as others have always done? He is plainly a great mediator even in all those things *that are for peace*, seeking it not in a perfunctory, but in an effective, way. Yes, he is an infant, but the infant Word, and not even his infancy is silent.[1]

2 Cor 1:3-4
*Eph 2:4
*Gal 4:4
°Mt 3:17;
†Rm 5:10, 1

*Lk 2:7

Ps 122 [121]:6

---

[1] *Infans* means 'without speech'; an 'infant' is therefore a child who has not yet learned to speak.

Be consoled, be consoled, says the Lord our God.   Is 40:1
Emmanuel, *God with us,* is saying this. The stable   Is 7:14, Mt 1:23
proclaims this, the manger proclaims it, the tears
proclaim it, the swaddling clothes proclaim it. The
stable proclaims that it is prepared for the healing of
the man who had fallen among thieves;[2] the manger
proclaims that food is being served to the same
man, who had been compared to beasts;* the tears   *Ps 49:12, 20
proclaim, the swaddling clothes proclaim that the   [48:13]
bloody wounds of this same person are being washed
and wiped clean.

In fact, Christ needed none of these things; none
of them are for his sake, but all are instead for the sake
of the elect.* *They will revere my son,*° says the Father   *2 Tm 2:10
of mercies. Yes indeed, Lord, they do revere him. But   °Mt 24:22;
who are they? Evidently not the Jews, to whom he   Mt 21:37
was sent, but the elect, for whose sake he was sent.

2. We ourselves revere him in the manger, we revere him on the gibbet, we revere him in the tomb.
Devoutly do we acknowledge that he was a tender
child for our sake, and blood-stained for our sake;
we revere him, pallid for our sake, buried for our
sake. Devoutly do we adore the Saviour's infancy
along with the wise men, devoutly do we embrace
him along with holy Simeon, as we receive your
mercy in the midst of your temple.*   *Mt 2:11;
[Christ] is the one of whom we read, *The mercy of*   Lk 2:28;
the Lord is from eternity.° What else is coeternal with   Ps 48:9 [47:10]
the Father except the Son and the Holy Spirit? And   °Ps 103 [102]:17
each of these two is not so much merciful as mercy
itself. Yet the Father is no less mercy—and these

---

[2] In Luke 10:34, the Good Samaritan story, the man who fell
among thieves was taken to a *stabulum,* an abode for persons or
animals, hence an 'inn' or a 'stable'. The nativity story, Luke 2:7,
does not mention a stable; the holy family found no room in a
deversorium—which is also the word used for the 'upper room'
in which Jesus chose to eat the last supper (Luke 22:11).

*Quicumque
(Athanasian
Creed)

*Collect, Mass for
the Dead

*Ps 36:6 [35:7]
*Ps 25 [24]:10
*Ps 101[100]:1

Rm 9:18

Ezk 18:23

*Ps 103:13

Ps 62:11-12
[61:12-13]

three are nothing else than one mercy, just as they are one essence, one wisdom, one divinity, one majesty.* Nevertheless, in that God is called the 'Father of mercies', does anyone not see the Son designated by his proper name? He whose nature is to have mercy and to spare* is well described as the 'Father of mercies'.

3. But perhaps someone may ask, 'How is it his nature to have mercy when his judgements are a great deep?* The psalm does not say, "All his ways are mercy" alone, but "are mercy and truth".* He whose mercy and judgement we sing* is not less just than merciful'.

That *he has mercy on the one he chooses, and hardens the one he chooses* is certainly true, but his nature is to have mercy. From himself he takes the matter and, as it were, the seedbed of showing mercy. What he judges and condemns we ourselves, to some extent, force him to judge and condemn, so that mercy and chastisement seem to proceed from his heart very differently. Listen to what he himself says: *Is it my will that sinners should die, says the Lord, and not rather turn from their ways and live?*

We are right, then, not to call him 'the Father of judgements', or 'of retributive justice', but the 'Father of mercies'. This is not only because mercy seems more natural to a father than outrage—and like a father he shows mercy to the children who fear him*—but still more because he takes the cause and source of showing mercy from his own nature, but that of judging and taking retribution more from ours.

4. But if for this reason he is the Father of mercy, why is he 'Father of mercies'? *God has spoken once,* says the Prophet, *these two things have I heard: that power belongs to God, and to you, Lord, mercy.* Furthermore, the Apostle commends to us this same mercy as twofold—in the one Word, in the one Son—

when he speaks of a Father not of only one mercy but of 'mercies',* and a God not of one but of '*all* consolation', who consoles us not just in this or that, but in '*all* our affliction'. *The Lord's mercies are many*, someone* has said, evidently because *many are the afflictions of the righteous, and from them all the Lord will rescue them.*

There is one Son of God, one Word, but our manifold misery looks not only for great mercy but for a multitude of mercies.* But perhaps on account of the twofold substance in which our human condition consists, since each of the two is so miserable, we may not inappropriately call human misery twofold, although it is manifold in each of the two. Indeed, the afflictions of both our body and our heart are multiplied,* but the one who healed a whole person* rescued that person from both constraints.

*[Ps 50:3]

*[Ps 24:17]
*Jn 7:23

Since, therefore, the one and only Son of God is even now coming for the sake of souls—that is, to take away the sins of the world*—and will come a second time for the sake of bodies, to revive them and conform them to the body of his glory,* perhaps it will not seem inappropriate if in blessing the 'Father of mercies' we confess this twofold mercy. Taking on both the body and soul of human nature, [he said] not once, 'Be consoled', but, as we recalled earlier, *Be consoled, be consoled, says the Lord your God.* Evidently we are to be certain that he who did not refuse either is going to save both.

*Jn 1:29

*Ph 3:21

5. But in whom, do you think? Clearly in his people. Even now *he will save* not everyone but *his people from their sins,* and later he will conform not every body but 'the body of our humiliation' to 'the body of his glory'.* In short, he is consoling his people, at least his humble people, whom he is going to save*—for he humbles the eyes of the proud.° Do you want to know his people? *To you are the poor*

*Ibid.

*Mt 1:21
°Ps 18:27 [17:28]

Ps 10:14 [9:35]
*David. 1 Sm
13:14;Ac 13:22
°Lk 6:24

committed, says the man after God's heart.* But he himself says in the Gospel, *Woe to you who are rich, you who have your consolation.*° Dearly beloved, if only we may always choose to be found among the people to whom he does not say 'Woe', but whom the Lord their God consoles!

Why should he console those who have their own consolation? The infancy of Christ offers no consolation to the talkative, the tears of Christ offer no consolation to those who roar with laughter, his swaddling clothes offer no consolation to those who strut about in fine garments, the stable and the manger offer no consolation to those who love the

*Mt 23:6

best seats in the synagogues*—but perhaps they will appear content to yield this universal consolation to

*Lam 3:26

those who wait silently for the Lord,* to mourners, and to the ragged poor.

Yet let them listen, because not even the angels themselves console the others. The joyful news of the new light is brought to shepherds who are watching and keeping watches by night; to them is the Sav-

*Lk 2:8-11

iour said to be born.* On the poor and those who toil—not on 'you who are rich, you who have your consolation' and your divine 'Woe'—has *a holy day dawned'³* amid these watches of the night; on them

*Ps 13 [138]:12

has the night become bright as the day*—or rather, been changed into day. As the angel says, *To you is*

*Lk 2:11
Rm 13:12

born a Saviour this day',* not this night. Indeed *the night is far gone, the day is near*—the true day of days,

*Lk 3:6

'the salvation of God',*
Jesus Christ our Lord,
who is over all, God blessed forever.

*Rm 9:5

Amen.*

---

³ Neh [2 Esd] 8:9, used in the responsory *Beata viscera* at Vigils on Christmas and in the *Alleluia* of the Day Mass of Christmas.

ON THE FEASTS OF SAINT STEPHEN, SAINT JOHN, AND THE HOLY INNOCENTS[1]

1. *B**LESSED IS HE who comes in the name of the Lord; the Lord is God, and he has shone upon us*. Blessed is the name of his glory, which is holy.* The Holy[2] that was born of Mary° has not come without purpose, but is copiously pouring forth both the name and the grace of holiness. This indeed is why Stephen is holy, why John is holy, and why even the Innocents are holy. That this threefold celebration accompanies the Lord's birthday is a helpful ordering of things—not only does an unbroken thread of devotion run through this series of feasts, but the fruit of the Lord's birth is also made known to us as by a trail of events quite clearly visible. In this way we may observe a threefold image of holiness in these three celebrations; nor, apart from these three kinds of holiness, do I think we can easily find a fourth among human beings. In blessed Stephen we have both the deed and the will of martyrdom; in blessed John we have only the will; in the blessed Innocents we have only the deed. All these drank from the cup of salvation,* either in both body and spirit, or only in spirit or only in body.

You will indeed drink my cup, the Lord said to James and John.* No doubt he was speaking of the cup of his passion. Then when he said to Peter, *Follow me*, evidently calling him to imitate his passion, Peter turned and saw the disciple whom Jesus loved following,* not so much with physical steps as with

Ps 118 [117]: 26, 27
*[Dn 3:52]; Prayer of Azariah 30
°Lk 1:35

*Ps 116 [114]:13

*Mt 20:23

*Jn 21:19-20

---

[1] Celebrated respectively on 26, 27, and 28 December.
[2] In Latin, the child born of Mary is *sanctum*, 'a holy thing'.

129

*affectus

an unwavering love* of ready devotion. Therefore John too drank the cup of salvation and followed the Lord—like Peter, although not in the same way as Peter. That he remained thus and did not follow the Lord in his physical suffering accorded with the divine plan, for the Lord himself said, *I will that he remain thus until I come,* as if to say, 'He too wants to follow, but I want him to remain thus'.

Jn 21:22

2. Does anyone have doubts concerning the Innocents' crowns? Someone who does not believe that those reborn in Christ are counted among the children of adoption* may doubt that the infants slaughtered in Christ's place are crowned among the martyrs. But would that child who was born for us° have allowed children of his own age to be killed on his account—something he could have prevented by a mere nod—if he was not providing something better for them? As circumcision was then—as baptism is now—enough to save other infants apart from any use of their own wills, would not the martyrdom they endured in his stead be enough for holiness? If you are looking for some merit before God why they should be crowned, look for their crime before Herod why they should be slaughtered! Is Christ's godliness less than Herod's ungodliness, so that he could have these blameless children killed, but Christ could not crown those struck down for his sake?

*Rm 8:15, 23; 9:4; Gal 4:5; Eph 1:5
°Is 9:6

Let Stephen be a martyr before human beings, then. That his suffering was voluntary appears especially clearly in this, that at the very moment of death he showed more concern for his persecutors than for himself.* The emotion° of inner compassion overcame in him the sensation of physical passion, so that he mourned their villainies more than his own injuries. Let John be a martyr before the angels, by whom, as spiritual things to spiritual creatures,* the signs of his devotion were quite certainly known.

*Ac 7:59-60
°affectus

*1 Cor 2:13

But these [Innocents] are clearly your martyrs, O God. As neither human beings nor angels find merit in them, they reveal more clearly the unique privilege of your grace. *Out of the mouths of Infants and sucklings you have perfected praise. Glory to God in the highest,*[3] say the angels, *and on earth peace to persons of good will.* This is great—but I dare say not yet perfect—praise, not until the One comes who says, *Let the little children come to me, for of such is the kingdom of heaven,* and *peace to persons* exists even apart from any use of their own wills, in the mystery of religion.*

Ps 8:2 [3]

Lk 2:14

Mt 19:14

*1 Tm 3:16

3. Let those who are used to employing their wills and actions in contentious arguments consider these things; let them consider and notice that, whenever the faculty is not impaired, they should neglect neither will nor action, especially since the one without the other—when the faculty is impaired—can bring not only salvation but also holiness. But let them also hold firmly to this, that action apart from will—but not contrary to will—can do good—so that what saves infants may condemn those who come with false claims.

No less does will apart from action—but not contrary to action—suffice in some. For example, someone is attacked whose will is good but not yet perfect, not yet capable of bearing martyrdom. Who would dare deny this person salvation on account of this imperfection? Perhaps such people are not allowed to come to so severe a temptation lest they fail and be condemned.* If people with such weak wills are led into a temptation that is beyond them, and their wills are not strengthened, who can doubt that they will fail, will deny, and, if they happen to die in that state, must even be condemned? *Someone who is ashamed of me in the presence of human beings,*

*1 Cor 10:13

---

[3] Lk 2:14, as in the *Gloria in excelsis* in the eucharistic liturgy.

I will be ashamed of, says the Lord, *in the presence of the angels of God*. But by the imperfect will which saves them when they lack the faculty for taking action they cannot now be saved, because of a failure of [taking] action, or an action of failure. The same thing might happen through ignorance.

Let us then strive for love and pursue good actions, my brothers, in no way making light of sins of weakness or ignorance. Instead let us with concern and fear give thanks to our most kind and generous Saviour. He—who wills everyone to be saved and to come to the knowledge of himself*—searches for opportunities for human salvation with such abundant divine love that he rejoices to find in some people will and action, in some will apart from action, and even in some action without will. This is eternal life, that we know the Father, true God, and

Jesus Christ whom he has sent,*

who is one with him,

the true God who is over all,

blessed forever.*

Lk 9:26 vl

*1 Tm 2:4

*Jn 17:3

*Rm 9:5

On the Lord's Circumcision, the Reason for Circumcision, and the Name 'Jesus'

1. *A**FTER EIGHT DAYS** had passed, that the child should be circumcised, his name was called Jesus.* From the beginning, God has approved of moderation,* and nothing immoderate has ever been acceptable to him who is perfect balance. Thus not only did he found all creation on weight and measure and number,* but from the very first he prescribed moderation for humankind: he gave a commandment, saying, *You shall eat of every tree of the garden, but of the tree of the knowledge of good and evil you may not eat.* Plainly this was the lightest of commandments and the most generous of measures! Human beings transgressed the restraint prescribed for them, however, and went beyond the limits set for them.

This made God turn away his face from them.* At length—and barely—in the days of Abraham his friend* God began to be appeased. Again he established moderation; he promulgated a Law—not altogether like the first. That one had been cautionary, this one was remedial; there a prohibition was made so that excess would not steal in, here a cutting away was declared so that the healing power of a sacrament

Lk 2:21

*modus

*Ws 11:20 [21]

Gen 2:16-17

*Ps 1 [12]3:1, 30 [29]:8 et al.

*[Jdt 8:22]

might remove what had crept in. Finally, the former was given concerning a tree, that its fruits were not to be eaten, while this one concerned a person's own body, that the flesh of the foreskin was to be cut away.* No doubt, too, that excess°—that Leviathan,[1] the poison of sinful desire and of unrestrained and disordered enticements to pleasure—would so take possession of the other members of the human body that a sort of general cutting away would seem to be needed in all of them.

*Gen 17:11
°additamentum

2. But the frailty of human flesh and the weakness of a child's age could by no means withstand the cutting away of each member. With caring restraint therefore the divine design provided that concupiscence would be checked most strongly in that part in which everyone knows it rages quite fiercely and does quite violent harm. Of all the rebellion of the members that oppose the Spirit this member alone is found defiant to the point that it rises in a shameful and unlawful movement despite every deliberation of the will.

*Gen 17:12

In that this circumcision took place on the eighth day* it offered hope of the heavenly kingdom, because, when the cycle of days has come round again to its beginning, it would seem to present a kind of likeness to a crown. This is why we especially celebrate the eighth day after principle feasts. Also, in the Lord's sermon, the eighth beatitude is coupled

*Mt 5:3 and 10

with the first,* so that the precisely repeated promise of the kingdom of heaven may plainly fashion for us a crown.

---

[1] Leviathan (Is 27:1) was understood to mean 'their excess' (Is 15:9). See Jerome, *Liber de nominibus hebraicis* (PL 23:839) and Isidore, *Etymologiarum.* 8.11.28 (PL 82:317), both of whom define Leviathan as *additamentum eorum*, 'their increase' or 'their addition'.

3. Rightly, then, while the Child who was born for us is being circumcised, is he called 'Saviour',* because from this moment on he is beginning the work of our salvation by pouring out for us his immaculate blood. Christians have no need now to ask why Christ the Lord chose to be circumcised. He was circumcised for the same reason that he was born and that he suffered. None of these was for his own sake, but all are for the sake of the elect. He was not begotten in sin, he was not circumcised from sin, he did not die for his own sin, but instead for our transgressions.*

What he was called, the Gospel says, *by the angel before he was conceived in the womb.* He 'was called'— the name was not imposed. This name was his from eternity. That he should be 'Saviour' follows from his very nature; this name is inborn in him, not imparted to him by any creatures, human or angelic.

4. But what do we say about the great Prophet who foretold that he would be called by many names seeming to have been silent about this one, which alone—as the angel advised beforehand and the Evangelist testifies—is called 'his name'?[2] Isaiah rejoiced that he would see this day: he saw it, and was glad.* And then he spoke, giving thanks and praising God: *A child has been born for us, and the government is on his shoulders. His name will be called Wonderful, Counselor, God, Strong One, Father of the World to Come, Prince of Peace.*

These are great names indeed—but where is the name that is above every name, the name of Jesus, at which every knee should bend?* Perhaps among all the others you will find this one name, but somehow suggested and spread out. Unmistakably this is

Is 9:6; Lk 2:11, 21; Mt 1:21

Mt 24:22; 2 Tm 2:10; Rm 4:25

Lk 2:21

Jn 8:56

Is 9:6

Ph 2:9-10

---

[2] The name 'Jesus' means 'Saviour' or 'salvation', according to Jerome, *De nominibus hebraicis* (PL 23:854).

the name of which the bride the song of love says,
Your name is oil poured out.

5. You have one Jesus in all these names, and he could absolutely neither be called, or be, the Saviour if any one of them should be missing. Has not every single one of us found him 'Wonderful', especially in the changing of our wills? This, of course, is the origin of our salvation, when we begin to reject what we used to love, to grieve where we used to laugh, to embrace what we used to fear, to pursue what we used to avoid, to long for what we used to despise. Wonderful indeed is the One who works these wonders!*

Yet even so he must also show that he is a 'Counselor' in the choice of repentance and the ordering of life. Otherwise our zeal might be without knowledge and our good will without prudence. Plainly we must also establish that he is 'God' by the forgiveness of our former sins,* because without this we can have no lasting salvation, and no one can set sins aside save God alone.* But not even that is enough for salvation if we do not also experience a 'Strong one' fighting against those who fight against us,* so that we are not overcome again by the same evil desires, and our last state be worst than the first.*

Do we see anything now lacking to the Saviour? Yes, the most important thing is lacking if he is not also 'Father of the World to Come' so that we who are begotten for death by the father of the present world may through him rise up into immortality. Nor is this enough if he is not also the 'Prince of Peace' who reconciles us to the Father, and to whom the kingdom is to be handed over,* so that we, as children of perdition* and not of salvation, may not seem destined to be raised up for punishment. *His authority shall grow continually*, surely, so that he may rightly be called 'Saviour' even on account of the

Sg 1:3

Si 48:15

Rm 3:25

Mk 2:7

Ps 35 [34]:1

Lk 11:21, 26

1 Cor 15:24

Jn 17:12

great number of those to be saved; *and there shall be endless peace,* so that you may know that genuine salvation which cannot dread failure.

Is 9:7

ON THE LORD'S CIRCUMCISION

SERMON TWO

On the Medicine of
Circumcision and Its Value

1. *A**FTER EIGHT DAYS** had passed, that
the child should be circumcised, his name was
called Jesus.* We have heard a great mystery of religious belief* expressed in few words. We
have heard a reading consistent with the abbreviated Word[1] that the Lord has made upon earth. In
flesh the Word was abbreviated, and he was further
abbreviated when that flesh received circumcision.
Made a little lower than the angels,* the Son of
God put on human nature; yet now, lest he reject
the medicine for human corruption, clearly he becomes much lower than they are.

Lk 2:21 (margin)

*1 Tm 3:16 (margin)

*Ps 8:5;
Heb 2:7, 9 (margin)

Here you have a great lesson for faith, and a manifest example of humility. What need have you of
circumcision, you who have never committed or
contacted sin? That you did nothing yourself, your
age makes clear; that you did not contract it, the
divinity of your father divinity and the integrity of
your mother prove much more surely. You are the
High Priest who—as prophesied rather than commanded in the Law—was not to be defiled because

---

[1] [Rom 9:28] See the First Christmas Sermon, fn. 1.

138

of your mother or your father.* You have a Father from eternity, but he is God whom no sin befalls. You have a mother from time, but she is a virgin, and incorruption cannot give birth to corruption. More than all this, the child who is circumcised is the Lamb without blemish;* even though he did not require it, nevertheless chose to be circumcised. Without any trace whatever of the wound, he did not flee the bandaging of the wound. *Not so are the wicked, not so;* not so does the perversity of human haughtiness behave. We blush for the bandage on our wounds even while we boast about the wounds! He whom no one can convict of sin*—He accepted medicine for sin, as shameful as it is sour, without any need to do so. Nor did he, on whom alone there was no ancient rust* to be scraped away, turn away from the flint knife.

We, on the other hand, who are shameless about the foulness of our faults, blush to repent—this is the height of madness! It is bad to be prone to wounds, but worse to be discomfited at the medicine. He who committed no sin* did not spurn being reputed a sinner,* what we want is to be sinners and not be thought to be so! Do the healthy need medicine, and not those who are ill?* Even more, does the doctor need the medicine, and not the sick person? Is any human being conscious, I will not say of such glory, but even of such innocence, as calmly to submit to the hand of the circumciser? Christ, however, who had come not to endure purification for transgressions, but to effect it,* patiently restored what he had not stolen.*

But you may ask, 'Why should the child not endure it?' Ask instead, why should one humble and meek not endure it? Why should one who was dumb before his shearer,* who was silent before his crucifier, not remain dumb before his circumciser?

*Lv 21:11

*Ex 12:5; Lv 14:10; 1 Pt 1:19 et al.

Ps 1:4

*Jn 8:46

*Jos 5:2; Ezk 24:6ff.

*1 Pt 2:22
*Lk 22:37

*Mt 9:12

*Heb 1:3
*Ps 69:4 [68:5]

*Is 53:7

Besides, to preserve his flesh intact, without being cut, was not difficult for him, who saw to it that the entrance to the virginal womb remained unopened as he passed through it. For the child to keep his flesh from being circumcised was not difficult when, even in death, to keep it from being corrupted* was not difficult.

Ps 16 [15]:10; Ac 13:35

2. *After eight days had passed, that the child should be circumcised,* then, *his name was called Jesus.* What a great and wonderful mystery! The boy is circumcised, and he is called Jesus. What does this connection mean? Circumcision seems to pertain more to the one being saved than to the Saviour, and for the Saviour to circumcise is more appropriate than for him to be circumcised. But recognize the mediator between God and humankind* who from the very beginning of his birth joins what is human to what is divine, the lowest to the highest. He is born of a woman,* but one to whom the fruit of fertility comes in such a way that the flower of virginity does not drop. He is wrapped in swaddling clothes, but those very clothes are honored by angelic praises. He is hidden away in a manger, but a star shining from heaven proclaims him.* Similarly, his circumcision proves the reality of the human nature he has taken on, and the name which is above all names* declares the glory of his majesty.*

1 Tm 2:5

Gal 4:4

Lk 2:7, 9; Mt 2:2

Ph 2:9

Is 2:10, 19

This, my Jesus, does not bear a meaningless and empty name, as did those who bore it in the past. In him is not the shadow of a great name, but the reality. The Evangelist tells us that the name *which he had been called by the angel before he was conceived in the womb* was given from heaven. And notice the depth of meaning in the word. After Jesus was born, he is called by humans beings what he was called by the angel before he was conceived in the womb: the same Jesus is Saviour of angels and of human beings,

Lk 2:21

but of humans by the incarnation, of angels from
the beginning of creation.* *2 Pt 3:4

3. *His name was called Jesus, which he had been called
by the angel. Let every word be confirmed by the evidence of two or three witnesses.* The abbreviated Word
of which we read in the Prophet,* having become
flesh,° is put before us more plainly in the Gospel.
We, my brothers, we are the ones this parable concerns. Christ needed neither angelic nor human
witness,* but, as is written, *everything is for the sake of
the elect.* Consequently we must look for a threefold
testimony for our own salvation, lest we seem to
have taken the name of God in vain.*

Lk 2:21

Mt 18:16
*Rm 9:28;
Is 10:22-23
°Jn 1:14

*Jn 5:34
2 Tm 2:10

*Ex 20:7

And we too, brothers, must be circumcised, and
so receive the name of salvation—circumcised not
literally, but in spirit and truth;* circumcised not in
one member, but in the whole body at once. For
although excess*—Leviathan, that creature of evil
that needs to be cut off*—reigns most of all in that
part the Jews were commanded to circumcise, yet it
is spread throughout all flesh. *From the sole of the foot
even to the top of the head no soundness is in us,* no part
that is not putrefying through this poison. Therefore
a people still childlike in faith and love received as
appropriate to it the commandment of a minor circumcision, so when it has grown to maturity* it was
ordered to be baptized in the entire body, which is
a perfect circumcision of the whole human person.
This is why our Saviour graciously allowed himself
to be circumcised on the eighth day, and to be crucified after his thirtieth year, when his whole body
was stretched out in pain. In the likeness of his death
we too have been planted together, as the Apostle
writes,* when we observe what has been handed
down to us most recently.

*Jn 4:23

*Is 15:9
*Is 27:1

Is 1:6

*Eph 4:13

*Rm 6:5

4. What, then, is our moral circumcision if not
what the same Apostle recommends: *If we have food*

1 Tm 6:8

and clothing, he says, *let us be content with these*? What circumcises us the best, and cuts away everything superfluous is voluntary poverty, the work of repentance, and the observance of regular discipline.

Moreover, in this circumcision we have to seek a threefold testimony of our salvation: from the angel, and Mary, and Joseph. Before all else, I say, the angel of great counsel[2] has to settle on us the name of salvation. Thereafter we need as well the testimony of the community, as it is the mother of each one of us—a mother, I say, and a virgin, like the one whom the Apostle promised in marriage to one husband,

*2 Cor 11:2

to present as a chaste virgin to Christ.* But anyone who seeks to imitate the Saviour's example must not take the testimony of his minister lightly. This is Joseph, who held the position of husband but was

*Lk 2:48

in actuality servant and steward; he is called father,* but is more a guardian.

*Ac 16:2

5. I will say this quite plainly. We must have good testimony,* my brothers, both from those who are without, and from him who is within. The whole community of brothers undoubtedly bears witness concerning their personal salvation to those who see their way of life is agreeable to everybody and irksome to none. It is plainly useless for that most

*Rv 12:10

wicked accuser of the brothers* to bring a case against those whom the entire community of brothers acquits—at least in regard to what is apparent. Anyone who lays bare the sins of their life in the world and the carelessness of this age in humble and pure confession, also have their testimony from the

Jas 3:2

church authorities—for *in many things we all offend*, unless perhaps we think ourselves holier than the

---

[2] Is 9:6 as in the Introit *Puer* for the Mass of the Feast of the Circumcision.

disciple whom Jesus loved.[3] They do this in order judged by them, and are eager to make satisfaction as they direct.

Now we need not fear an open accusation by the evil one even in these things since *God will not judge the same things twice.* But perhaps he will want to accuse you of a criminal intention and will contrive to fabricate a calumny in a case where neither the testimony of the brothers nor of the father himself seems effective enough. In this case, then, an inner witness must be of use to us, one who looks on the heart rather than the face.* From this [inner witness] we must begin, so that we conceive nothing in the mind before it receives from him the name of salvation. When it issues in visible action, however, it is expedient in gaining external testimonies to itself as well—as the Apostle says: *providing good things, not only in the sight of God, but also in the sight of human beings.*

Na 1:9 VL

**1 Sm [K] 16:7 VL*

[Rm 12:17]

---

[3] Bernard seems to attribute the words from James to John, who was taken to be the 'beloved disciple' of John 13:23.

On Spiritual Circumcision

1. IN THE LORD'S CIRCUMCISION, my brothers, we have something to love and to wonder at, and we have also something to imitate. There is disclosed in it a great gift of dignity, for which we give thanks; there is concealed something hidden, which we must fulfill in ourselves. The Lord has come for our sake, not only to redeem us by shedding his blood, but also to teach us by his words, and, no less, to instruct us by his example. As knowing the way was altogether useless if we were detained in prison, so being redeemed would be of no advantage if the first to find us ignorant of the way would be the first to lead us back to be thrust back into prison. Therefore in his maturity the Saviour gave us clear examples of patience and humility, and, above all, of divine love, and the other virtues; in his infancy these were veiled in symbols.

2. But before we come to discuss these things, I take pleasure in first saying something about so great and so manifest a dignity. The angels possess glory pure and perfect—but nor are we to be without glory. We see his glory, the glory as of the Only-begotten of the Father,* the glory of mercy and true parental affection, the glory of one coming forth from the Father's heart and revealing clearly his deepest parental depth of love.*

*Jn 1:14

*viscera

144

All have sinned, says the Apostle, *and fall short of the glory of God,* and in another place he says, *May I never glory in anything except in the cross of our Lord Jesus Christ.* What is more glorious than for God to value us so highly? What greater glory for him than such great dignity and such great kindness, which are all the sweeter for being so freely given?—for assuredly he died for the ungodly.*

You see how much he did, and for what kind of people he did it: for what kind of people, so that we may not be proud; how much, so that we may not despair. Consequently, that you may be found to have not the spirit of this world but the Spirit that is from God,* and may know what has been given you by God, I beg you not to become like horse and mule,* but rather like the loyal beast that says, *I have become like a beast in your presence, and I am always with you.* Such beasts know their owner* and their master's manger, into which is put for them the very tenderest grass—the One who is the bread of angels.* He is the living bread° on which humans ought to live, but, because human beings have become beasts, bread has been made into grass, so that in this way humanity may live on it.

3. The mystery of this change we celebrate on the day of his birth when *the Word was made flesh,* while *all flesh is grass.* On that day he became lower than the angels* and was found in human condition.° Yet today I hear something more wonderful. Now the One has become much lower than the angels,* who takes the form not only of a human being, but the form of a sinner, and is, as it were, branded as a criminal!

What is circumcision if not evidence of excess and sin? In you, Lord Jesus, what is excessive that can be circumcised? Are you not true God from God the Father,* true man without any sin from

Rm 3:23

Gal 6:14

*Rm 5:6

*1 Cor 2:12

*Ps 32 [31]:9

Ps 73 [72]:22-23
*Is 1:3

*Ps 78 [77]:25
°Jn 6:41, 51

Jn 1:14
Is 40:6
*Ps 8:5
°Phil 2:7

*Heb 2:9

*Nicene Creed

the Virgin your mother? What are you doing, circumcising him? Do you think that this judgement can fall upon him: *A male, the flesh of whose foreskin is not circumcised, that soul shall perish from among his people?* Can the Father forget the child of his womb?[1] Would He fail to recognize him if he lacked the mark of circumcision? On the contrary, if he could somehow fail to recognize the Son in whom he was well pleased,* he could mistake him especially on account of this mark—the circumcision found in him—which he had provided for sinners, precisely for the purification of transgressions.*

What wonder if the Head has accepted on behalf of his members the healing he did not need in himself? Among our own members, do we not often apply healing to one member for the weakness of another? The head aches, and we put a poultice on the arm; the kidneys suffer pain and we put it on the shin; so today, we apply a hot iron to the Head for the festering of the entire body.

4. What wonder is it then if he deigned to be circumcised for us who deigned to die for us? He gave himself wholly to me, and spent himself wholly for my benefit. As for me, when I heard that the Son of the Great King was passing by my prison, I began to groan loudly and to call out piteously, saying, 'Son of God, have mercy on me!'* And he, all kindness as he is, said, 'What is that weeping and wailing that I hear?' And they say to him, 'It is Adam, the traitor, whom your Father caused to be thrown into prison while he ponders by what torments he will put him to death'.

What was he to do, the One whose nature is goodness, whose distinguishing trait is always to have mercy and to spare?* He descends into the

Gen 17:14

*Mt 3:17

*Heb 1:3

**Mk 10:47;
Lk 18:38*

**Collect, Mass
for the Dead*

---

[1] Bernard has abridged Is 49:15, which refers to 'a woman'.

prison, he comes to bring the prisoner out from
the dungeon.* The Jews, however, not unmindful of
the hatred with which they hate the Father, bring it
to bear against the Son; this is why he himself says,
They have hated both me and my Father.

What have the ungodly done, then, for whom
even to see this is grievous? *This is the heir,* they say;
come on, let's kill him. And so they killed the Lamb
of God,* to their own ruination, but to our salvation. They poured out the blood of the Lamb,*
and we drew near and drank it. We have received
the cup of salvation*—*the cup that inebriates, how
splendid it is!* See why we give thanks! A few days
ago we celebrated his coming into the prison of
this world—that is, the day of his birth; today we
celebrate because he took on our chains and fetters.
Today he who committed no sin* put his innocent
hands into the fetters of the guilty so as to set them
free; today the One who gave the Law was born
under the Law.*

5. But now we must state what is indicated spiritually by this circumcision for us to do. The Law does
not prescribe that circumcision be performed on the
eighth day* without a reason, nor without a reason
does the Lord fulfill it.* *Who has known the mind of
the Lord, or who has been his counselor?* May the Spirit,
the Advocate—the One who searches the depths of
God*—be present in answer to your prayers, and
unfold for us this mystery of the eighth day.

We are not unaware nowadays that human beings
must be born anew, since to this end the Son of God
was born a second time. We are all born in sins,*
and we have to be born again in grace—something
we did indeed receive in baptism, but has totally
perished in the life of this world. Now, for the first
time, by God's mercy, the power of grace is at work
in us *so that we may walk in newness of life.* A human

*Is 42:7

Jn 15:24

Mt 21:38
*Jn 1:29, 36
*Rv 7:14

*Ps 116 [114]:13
[Ps 22:5]

*1 Pt 2:22

*Gal 4:4

*Gen 17:12
*Lk 2:21
Rm 11:34

*1 Cor 2:10

*Jn 9:34

Rm 6:4

*Mal 4:2
*Ps 8:28 [17:29]

Gen 1:5

*Mt 16:27

*Lit. 'the mind'
*Gal 1:4

Ps 26:4 [25:5]

being is, then, when the Sun of righteousness,* having risen in the soul, sheds light on the darkness* of sins and brings the dread judgement of God before the inner gaze, while adding to the bond of fear the short number of our days and our uncertain end. Clearly, this is the evening where weeping lingers, to which the joy of morning must be added so that he may cause us to hear his mercy. Thus comes *evening and morning, one day.* This is the day of righteousness,[2] which repays each one what belongs to each,* misery to us, mercy to God. On this day a child is born when the things we have spoken about rouse the soul to love of penance and hatred of sin.

6. But there is a danger if we should want to do penance amid the crowds of the world, where all around us, as we know, some by toxic opinions and others by the bad examples may entice us to sin; some may demean our minds to vainglory by their flatteries, others to impatience by their slanders.

Now must the beam of prudence come forth! Let it show how many and how insistent are the occasions and opportunities of sin which the world presents, especially in this generation. Let it press home how feeble is the human mind in responding to them, especially one that has been reared in the habit of sin. On this day of prudence, then, let us* elect to flee the present evil age,* saying with the Prophet, *I hate the company of evildoers, and I will not sit with the ungodly.* But even this is still not enough. Perhaps we want to choose solitude, but do not take enough account of our own weakness and of the devil's dangerous wrestling. What is more dangerous than to wrestle alone against the wiles of the ancient

[2] The 'day of righteousness' is the first day. The days of prudence, might, moderation, patience, humility, devotion, and discretion (the eighth day) follow.

foe, who sees us, but whom we cannot see? Now we
need the day of might, so that we may know that
our fortitude must be kept safe for the Lord, and we
have to seek it in the ranks* of the many who are   *RB 1:5*
fighting side by side. Here we have as many auxilia-
ries as we have allies, people who can say with the
Apostle that *we are not ignorant of the enemy's devices.* A   *2 Cor 2:11*
community is as terrible in its might as an army in
battle array.* *Woe to those who are alone, because if they*   *Sg 6:4 [3]*
fall they have no one to lift them up. Even if we have   *Qo 4:10*
heard that this grace [of solitude] was granted to
some among the early Fathers, to commit ourselves
rashly to this danger does us no good, nor should
we put God to the test.* Our Teacher too speaks of   *Dt 6:16; Mt 4:7*
anchorites *who, not in the first fervor of monastic life,* and
so on.³ And so, on this day of fortitude, to what we
have already begun—that is, *I hate the company of the*
ungodly—we add what follows, *I will wash my hands*
among the innocent.   *Ps 26 [25]:5, 6*

7. When one chooses to be in a community of
many people, is someone who has not yet been a disciple going to choose to be the leader and to teach
what he has never learned? How will he be able to
moderate irrational impulses either in himself or in
others? *No one ever hated his own body.* If someone   *Eph 5:29*
is already his own teacher, how then, do you think,
will he avoid easily giving in to himself sometimes as
generously as [he knows himself] familiarly?

Let the day of temperance dawn,* then, so that   *Pr 7:18*
[the monk] may seek how to temper and rein in
the unrestrained impulses of pleasure, the brutish
impulses of curiosity, and the hard-necked impulses
of his own pride. Let him choose to be abject in

---

³ RB 1.3–5, which continues . . . *but after long probation in a*
monastery, they go forth well-armed from the ranks of the brothers to
the solitary combat of the desert.

Ps 84:9 [83:11]

the house of our God,* and subject to a teacher under whom his will may be broken and his concupiscence restrained by the bridle of obedience. Let it be as the Prophet says: *You have placed people*

Ps 66 [65]:12;
RB 7:41

over our heads. Servants should not look down on doing what the Lord has done before them; indeed

Jn 13:16

servants are not greater than their master. [Jesus] himself, when he had already grown in age, wisdom, and

Lk 2:40

favor with God and human beings,* when he was already twelve years old and had stayed behind in Jerusalem, was found by the blessed Virgin and by

Lk 3:23

Joseph—whose son he was thought to be*—they found him among the teachers, listening to them and asking them questions, but all the same, he went

Lk 2:41-52

down with them, and *he was subject to them.* You too—be subject, for his sake.

8. But now perhaps some 'hardships and difficul-

RB 58.8
°RB 71.2

ties'* can come to you in this way of obedience,° so that you may accept, now and then, various precepts which, although salutary, yet seem less than pleasant. If you begin to put up with these with difficulty, if you begin to criticize your superior, if you begin

[Na 2:7];
RB 5.18

to grumble in your heart,* even though outwardly you do what you are told to do, this is not the virtue of patience but a veil for malice.

The day of patience therefore must dawn, through which you may embrace the 'hardships and diffi-

RB 58.8; 7.35

culties' with a quiet mind,* criticizing yourself instead, and accusing yourself harshly whenever what is salutary displeases you. In your thoughts always take the side of your master against yourself because what is salutary displeases you. In your thoughts always take the side of your teacher against yourself, as far as you can, striving in everything to accuse yourself and to excuse him.

9. And now we come to the place where I think I have to warn you against pride: to overcome your-

self in this way is a very great thing. *The patient,* says Solomon, *are better than the mighty, and those who rule their own spirits than those who take cities by storm.* *Pr 16:32* Consider, then, how clearly the Prophet teaches the necessity—after patience—of humility when he says, *But be subject to God, my soul, for my patience is from him.* Does it not seem that in the exercise of *[Ps 61:6]* patience he felt a temptation to pride? This is why it is necessary that the beam of humility light up your heart* and make clear what you are of yourself **Si 2:10* and what you are from God, so that you will not be high-minded,* for *God opposes the proud, but gives* **Rm 11:20* *grace to the humble.* *Jas 4:6*

10. Now, when you have been exercised in these things for a long time, ask to be given the light of devotion, the fairest day, and a sabbath of the mind. In these, like a soldier who has served his time, you may live without labor in the midst of all labors, running with your hearts enlarged in the way of God's commandments.* What you did at first with **RB Prol. 49* bitterness and by coercing your spirit, you now carry out with the utmost sweetness and delight. This, if I am not mistaken, is what he was asking who said, *Forgive me, that I may be refreshed*—as if to *[Ps 38:14]* say, 'Why am I tormented with this toil and pain,* **Gen 3:17, 16;* and put to death all the day long?° Forgive me, that *Ps 89 [90]:10* I may be refreshed'. *°Ps 44 [43]:22*

Few attain this perfection in this life, if I am not mistaken. If anyone seems at some time to possess it, he must not immediately trust himself, especially if he is a novice and has not mounted the steps I have mentioned. The good Lord usually attracts the feeble-hearted with this sort of coaxing. Such people should be aware that this grace is lent to them, not given, so that in the day of good things they may be mindful of evils, and in the day of evil things they may not be unmindful of good things.

Far different are those whose senses have been trained.* They enjoy the happy pleasure of this devotion. Many, however, reach out for it their whole life long and never reach it. Nevertheless, if they have striven religiously and relentlessly, as soon as they leave their bodies they are given what in this life was denied them for their own good. Grace alone leads them to the place they formerly reached out for with the help of grace, so that, being perfected in a short time, they may fulfill long years.*

Heb 5:14

Ws 4:13

11. One danger seems to remain for those who reach this grace of devotion. They must fear absolutely the noonday demon.* *Satan transforms himself into an angel of light.* Someone who does everything with great delight must fear this: that while following what he loves to do, he may weaken his body through immoderate exertion. Then he will be forced, not without great harm to his spiritual discipline, to spend his time taking care of a weakened body.[4]

Ps 91 [90]:6
2 Cor 11:14

Therefore, so that those who run may not run into trouble, they must be enlightened by the light of discretion, which is the mother of virtues and the sum of perfection. The teaching of discretion is, 'Avoid extremes.'[5] And this is the eighth day, on which the child is circumcised, because discretion truly circumcises, with the result that there is neither too much nor too little. Someone who exceeds the measure[6] excises rather than circumcises the fruit of a good work; similarly he is lukewarm if he does too little.

---

[4] On Bernard's own excessive austerities, see William of Saint Thierry, *Vita Prima Bernardi* I.4.22; PL 185:239D–240A.

[5] *Ne quid nimis*: RB 64.12; Terence, *Andria* 1.1.34.

[6] Reading *nimius* with Mabillon, rather than *minus*, 'too little', with Leclercq, SBOp 4:291.

On this day, then, the name is given, and it is the name of salvation.* Nor have I any hesitation in saying of those who live in this way that they are working out their own salvation. Until this day the angels, who know the secrets of heaven, can say the name of salvation; but now I first confidently bestow it on him. But in truth, because this bird is very rare on earth,[7] let the virtue of obedience fill up the place of this discretion in you, brothers, so that you may do nothing too much, nothing too little, nothing otherwise than you are told to do.

*Lk 2:21

[7] Juvenal, *Satires* 6.165.

ON THE LORD'S EPIPHANY

SERMON ONE

On the Three Appearances[1]

1. *THE GRACIOUSNESS and humanity of God our Saviour have appeared.*[2] Thanks be to God, through whom our consolation is so abundant* in this pilgrimage, in this exile, in this misery. We are careful to remind you quite often of these things so that it may never slip your mind that you are pilgrims, made to live far from your homeland,* driven from your inheritance. Someone who does not know desolation cannot recognize consolation either. Someone who does not realize that consolation is necessary shows that he lacks the grace for it. Thus worldly people who are entangled in everyday affairs* and vices do not look for mercy as long as they do not feel misery. But you who are not told in vain, *Be still, and see that the Lord is good,* and of whom the same Prophet says, *He will show forth to his people the power of his works*—you, I say, who are not held back by worldly occupations, heed what spiritual consolation is. You who are not unaware of your exile, hear that help has come from heaven.*

*2 Cor 1:5

*Heb 11:13-14

*2 Tm 2:4

Pss 46:10 [45:11] & 34:8 (33:9)

Ps 111 [110]:6

*1 Mc 16:3

[1] On Epiphany, 6 January, three 'manifestations' or 'appearances' of Christ were celebrated: the coming of the Magi, the baptism of Christ, and the first miracle at the wedding at Cana.
[2] Ti 3:4, as in the Epistle for the Dawn Mass of Christmas.

154

*The graciousness and humanity of God our Saviour
have appeared.* Before his humanity appeared, his
generosity was concealed—even if it was prior, since
the mercy of the Lord is from eternity. But how could   Ps 103 [102]:17
people recognize something so great? It was prom-
ised, but not experienced, and as a result many did
not believe. At various times and in many ways the
Lord spoke by the prophets.* *I think thoughts of peace,*   *Heb 1:1
he said, *and not of affliction.*[3] But what did the people
experiencing affliction, and not knowing peace, answer? 'How long will you go on saying, "*Peace, peace*",
and there is no peace?' This is what made the angels of   Jer 6:14
peace weep bitterly* and ask, *Lord, who has believed*   *Is 33:7
our message? But now let people give credit to their   Is 53:1; Jn 12:38;
own sight because the testimonies of God have be-   Rm 10:16
come very credible.* So that not even a troubled eye   *Ps 93 [92]:5
can miss it, *he has set his tabernacle in the sun.*[m]   [Ps 6:8]; Ps 19:4
 2. Behold peace, not promised but present, not de-   [18:6]
ferred but conferred, not prophesied but presented.
Behold, God the Father has sent to the earth, as it
were, a sack filled with his mercy, a sack that must be
cut to pieces* in the passion so that it can pour out   *[Ps 29:12]
what is concealed in it for our ransom; a small sack,
indeed, but stuffed full. A child has been given us,*   *Is 9:6
but in him dwells the whole fullness of divinity.* He   *Col 2:9
came in the flesh* so that in this way he might be   *1 Jn 4:2
shown to those made of flesh, and his the likeness
of humanity so that his graciousness might be recognized. When God's humanity becomes known, his
graciousness can no longer be concealed.
 How could he better commend his graciousness than by taking my flesh? My flesh, I repeat, not
Adam's flesh as it was before the fall. What could better demonstrate this mercy than his taking on misery

---

[3] Jer 29:11, as in the introit *Dicit Dominus: Ergo*, for the
Twenty-third Sunday after Pentecost.

itself? What is as replete with loving-kindness as that
the Word of God became grass for our sake?* *Lord,*
what are human beings that you make so much of them?°
Or why do you set your heart on them?'†

*Is 40:6, Ps 103
[102]:15
°Ps 144 [143]:3
†Jb 7:17

This should enable humankind to realize the great
care God has for them; from this they should be able
to realize his thoughts and feelings about them. Do
not ask questions, O human being, about what *you*
are suffering but about what *he* suffered. Recognize
how great he made you from what he became for
you, so that his graciousness may be apparent to you
from his humanity. The less he has made himself in
his humanity the greater has he shown himself in
goodness; and the more he debased himself for me
the dearer he is to me. *The graciousness and humanity of God our Saviour have appeared,* says the Apostle.
Clearly great and manifest are God's graciousness
and humanity! He who took the pains to join the
name of God to humanity has given a strong indication of his graciousness.

3. The angel Gabriel, sent to Mary, speaks of the
Son of God but does not call him God.* Blessed be
God, who has given us such an angel from our very
selves, so that our angel may supply what the other
did not say.[4] He too had the Spirit of God,* and he
spoke in his Spirit what was extremely necessary
for us. What can so instruct our faith, strengthen
our hope, and inflame our love as God's humanity? What the others left unspoken was reserved for
our angel. Nor was it appropriate for all of them
to say everything; consequently we can rejoice in
gathering different things from different people, and
return to each one the thanks we owe.

In one point the Apostle and the Angel, who both
speak of Christ's birth, are in agreement, and that is in

*Lk 1:26ff.

*1 Cor 7:40

---

[4] *Angelus*, meaning messenger, is applied here to Saint Paul.

the name 'Saviour'. Gabriel, when speaking to Mary, as to one fully taught by the Spirit, mentions only a name: *And you will call his name Jesus.* When he went to Joseph, the Angel not only uttered the name but also taught its meaning: *And you will call his name Jesus,* he says, *for he shall save his people from their sins.* Yet to the shepherds too he announced a great joy, that a Saviour, Christ the Lord, was born to them.*

Lk 1:31

Mt 1:21

*Lk 2:8-11

Paul says something similar: *The graciousness and humanity of God our Saviour have appeared.* Both did well not to leave that sweet name unspoken, because it was to the highest degree necessary for me. Otherwise, what should I do on hearing that the Lord is coming? Should I flee, like Adam—who fled from his face* but did not get away? Should I not despair, hearing that He is coming whose law I have so transgressed, whose patience I have so abused, for whose kindness I have been found so ungrateful? What greater consolation could there be than in this sweet word, this consoling name?

*Gen 3:8

This, too, is why he says that he comes, not to judge the world, but that the world may be saved through him.* Now I can approach with assurance, now I can plead with confidence. What shall I fear when the Saviour comes into my house? Against him alone have I sinned;* whatever he is inclined to will shall be granted; he may do as he *wills.** It is *God who justifies; who is to condemn? Who will bring any charge against God's elect?* On this account must we rejoice, that he is coming among us; for now he will be ready to overlook faults.

*Jn 3:17

*Ps 51:4 [50:6]
*Mt 20:15

Rm 8:34, 33

4. Moreover, he is a child, he can easily be pleased. Does anyone not know how easily a child overlooks things? Look, if he is not very little for us we can be reconciled for very little. For very little, repeat; not without repentance, but our repentance itself is something very little. We are poor, we can give only

a little; yet we can be reconciled for that little, if we choose. All that I can give is this wretched body. If I give it, that is enough. If it is less than enough, I add his body, for it came from mine, and is mine. *A child has been born for us, and a son has been given to* *Is 9:6* *us.* From you, O Lord, I will supply what is wanting in myself. O sweetest reconciliation! O gentlest satisfaction! O reconciliation, easy but very useful; O satisfaction, little but not to be belittled!

As this is easy now, so it will be difficult later. As now there is no one who cannot be reconciled, so after a little while there will be no one who can, for just as graciousness beyond all hope and beyond all conjecturing has appeared, we can expect a like severity of judgement. Do not then despise God's mercy if you do not want to experience his justice, *Rm 2:4* his wrath, his indignation, his jealousy, his rage.* *Lord, rebuke me not in your rage, nor discipline me in* *Ps 6:1[2]* *your wrath.* To let you know the degree of the severity that is coming, gentleness equally great has preceded it. From the magnitude of the indulgence reckon the magnitude of the chastisement!

God is immeasurable and boundless in righteousness as well as in mercy, abundant in pardoning,* *Is 55:7* abundant in chastising. Yet mercy claims the first place for itself, so that, if we choose, severity will be unable to find anyone against whom to rage. This is why he gave precedence to graciousness—that once reconciled by it, we may see ourselves safe from severity. He wanted not only to come down to earth, then, but also to be known; not only to be born, but to be recognized.

5. For the sake of this recognition we have this festive day, the great day of his appearance. Today *Mt 2:1* the Magi came from the East* seeking the risen Sun *Mal 4:2* of Righteousness,* the one of whom we read, *Here* *[Zec 6:12]* *is a man, the East is his name!* Today they worshiped

the Virgin's newborn, following the leading of a new star. Is there not a great consolation for us here, just as there is in the Apostle's words, of which we have spoken? He spoke [the word] God; they say it with their action, not their voice.

What are you doing, O Magi, what are you doing? Are you worshiping a suckling child in a shabby hovel, in shabby rags? Is he then God? Surely *God is in his holy temple, the Lord's throne is in heaven'*, and are you looking for him in a shabby stable, in his mother's lap? What are you doing, offering gold?* Is he then a king? And where is the royal palace, where is the throne, where the crowd of royal courtiers? Is the stable his palace, the manger his throne, Mary and Joseph the throng of courtiers? What has made these wise men so foolish as to worship a child as contemptible for his age as for the poverty of his family?

They became foolish so that they might become wise; the Spirit had already taught them what the Apostle later proclaimed: *Let those who want to be wise become foolish so that they may be wise. Since the world in its wisdom could not know God through wisdom, God was pleased through the foolishness of our proclamation to save those who believe.*

Was it not to be feared, brothers, that those men would be offended, and believe that they had been made sport of, when they saw such unseemly things? From the royal city, where they guessed they should seek the King, they are directed to the insignificant village of Bethlehem; they enter a stable, they find a tiny infant wrapped in swaddling clothes.* For them, the stable is not mean, the swaddling clothes are not displeasing, the suckling child does not cause offense! They fall prostrate, they venerate him as King, they worship him as God. In reality, the One who led them there also instructed them; the One who

Ps 11:4 [10:5]

**Mt 2:11*

1 Cor 3:18; 1:21

**Lk 2:7*

guided them outwardly by a star taught them secretly in their hearts. This disclosure of the Lord has made this day illustrious, and the holy veneration of the Magi has made it holy and venerable.

6. This is not the only appearance we celebrate today. Another—as we learn from our Fathers—is believed to have happened on this same day, although some time later. When [Jesus] had already completed thirty years in the flesh—who with respect to his divinity is ever the same, and whose years will never end*—he came to the baptism of John among crowds of people. He came like one of the people, he who alone was without sin.* Who would then have believed that he was the Son of God? Who would have thought that he was the Lord of majesty?*

You humble yourself profoundly, Lord; you conceal yourself very well, but you cannot hide from John. Is he not the one who recognized you through his mother's womb; you, not yet born, [were recognized] by him, not yet born? Is he not the one who recognized you through the walls of both mother's wombs, and because he could not cry out to the crowds, he enlightened at least his own mother with a joyful movement?*

But now what happens? *John saw him coming toward him*, says the Evangelist, *and said, Behold the Lamb of God who takes away the sins of the world.* Behold the One who is going to bring about the purging of transgressions; he is coming to purge away our dregs—and yet, after this testimony, he chooses to be baptized by John.

[John] trembles. Is it any wonder? Is it, I ask, any wonder if a person trembles and does not dare to touch God's holy head, the head to be adored by angels, revered by powers, held in awe by principalities?* You choose to be baptized, Lord Jesus? But

*Heb 1:12

*Jn 8:7

*Ps 29 [28]:3

*Lk 1:41

Jn 1:29

*Eph 3:10

why? What need have you of baptism? Have the healthy a need of medicine, and the clean of cleansing?* Where did you contact sin that you need to be baptized? From your Father? But you have God for a Father, and you are his equal, God from God, Light from Light.* Everyone knows that no sin can befall God. From your Mother? You have a mother as well, but she is a virgin. What sin, then, could you have derived from her who conceived you without iniquity and bore you without loss of integrity? What blemish can a lamb without blemish* have?

[Mt 9:12]

[Nicene Creed]

[Ps 50:7]; Lv 9:3

I ought to be baptized by you, says John, *and do you come to me?* Great humility is on both sides, but they cannot be compared. How can a human being not be humbled in the presence of the humble God? *Let it be so now*, the Lord says, *for it is right for us so to fulfill all righteousness.* John consented and obeyed; he baptized the Lamb of God, and washed the waters. *We* have been washed clean, not *he*, because the waters, now washed clean, are understood to be for washing us.

Mt 3:14

Mt 2:15

7. But perhaps you mistrust the testimony of John because he is only a human being and you can hold him suspect. He is a relative of the one to whom he gives testimony. Look, there is a greater testimony than John's, the testimony of the coming of the dove.* It was not unfitting that a dove came to point out the Lamb of God, because nothing befits a lamb better than a dove. A dove is among birds what a lamb is among mammals—in both, perfect innocence, perfect meekness, perfect simplicity. What is further from all malice than a lamb and a dove? They do not know how to harm anyone, they have not learned how to wound.

[Mt 3:16; Jn 1:32]

If you should allege that this happened by accident, here is the testimony of God the Father: *Behold, the God of majesty has thundered, the Lord is over*

Ps 29 [28]:3

Mt 3:17, 17:5

*Is 3:8

Jn 8:29

Mt 17:5

*[Jb 3:26]

*1 Cor 1:24

*Mt 13:55

*Lk 3:23

*Jas 1:19

Mt 11:29

many waters, and the *Father's* voice *was heard, This is my beloved Son, with whom I am well pleased.* Truly this is he in whom there is nothing that displeases the Father, nothing that offends the eyes of majesty.* That is why he himself says, *I always do what is pleasing to him.*

Listen to him, it says. Now at last, Lord Jesus, you will speak! How long will you be silent? How long will you dissemble?* For a long time you have kept silent, a very long time. Now at last, you have license to speak from the Father. Power of God and Wisdom of God,* how long will you hide among the people as someone weak and foolish? How long, noble King and King of heaven, will you let yourself be called and thought to be the son of a carpenter?* Even Luke the evangelist testifies that he was still thought to be the son of Joseph.*

O humility, moral excellence of Christ, how you confound our pride and vanity! I know a little something, or rather, I seem to myself to know something, and already I cannot keep silence, I thrust myself forward and show off impudently and imprudently, ever ready to speak, quick to instruct, slow to listen!*

And Christ, when he was silent so long, when he concealed himself, did he fear vainglory? Why should he be afraid of vainglory, who is the Father's true glory? Nevertheless he was afraid—but not for himself. He was afraid for us, for whom he knew he had to be afraid. He was alerting us, he was instructing us. His mouth was silent, but his works were teaching us, and what he later taught by words he now cried aloud by example: *Learn of me, for I am meek and humble in heart.* About the Lord's infancy I hear very little; from then until his thirtieth year I discover nothing. But now he who is so clearly pointed out by the Father can no longer conceal himself. In his first appearance he chose to appear with his virgin Mother because by virginity is represented a certain kind of modesty.

8. His third appearance too is found in the Gospel, and we celebrate this today no less. The Lord was invited to a wedding, and when the wine ran out he pitied their embarrassment and changed water into wine. *This*, as the Evangelist says, *was the first of his signs.* So, in his first appearance, when he appeared as an infant at his mother's breasts, he became known as a true human being. In the second, the Father's testimony points out that he is the true Son of God. In the third, he is revealed as the true God at whose command nature is changed. By these several testimonies today our faith is confirmed; by these many proofs our hope is strengthened; by these many inducements our godly love is inflamed.

Jn 2:11

SERMON TWO

On the First Appearance

1. WE READ OF THREE appearances of the Lord all on the same day, but not at the same time. The second is surely wonderful, the third is wonderful, but the first, still more wonderful, is to be admired. The changing of the waters was wonderful,* the simultaneous testimonies of John, of the dove, and of the Father's voice were wonderful,* but the greatest wonder was the Magi's recognition of him.* Their worship and their offering of frankincense show that they recognize God. They recognize that he is not only God but also a King, and this is represented by the gold. Moreover, the great mystery of divine loving-kindness is not concealed from them, and the myrrh indicates that he is going to die. The Magi worship and offer gifts to One still suckling the breasts of his mother.*

But where, O Magi, where is the royal purple of this King? Surely not in those shabby swaddling clothes in which he is wrapped?* If he is a king, where is his diadem? But you see him truly in the diadem with which his mother crowned him, wearing the sackcloth of mortality. Of this he says, as he is rising [from the dead], that *you have cut away my sackcloth and clothed me with joy! Come out, O daughters*

*Jn 2:2-11

*Mt 3:13-17
*Mt 2:1-12

*1 Tm 3:16;
Sg 8:1

*Lk 2:7

Ps 30 [29]:12

164

of Zion, and see King Solomon in the diadem with which his mother crowned him, and so on. *Come out*, angelic powers, inhabitants of the heavenly city! *Behold your king*, but in our crown, *in the diadem with which his mother crowned him*. Until now you have lacked these delights, you do not yet taste this sweetness. You know his loftiness, but you do not see his lowliness. *Come out*, then, *and see King Solomon in the diadem with which his mother crowned him*.

2. But they have no need of our exhortation because they are the ones who long to gaze upon him. The more familiar they are with his loftiness the more precious and lovable is his lowliness. This is why, although it is a greater cause of joy for us—he has been born for us, and has been given to us*— nevertheless they anticipate us, they exhort us. The angel who proclaims great joy to the shepherds is proof of this, and with him was a great multitude of the heavenly host.*

To you, then, daughters of Zion—you worldly souls, feeble, pampered daughters and not sons, who possess no fortitude, no virility of spirit—we say, *Come out, daughters of Zion!* Come out from the sense of the flesh* to the understanding of the mind, from the slavery of fleshly cravings to the liberty of spiritual insights. Come out from your country, your kindred, and your father's house,* *and see King Solomon*. Otherwise, to see him as Ecclesiastes[1] will not be safe for you.[2] The one who is Solomon—that is, the peacemaker*—in [this time of] exile will be

Sg 3:11

Jn 19:14

*Is 9:6

*Lk 2:10, 13

*Col 2:18

*Gen 12:1

*1 Chr 22:9

---

[1] The scriptural book of Ecclesiastes is known as Quohelth or Koheleth in modern translations.

[2] In assigning these three titles to Solomon, Bernard follows Jerome, *Commentarius in Ecclesiasten, ad Paulam et Eustochium*; PL 23:1011B.

Ecclesiastes—the haranguer³—at the judgement, and, in the kingdom, Idida*—the Lord's beloved.⁴ In exile he is mild and lovable, at the judgement he will be just and terrible, in the kingdom he will be glorious and wonderful.

*2 [4] K 22:1

Come out, then, *and see King Solomon*—for he is everywhere king. Even though his kingdom is not of this world he is still a king, even in this world. What is more, when he is asked, *So you are a king?*, he says, *For this I was born, and for this I came into the world.* Here, then, he is director of morals, at the judgement he will be discerner of merits, in the kingdom he will be distributor of rewards.

Jn 18:36, 37

3. *Come out*, then, *O daughters of Zion, and see him in the diadem with which his mother crowned him*, in the crown of poverty, the crown of misery. He was also crowned by his stepmother with a crown of thorns,* a crown of misery. He is to be crowned by his close associates* with a crown of righteousness° when the angels will come and collect out of his kingdom all stumbling blocks,* when he shall enter into judgement with the leaders of his people,* and when the whole world will fight with him against the frenzied.* And the Father crowns him with a crown of glory;* as the Psalmist says, *You have crowned him with glory and honor!*

*Jn 19:2, 5

*familia
°2 Tm 4:8

*Mt 13:49, 41
*Is 3:14

*Ws 5:20 [21]
*Is 28:5, 62:3
Ps 8:5 [6]

See him, daughters of Zion, in the diadem with which his mother crowned him. Take up the crown of your King, a child for your sake. Still more, adore his humility, in company with the Magi, whose faithful devotion is set before you today as a model. To what shall we compare these men, and to what shall we liken them?* If I reflect on the faith of the thief and

*Is 46:5;
Lam 2:13

---

³ In *De nominibus hebraicis* (PL 23:854) Jerome also identifies *Ecclesiastes* as *concionator*, 'haranguer' or 'demagogue'.

⁴ Jedidah in modern translations.

the confession of the centurion, [the Magi] seem to surpass them, because by their time [Jesus] had already performed miracles, by then many people had already proclaimed him, and many had already worshiped him. Let us also reflect on what they said. The thief cried out from the cross, *Lord, remember me when you come into your kingdom.* Is he going to come into the kingdom through his petition then? Who told you that Christ had to suffer and so enter into his kingdom?* And you, centurion, how did you recognize him? Seeing what he cried out as he breathed his last, [the centurion] said, *Truly this man was the Son of God!* This is a wonderful thing, and worthy of all our wonder!

4. For this reason I ask you to reflect and to see how clear-sighted faith is; consider carefully what sharp eyes[5] it has. It recognizes the Son of God as he sucks milk, it recognizes him as he hangs on the cross, it recognizes him as he dies. The thief recognized him on the gibbet, the Magi in a stable; the one [recognized him] pierced by nails, the Magi, wrapped in swaddling clothes, while the centurion knew him as life in death. They [recognized] the power of God* in the weakness of a youthful body, and he [recognized] the supreme Spirit as he breathed his last.* The Magi recognized the Word of God in a speechless baby—whatever the others confess by their utterances, they confess by their gifts. The thief pronounces him a king, the centurion both the Son of God and a human being. The Magi's gifts declare all these three—although by the frankincense they point less to the Son of God than God.

Lk 23:42

*Lk 24:26

Mk 15:39

*Rm 1:16 et al.

*Mk 15:39

---

[5] *lynceos oculos*—like the eyes of Lynceus, in greek mythology, one of the Argonauts and known for his preternaturally keen sight.

We therefore pray, dearly beloved, that these may benefit you: the great godly love which the God of majesty has shown you, the great humility which he took on, and the great graciousness which has become apparent to you through the humility of Christ. Let us give thanks to our Redeemer and Mediator, through whom we have come to know the good will of God the Father towards us. We now know that his disposition* is such that we can rightly say that *we so run, not as at an uncertainty.*

*animus

1 Cor 9:26

On the Three Appearances, but Chiefly on the First

1. IT APPEARS NECESSARY, my brothers, in accord with the custom on other solemnities, to explain to you as well the meaning of today's solemnity. Sometimes we preach against vices, and that kind of sermon is very useful, but it seems more appropriate for other days. On feast days, and particularly on the great solemnities, it seems more suitable to dwell on the subject of the solemnity, simultaneously to instruct the mind* and to stir the feelings.* How can you celebrate what you do not know, and how can you know unless you are told?*

So it should not be irksome for those who are experts in the law if we bear especially in mind the less learned—as the logic of love demands. I believe that they will not be deprived of their own fine banquet if they serve coarser food first to the less educated, to the common crowd, so to speak. They will serve it this way if, through the perceptiveness of brotherly love, they accept contentedly what is needed from those whose understanding is not equal to theirs, even if it does not seem as requisite to themselves. Let them gather up the fragments for themselves later,* carefully pondering points of greater subtlety, like clean animals* ruminating on

*animus
*affectus
*Rm 10:14-15

*Jn 6:12
*Lv 11:2ff

169

what, because of its subtlety, may have escaped the less intellectually gifted.

2. Today's solemnity receives its name from 'appearance'. Epiphany, of course, means appearance. Today, therefore, we celebrate the Lord's Appearance—not just one, but three, as we have it from our forebears. Today our child-King, only a few days after his birth, appeared to the first fruits of the Gentiles, heralded by a star.* Today, too, when he had already spent nearly thirty years in his condition of flesh, he—who with respect to his divinity is ever the same and whose years never end*—came to the Jordan to be baptized, concealed among crowds of people, but made known by the testimony of God the Father.* Today, again, invited with his disciples to a wedding, when the wine gave out, he changed water into wine* as a sign of his astonishing powers.[1] I take pleasure in reflecting particularly on that quite delightful appearance that took place in the Saviour's infancy, because it is utterly endearing and the one particularly associated with today's celebration.

3. Today, then, as we heard in the Gospel reading, the Magi came to Jerusalem from the East.* Rightly do they come from the East, those who proclaim to us a new rising of the Sun of Righteousness* and who illumine the whole world with joyous reports. Only unhappy Judea, because it hated the light, was darkened to the brilliance of a new splendor, and Judea's dimmed eyes* become still blinder in the dazzling rays of the eternal Sun.

Let us listen to what they say, these Magi coming from the east. *Where is he who has been born king of the Jews?* What certain faith, never wavering at all!* They do not ask *whether* he is born, but they

*Mt 2:1-12

*Ps 102:27
[101:28]

*Mt 3:13-17

*Jn 2:2-11

*Mt 2:1-2

*Mal 4:2

*Gen 27:1

Mt 2:2
*Jas 1:6

---

[1] 'As a sign. . .'. From the preface to the blessing of the font at Easter Vigils.

speak confidently and ask without any uncertainty, *where* he is who has been born king of the Jews. But at hearing the word 'king', King Herod, who suspects the arrival of a successor, takes fright. No wonder Herod is troubled! But can anyone not be surprised that Jerusalem, the city of God,* the vision of peace,* is troubled along with Herod? See, my brothers, what great harm unjust power can do, and how a godless head molds his subjects to his own ungodliness. It is indeed a wretched city where Herod reigns, because it will beyond a doubt share in Herod's evil doings and be stirred up by Herod's alarm at the rising of the new salvation. *Tb 13:11 *Ps 87:3

As for me, I trust in the Lord* that [Herod] will reign but little among us, even if he should happen to be present; may God prevent both that and him! Herod's evil doing is also Babylon's cruelty, the will to snuff out the newborn religion and to dash the little ones of Israel against a rock.* If anything touching on salvation, if anything concerning religion, arises, those who resist it, those who fight against it, are plainly trying, with the Egyptians, to slay the little ones of the stock of Israel,* or rather, with Herod, to persecute the newborn Saviour. *Rm 14:14; Ph 2:24 *Ps 137 [136]:9 *Ex 1:15ff.

But now let us go on with the story we have begun. I believe that anyone conscious of this thing in themselves will hereafter take great pains to put away the temperament of Herod and dread coming to a similar end.* *Ws 7:6

4. While the Magi were seeking the King of the Jews, Herod inquired of the scribes the place of the Lord's birth, and they declared the name of the city as the Prophet had given it.* When the Magi had gone and left the Jews behind, *there, ahead of them went the star they had seen in the East.* In this we are plainly given to understand that in seeking human counsel they had lost divine guidance, and that when *Mi 5:2; Mt 2:4-5 Mt 2:9

they turned to earthly evidence the heavenly sign deserted them. This is why, when they left Herod, at once *they rejoiced with exceeding great joy for the star went ahead of them until it came and stopped over the place where the child was. On entering the house they found the child with Mary his mother, and falling down,* Mt 2:9-10 *they worshipped him.* How did this come to you, foreigners? We do not find such faith in Israel!* Does *Mt 8:10 the common dwelling, the stable, or the poor cradle, the manger, not offend you? Does the presence of a poor mother and a suckling baby not shock you?

5. Then, *opening their treasures*, says the Evangelist, *they offered him gifts, gold, frankincense, and myrrh.* If they Mt 2:11 had offered only the gold they would have seemed, perhaps, to have wanted to help the poverty-stricken mother so she might have something with which to bring up her infant son. As it is, since they offered frankincense and myrrh along with it, they unmistakably intended a kind of spiritual offering. Gold is regarded as the most precious of earthly riches—something we have all of us offered devoutly to the Saviour through his grace when, for his name's sake, we renounced entirely the world's goods.

Now, however, it is necessary that we who have utterly scorned the things of earth seek those of heaven with a burning desire. This is how we offer the aroma of frankincense, which of course—as you read in the Apocalypse of blessed John—represents the prayers of the saints.* This is why the Prophet *Rv 5:8 too asks in the psalm, *Let my prayer be directed as incense in your sight.* And you read in another place that Ps 141 [140]:2 *the prayer of the righteous pierces the heavens*—not just Si 35:21 anyone's prayer, but *the prayer of the righteous*, for *the prayer of someone who turns away from hearing the Law will be an abomination.* Pr 28:9

6. Moreover, if you want to be righteous and not turn your ear away from the Lord's commandment,* *Lam 3:56

so that he will not turn away from hearing your prayers, you must not only despise the present world but also chastise your flesh and bring it into subjection.* The One who said, *If you do not give up all you possess, none of you can be my disciple,* and again, *If you want to be perfect, go, sell all that you have and give to the poor, and come, follow me,* said the same thing in another place: *Anyone who wants to come after me, let him deny himself and take up his cross and follow me.* The Apostle expounds this, saying, *Those who belong to Christ have crucified their flesh with its vices and desires.*

1 Cor 9:27

Lk 14:33

Mt 19:21

Mk 16:24

Gal 5:24

Let our prayer have two wings, then: contempt for the world and affliction of the flesh, and surely it will pierce the heavens and be directed as incense in God's sight. Our sacrifice will be pleasing and our offering acceptable which has myrrh along with the gold and frankincense. Myrrh, although bitter, is very useful and preserves the body which is dead because of sin from dissolving into vice and rotting. I say this briefly so that we may imitate the offering of the Magi.

Qo 12:12

Rm 8:10

7. Yet since we have said that this is an appearance, we may rightly ask what appeared in it. Surely, in the words of the Apostle, *The goodness and humanity of God our Saviour have appeared.*[2] Notice how we heard in the Gospel reading that on entering the house, the Magi found the child with Mary his mother. In the infant body, which his mother was caressing on her virginal lap, what appeared if not the reality of the flesh he had taken on? What appears in the child's being found with his mother, if not a declaration that he is a real human being and the real son of a human being?

Ti 3:4

---

[2] Read out in the epistle at the second, dawn, Mass of Christmas.

But see in the second appearance whether he is not clearly proven to be the Son of God by the testimony of the Father's voice. The heavens were opened over him, the Holy Spirit descended on him in bodily form as a dove, and the Father's voice was heard: *This is my beloved Son, with whom I am well pleased.* It is clear enough from this, plain enough and beyond all doubt, that God's Son must be God. No one doubts that the children of human beings are human, and that the offspring of animals are of the same kind as they are. Yet, to leave no room for sacrilegious error, the One who in the first appearance was declared to be a real human being and the son of a human being, is nonetheless declared in the second to be the true Son of God, and in the third is now proven to be true God and the author of nature, at whose pleasure nature is changed.

As for us, dearly beloved, let us love Christ Jesus as a real human being and our brother. Let us honor him as the Son of God. Let us worship him as God. Let us confidently trust in him, my brothers. Let us confidently entrust ourselves to him. He lacks neither the power to save us—because he is true God and Son of God—nor the good will—because he is like one of us,* a real human being and the son of a human being. How will he be capable of remorselessness with us when for our sake he became like us, capable of suffering.*

8. If now, for the improvement of your way of life, you would now like to hear something about these appearances, observe that Christ appears first of all as a child with his virgin mother, teaching us that before everything else we have to seek simplicity and modesty. Simplicity is natural to children, and modesty is characteristic of virgins. For all of us, then, at the beginning of our conversion no virtue

Mt 3:16-17

*Gen 3:22

*Jm 5:17

is more essential than humble simplicity and modest serious-mindedness.

In his second appearance the Saviour came to the waters of baptism, not to be washed, but to receive testimony from his Father. These [waters] are the tears of devotion with which we are seeking not the pardon of sins, but the good pleasure of God the Father, when the Spirit of adoption as children comes down on us, giving testimony to our spirit that we are children of God.* Thus we may seem to hear a mellifluous voice from heaven, because God the Father is truly well pleased with us.* A vast distance separates these tears of devotion and of adulthood from those that childhood sheds with infantile wailing—the tears, I mean, of repentance and shame. Far more excellent than either of these are those tears infused with the savor of wine. These tears, I would say, are truly changed into wine, tears brought forth in the fervor of love by the feeling of brotherly compassion. Because of them you may seem to forget yourself for an hour in a kind of sober intoxication!

*Rm 8:15-16

*Lk 3:22

On the Second Appearance

*Ex 32:9
°Ezk 11:19;
36:26
†Jos 5:2
*Jer 11:9

1. FOR A STIFF-NECKED people, a knife was needed* and for hearts of stone° were knives of stone, of the kind we recall were used for circumcision† by Joshua son of Nun.[1] Our Jesus, however, like a gentle lamb,* bore all the harshness. Lord, you are a lamb, coming with wool and milk: take from me, I beseech you, this knife. It seems hard and cruel to use a stone knife on a newborn child. This is what mercy does. You have changed the hardness appropriate to hardened servants into the gentleness appropriate to children. So from now on, water and the anointing of grace wash away the corrosion of original sin which the knife could scarcely scrape away. No wonder that sacred mysteries were changed because of changing time, so that each might be given what best suited it. Christ himself submitted to both [circumcision and baptism] so that he might join the

*Is 28:16;
Eph 2:20

two walls as the cornerstone,* and, as if stitching together the ends of two straps, he fulfilled the symbolic Passover and immediately began the real one.

2. He chose therefore to be circumcised to show that he is the source of the old Law just as he is of the Gospel. The One who says, *Unless a person is*

Jn 3:5

born again of water and the Holy Spirit, and so on, had

---

[1] In Latin, Joshua son of Nun is *Jesus Nave* (see Si 46:1), which allows Bernard to compare Joshua and Jesus.

176

earlier said through his servant, *Every soul, the flesh of whose foreskin is not circumcised shall perish out of his people.* Yet if he had submitted only to baptism he might have seemed to be rejecting circumcision as having nothing to do with him. If, however, he was circumcised and not baptized what could persuade me to be baptized and to abandon circumcision? As it is, by receiving baptism after circumcision, he instructed me to observe what he submitted to last.

Gen 17:14

3. And then, how could the lover of community and its advocate, the One who makes those of one mind to dwell in a home,* abandon the community and give scandal to others? Those who saw that he was not circumcised would have been scandalized, just as today the Church would be scandalized if it saw that a child was not baptized. He wanted not only to commend the value of community and of unity, but also to give an example of humility. Consequently, he who alone was without a wound submitted to the bandages worn by the wounded. Hence the Apostle says, *God sent his Son into the world, born of a woman, born under the Law.*

*[Ps 67:7]

Gal 4:4

4. But lest anyone say, 'That he was circumcised, his parent brought about; he was only a baby', he proceeded to be baptized when he reached thirty years of age. Bent beneath the Baptist's hands is the head before which Powers must quake and Principalities adore. What wonder if the Baptist trembled? Is there anyone who would not tremble even at the thought of it? O, how high will that head be at the judgement that is now bent so low? And the brow that now seems so lowly, how high and lofty it will then appear! *Let it be so now,* he says, *for it is right for us to fulfill all righteousness.* Indeed the one who comes in the fullness of time and in whom dwells the fullness of divinity, knows nothing except fullness. He came, not to abolish the Law but to fulfill it.*

Mt 3:15

*Mt 5:17

Now there is a righteousness which is so extremely strict and narrow that as soon as you take a step you fall into the pit of sin—neither to put oneself over an equal nor to make oneself equal to a superior. This is defined as rendering to each person what is his.* There is another wider and broader righteousness: neither to make oneself equal to an equal nor to put oneself over an inferior. Just as preferring oneself to an equal and making oneself equal to a superior are proof of great and perilous pride, so showing oneself inferior to an equal and equal to an inferior is proof of profound humility.

The greatest and full righteousness is to show oneself inferior to an inferior. As supreme and unendurable pride is to put oneself over a superior, so supreme and full righteousness to put oneself under an inferior. What John said, *I ought to be baptized by you,* was of the first kind in that he put himself under a superior; what Christ did, he did from full righteousness: he bent beneath the hands of his own servant.

5. Now let each of us see whom we should imitate: Christ, or the one who exalts himself above everything regarded or worshiped as a god.* As for us, I beseech you, my brothers, let us strive to fulfill all righteousness.* This is the way° that leads to joy. Joy is the reward, but righteousness is its merit and material. Our joy will come from that righteousness when Christ, who is our life, shall appear, and we shall be with him in glory,* because he became for us righteousness from God the Father.*

Happy are those who even now rejoice in righteousness and whose consciences cheer them as they *suck honey from stone and oil from the hardest rock.* Now righteousness seems hard work, but a time will come when it will be desired and possessed, loved and embraced, in complete sweetness and gladness, without any effort. Then shall we enjoy righteousness itself.

*Mt 16:27

Mt 3:14

*2 Thes 2:4

*Mt 3:15
°Jn 14:6

*Col 3:4
*1 Cor 1:30

Dt 32:13

Woe to those who pass by the way,* who, aban-
doning righteousness, seek some vain and passing
joy. When they seek joy from things that pass away,
it cannot not pass away with the passing things that
were its source. Just as fire goes out once the wood
gives out, so do *the world and its desires* pass away, and
so without a doubt does joy as well.

Ps 80:12 [79:13]

On the Gospel Reading, Which Includes the Miracle Performed at the Wedding; and, Before That, On What the Lord Said: *You must be like those waiting for their Lord when he returns from the wedding*

1. IN THE READING from the holy Gospel today, brothers, we heard that our Lord went to a wedding.* Let us do what he advises in another place and strive to become *like those waiting for their lord when he returns from a wedding*. If someone is holding on to a plough in a field or buying or selling something in the market, we do not say, 'What are you waiting for?' They are not like people who are waiting. If, however, we see a person standing at a gate, knocking repeatedly and frequently peering in at the windows,* it is no wonder we ask, 'What are you waiting for?' People who are not deaf to the words, *Be still and see that I am God*, are like those waiting.

The Lord will come to those really and truly waiting for him—those like the person who says,

*Jn 2:1-11

Lk 12:36

*Sg 2:9

Ps 46:10 [45:11]

Waiting, I waited for the Lord. He will come like the person returning from a wedding, drunk with the wine of love and forgetful of our iniquities. He will come to those who are not waiting for him like the one returning from a wedding, like a burly man besotted with wine;* truly drunk and forgetful of his mercies. Then, as far as they are concerned, *God will forget to show mercy.* He will come in wrath and indignation, like one enraged: *Lord, do not rebuke me in your anger!* These things I have not said about the wedding that is our subject, but for the occasion.

Ps 40 [39]:1

*Ps 78 [77]:65

Ps 77:9 [76:10]

Pss 6:1[2]; 38:1 [37:2]

2. Let us, along with the disciples, now follow the Lord as he goes to the wedding. Then, as we see what he was going to do, we may believe along with them. *When the wine gave out, the mother of Jesus said to him, 'They have no wine'.* Being merciful, being extremely kind, she felt compassion for their embarrassment. What issues from the fountain of loving-kindness if not loving-kindness? What wonder, I ask, if the inner depths of loving-kindness show loving-kindness? If someone's hand holds an apple for half a day, does it not keep the scent of the apple for the rest of the day? How much, then, did the power of loving-kindness affect the womb in which it rested for nine months? It filled her mind before it filled her body, and when it proceeded from her womb it did not recede from her mind.

Jn 2:3

The Lord's reply may seem rather harsh and severe, but he knew to whom he was speaking and she was not unaware of who it was who was speaking to her. Then, that you may know how she received his answer and how much she counted on her Son's generosity, she told the servants, *Do whatever he tells you.*

Jn 2:5

3. *There were six stone water jars standing here.* We need now to show the connection of these water jars to the purification of true Jews, not in letter but in spirit*—or rather, to show how they have been

Jn 2:6

*2 Cor 3:6

connected. The Church has not yet reached that state of perfect purity when Christ will present her to himself resplendent, without spot or wrinkle or anything of the kind.* In the meantime she has need of many purifications, so that, as sin abounds, leniency too may abound, and as misery increases, so too may mercy.* But *the gift is not like the trespass.* Grace not only washes away sins, it also bestows merits.

*Eph 5:26-27

*Rm 5:20
Rm 5:15

Six water jugs were set out there, then, for those who relapse into sin after baptism—we are speaking of these people because we are among them. We have put off our old garment, but unfortunately we have put it on again, the worse for wear;* we have washed our feet, but we have soiled them worse than before.

*Sg 5:3

As what one has soiled another washes,[1] so those soiled by us must also be washed by us. Water not their own washes those soiled by guilt not their own. Yet I do not say [guilt] 'not their own' to deny that it is our own—otherwise it would not cause soiling. It is 'not our own' because we all sinned unknowingly in Adam;* it is our own because we have all sinned, even if in another person, and it was imputed to us by God's just, yet hidden, judgement.

*Rm 5:12, 14

But now, to leave you with nothing to complain of, O human being, in contrast to the disobedience of Adam you are given the obedience of Christ, so that as you were sold for nothing you are also bought back for nothing.* If you perished in Adam without being aware of it, you are made alive in Christ without being aware of it.* You were not aware of it when the old Adam stretched out his guilty hands to the forbidden bough; no more were you aware of it when Christ stretched out his innocent hands on the bough of salvation. A stain which soiled you

*Is 52:3

*1 Cor 15:22

---

[1] That is, Christ washes what Adam soiled.

has flowed to you from the first man; water which
cleanses you has flowed from Christ's side.* Now
that you have been soiled by your own fault you
will be cleansed even so by water that is your own,
by him and through him who alone makes purification for transgressions.*

4. The first water jar and the first purification*
consists in compunction. Of this we read that *in
whatever hour a sinner groans in compunction, I shall
not remember all his iniquities.* The second is confession—everything is washed away in confession. The
third is almsgiving—so you have in the Gospel, *Give
alms, and everything is clean for you.* The fourth is the
forgiveness of wrongs—which is why we say when
we pray, *Forgive us our debts as we also forgive our debt-
ors.* The fifth is physical affliction—and so we pray
that 'once purified by abstinence we may sing glory
to God'.[2] The sixth is obedience to the precepts—if
only we might deserve to hear what the disciples
heard: *You are clean because of the word I spoke to you*—
for they were not like those to whom it was said,
My word has no place in you—but at hearing the word
they obeyed him.

These are the six water jars set out for our purification, but they are empty and full of air if they
are used for vainglory. They are filled with water if
they are safeguarded by the fear of God, for *the fear
of the Lord is a fountain of life.* Yes, I say, the fear of the
Lord is water—not very tasty, but the best source of
refreshment for a soul burning with harmful desires.
Water is it that can extinguish the enemy's fiery
darts.* Nor does it belie this that water always seeks
the lowest level and fear leads thought down to the
lowest level; and it stays in the lower regions and

*Jn 19:34

*Heb 1:3

*Purgatio

Ezk 18:22 VL

Lk 11:41

Mt 6:12

Jn 15:3
Jn 8:37
2 Sm 22:45;
Ps 18:44 [17:45]

Pr 14:27

*Eph 6:16

[2] From *Jam lucis orto sidere*, the hymn at the office of Prime.
Deo has been substituted for the hymn's *ipsi*.

surveys the dreadful places with a terrified mind, in accord with the verse: *I shall go to the gates of hell.* By divine power, however, water is changed into wine when *perfect love casts out fear.*

Is 38:10; 2 Pt 1:3

1 Jn 4:18

5. These water jars are said to be of stone not so much for their hardness as for the stability. *They contained two or three measures apiece.* 'Two measures'—the twofold fear that one may perhaps be thrust down into hell, or that one may perhaps be shut out from eternal life. But because these belong to the uncertain future and the soul can delude itself and say, 'After you have lived a while in pleasures you can repent, and then you will neither lose [heaven] nor perish in hell', it is good also to add a third with which spiritual persons are familiar and which is all the more useful in that it concerns the present. Those who are familiar with spiritual food are afraid that they may at some time be deprived of it. Those who put their hand to strong things need strong food.* Let those who slave at works of mud and brick live on the straw of Egypt;* we need stronger food because a long road stretches ahead of us and we must walk in the strength of this food.* It is the bread of angels,* our daily bread.°

Jn 2:6

[Pr 31:19]
Ex 5:7

1 [3] K 19:7-8
Ps 78 [77]:25
°Lk 11:3

This is the hundredfold which we have been promised we will receive in this age.* As food is given to hired workers every day at their work—while their pay is kept to the end—so shall the Lord bestow eternal life at the end, but meanwhile he promises a hundredfold—and he delivers it. What wonder then if someone who has already received this grace should be afraid of losing it? This is the third measure, which he has purposely distinguished from the others. It does not belong to everyone, in that the hundredfold is not promised to everyone, but only to those who have left everything.*

Mk 10:30

Mk 10:29

On Changing Water into Wine

1. WITH REGARD TO the Lord's deeds, brothers, reflection on their outward appearance nourishes less able minds while at the same time those with more practiced minds find food more solid and sweeter inside*—the best and finest wheat.* His deeds are delightful on the outside and far more delightful in their inner power, just as he was outwardly attractive in form beyond all the offspring of human beings,* but inwardly, like the brightness of eternal light,* surpassing even the faces of angels.

*Heb 5:14, 12
*Nm 18:12;
Pss 81:16
[80:17]; 147:14

*Ps 45:2 [44:3]
*Ws 7:26

Christ appeared from outside as a faultless human being, a sinless flesh, as a lamb without blemish.* How beautiful are the feet of the messenger of peace, of the messenger of good things!* Yet much more beautiful and more precious is his head, because the head of Christ is God.* Delightful is the appearance of a human being whom sin has not befallen and blessed are the eyes that see; but much more *blessed are the pure in heart, for they will see God.*

*Ex 12:5

*Rm 10:15;
Is 52:7

*1 Cor 11:3

Lk 10:23; Mk 5:8

Once the Apostle had reached the kernel he thought no more of the husk, despite its great beauty. He said, *Although we once knew Christ according to the flesh, now we know him so no longer,* surely because

2 Cor 5:16

185

the Lord himself proclaimed that *the flesh is useless; it is the Spirit that gives life.* This is the wisdom which Paul preached among the mature, not among those to whom, we read, he said: *I decided to know nothing among you except Jesus Christ, and him crucified.* He is, in the words of the bride, altogether sweet, altogether wholesome, altogether delightful, altogether desirable.* As he is revealed in himself, so will you find him in his deeds. Their surface appearance, regarded from outside, is very beautiful, and if anyone breaks open the shell he will find inside something more pleasing and far more delightful.

You will not find this so with our forebears of the Old Testament. The mystical meaning of their deeds is beautiful and delightful, but the actual deeds, considered in themselves, will sometimes be found less worthy—like Jacob's actions,* David's adultery,° and more like these. The food is precious; the dishes not so precious. This may be why Scripture speaks of *dark water in the clouds of air*—because those clouds were dark—and then adds concerning the Lord: *At the brightness before him the clouds passed away.*

2. I believe you already realize what it is I want to say. You have heard today of the miracle performed at the wedding—that is, the beginning of the Lord's signs.* The story is wonderful enough, and its meaning is still more delightful. For water to be turned into wine at the Lord's word was important evidence of divine majesty, but another—and in it was prefigured a far better—change of the right hand of the Most High.*

All of us have been summoned to the spiritual wedding* in which the bridegroom is Christ the Lord. This is why we sing in the psalm, *He comes out like a bridegroom from his wedding chamber.* We ourselves are the bride—if that does not seem incredible to you—and all of us together are one bride, and the

Jn 6:63 [64]

1 Cor 2:6,2

*Sg 5:16

*Gen 27; 30
°2 Sm 11

[Ps 17:12-13]

*Jn 2:1-11

*Ps 77:10 [76:11]

*Mt 22:9

Ps 19:5 [18:6]

souls of each individually are like the soul of an individual bride. When will our frailty be able to sense
this about our God: that he loves us with the same
deep affection that a bridegroom has for his bride?

This bride is very much inferior to her bridegroom—inferior in nature, in beauty, in dignity.
Nevertheless, the Son of the eternal King came from
afar for the sake of this ethiopian woman,[1] and in
order to betroth her to himself he was not afraid even
to die for her. Moses took an ethiopian wife, but he
could not change the ethiopian woman's color.* Yet   *t. Nm 12:1 (Ex*
Christ is going to present to himself as a glorious   *2:21); Jer 13:23*
Church, without spot or wrinkle,* the woman he   **Eph 5:27*
deeply loved while she was still base and ugly. Aaron
complained, and Mary complained,*—not the new,   **Nm 12:1*
but the old Mary,[2] not the Lord's mother but Moses'
sister. Not our Mary, I say: she was concerned* that   **Lk 10:41*
something might be lacking at the wedding. You,
however, as is proper, must turn to thanksgiving
with your full and deep affection while the priests
are complaining and the synagogue is complaining.

3. Why should this happen to you, O human soul,
why to you? Why to you has this inestimable glory
come—to be counted worthy to be the bride of Him
on whom the angels long to gaze? Why to you that your   *1 Pt 1:12*
bridegroom should be the One at whose beauty sun
and moon are astonished, at whose nod all creation
is changed? What will you render to the Lord for all
the things he has rendered to you,* making you his   **Ps 116 [115]:12*
companion at table, his companion in sovereignty, his
companion not least in his marriage bed, so that the
King leads you into his wedding chamber?

See now what you are to feel about our God,
see how much you are to anticipate from him, see

---

[1] 'Cushite woman' is the modern translation.

[2] 'Miriam' in modern translations.

how you are to love him in return and embrace with the arms of vicarious love the One who has thought so much of you—indeed who has done *Gen 2:21-22* so much for you! Out of his own side[z] he formed *Jn 19:34* you, when for you he fell asleep on the cross* and accepted the sleep of death. For your sake he went *Jn 16:28* out from God his Father* and left the synagogue his mother, so that, being united to him, you might *1 Cor 6:16* become one spirit with him.* For your part, then, *listen, O daughter, and see*—ponder how great is your God's condescension toward you—*and forget your* Ps 45:10 [44:11] *people and your father's house.* Abandon your carnal affections, unlearn your worldly ways, give up your former sins, forget your self-destructive habits. What do you think? Is the Lord's angel not standing ready *Susannah 59* to cut you in half* if by chance—God forbid!—you [Dan 13:59] should take another lover?

4. Now you have been betrothed to him. Now the wedding feast is being celebrated; for indeed a banquet is being prepared in heaven and the eternal *Jn 2:3* court. Will the wine give out there?* Never think it! There we will be inebriated with the abundance of God's house and we will drink from the torrent of *Ps 36:8 [35:9]* his delight.* A river of wine has been prepared for *Ps 104 [103]:15* this wedding—yes, of wine that gladdens the heart.* Ps 46:4 [45:5] Just as *the current of the river gladdens God's city.*

Now, however, a long road stretches ahead of us. We do take a meal here, but not in such abundance, because plenteousness and contentment are reserved for the eternal banquet. Here the wine—that is to say, the grace of devotion and the fervor of love—sometimes does give out. How often, my brothers, after your tearful complaints, must I beseech the Mother of mercy[3] to point out to her ever gracious

---

[3] A marian title used in the hymn-antiphon *Salve Regina*.

Son that you have no wine? And she, I assure you, dearly beloved, if we respectfully entreat her, will not fail us in our need, for she is merciful and the Mother of mercy. If she sympathized with the embarrassment of those who had invited her, much more will she be sympathetic to us if we respectfully call on her. Our wedding pleases her. It concerns her far more than that other, not least because it was from her womb, as from a wedding chamber, that the heavenly bridegroom came forth.* *Ps 19:5 [18:6]*

5. But who is not disturbed that at that wedding the Lord answered his most gracious and most holy mother by saying, *Woman, what is it to me and to you?* *Jn 2:4* What is that to you and to her, Lord? Is that not to a child and his mother? Why do you ask what you have to do with her, when you are the blessed fruit of her immaculate womb?* Did she not conceive *Lk 1:42* you with her modesty intact and bear you without detriment? Did you not spend nine months in her womb, suck at her virginal breasts, and at twelve years of age go down from Jerusalem with her and be subject to her?* Now then, Lord, why do you *Lk 2:42, 51* trouble her and ask, *What is that to me and to you?*

Much in every way. Now I see clearly that you said, *Rm 3:2* *What is that to me and to you*, not as if you were displeased or wanting to disturb your virgin mother's tender modesty. No, when the servants came to you at your mother's bidding you did not hesitate to do what she was prompting you to do. Why then, brothers, did he first respond as he did? For our sake, surely, so now that we have turned to the Lord, concern for our kinsfolk according to the flesh may no longer make us uneasy and their needs may not hinder our spiritual exertion. As long as we are of the world we are assuredly responsible for our kinsfolk. But after we have renounced ourselves, to a much greater extent have we been freed from responsibility for them. So we read about a brother who was living in the desert that when his blood brother came to ask him for help, he replied that he should go to another brother, even though the other had already died. To the astonished brother who pointed out that he was dead, [the hermit] replied that he too was dead.*

*Cassian, Conf.
24.9

So then, when he answered his mother—and such a mother—*What is that to me and to you?* the Lord was teaching us in the best way that we should not be more concerned for our blood relatives than religion requires. So too, in another place, when someone told him that she was standing outside with the Lord's brothers, asking to speak to him, he replied, *Who are my mother and my brothers?** Where now are those who are accustomed to have as much family and fruitless anxiety for their blood relatives as if they were still living with them?

*Mk 3:33

6. Let us see what comes next. *Six stone water jars were standing there*, says the Evangelist, *for the jewish rites of purification.* From this you can see quite plainly that when purification is still needed this is not the culmination of, but the preparation for, the wedding. This then is a wedding of betrothal and not of consummation. God forbid that vessels for purification should be present at the wedding when Christ presents the glorious Church to himself without spot or wrinkle or anything of the kind!* What purification will be needed when no spot exists? Now is the time for washing, the need for purification is obvious now, when *no one is clean from filth, not even a child who has lived one day on earth.* Now is the bride being cleansed, now she is being purified, so that at the heavenly wedding she may be presented immaculate to her bridegroom.

*Eph 5:27

Jb 14:4 vᴸ

Let us then seek six water jars in which this cleansing and the purification rite of the Jews—that is, of those who confess[4]—may take place. *If we say that we have no sin, we deceive ourselves and the truth is not in us*—the truth that alone sets us free, that alone saves us, that alone washes us clean. *If we confess our sins*, then true Jews will not lack water jars for purification because faithful is the God who forgives us our sins and cleans us from all iniquity.*

1 Jn 1:8

*1 Cor 10:13;
1 Jn 1:9

7. For my part, I think that the six water jars are six observances which our holy forebears instituted to purify the hearts of those who confess, and all of them—if I am not mistaken—we can find right here. The first water jar is the restraining influence[5] of chastity, which washes clean whatever self-indulgence has previously stained.* The second is fasting, so that abstinence now cleanses what over-indulgence* has spotted. By sloth and idleness—which is the enemy of the soul*—we have amassed a great deal of grime, as, contrary to God's judgement, we munch our bread in the sweat of another's brow, not our own.* This is why a third water jar is provided for us, so we can wash away this grime by manual labor.* So too we are remiss about many things through sleepiness and other works of the night and of darkness.* Therefore a fourth water jar, the regular observance of vigils, is also set before us. By rising at night to praise the Lord* then we may redeem the nights of the past that were not good.

*RB 4.64

*RB 39.7-9
*RB 48.1

*Gen 3:19

*RB 48.1, 8

*Rm 13:12

**RB 16.5; Ps
119 [118]:62*

Now, about the tongue:* who is unaware of how much it defiles us through idle talk and lies, through slander and flattery, through malicious words and boastful words? For all of these we need a fifth water jar—silence—which is the safeguard of religious life and in which lies our strength. And the sixth

*Jas 3:5ff.

---

[4] Jerome, *Liber interpretationis hebraicorum nominum*; PL 23:825; CCSL 72:67,19.

[5] *Continentia castitatis . . . luxuria.*

water jar is discipline, by which we live not by our
own volition but by another's* so that the faults we
have committed by living without discipline may
be washed away. These jars are stone; they are hard.
But we have to be washed in them unless we want
to receive a bill of divorcement* from the Lord on
account of our filthiness. Nevertheless, their being
described as stone lets us grasp not just their hardness but, far more, their solidity. Unless they remain
firm and stable they do not wash these things.

8. The Lord said to the servants: *Fill the jars with
water.* What does this mean, Lord? The servants are
worried about the lack of wine and you say, 'Fill the
jars with water'! They are thinking of goblets and
you tell them to fill jars for purification rites? This
is just like Leah's father substituting her when Jacob
was panting for Rachel's embraces.*

We, brothers, we who are your ministers and servants are commanded by Christ to fill the jars with
water as often as there is a shortage of wine. It is as
if he is saying, 'These people long for devotion, they
ask for wine; they are demanding fervor, but *my hour
has not yet come. Fill the jars with water*'. What is the
water of wisdom*—wholesome though not overly
sweet—if not the fountain of life* and *the beginning
of wisdom, the fear of the Lord*?° The servants are therefore told, 'Inspire awe, and fill with the spirit of fear,†
not jars so much as hearts'. If they are ever to arrive
at God's love, they must begin with fear,* so that
they too can say, *By your fear, O Lord, have we conceived
and we have give birth to the spirit of salvation.*

But how will the water jars be filled? The Evangelist stated that *they contained two or three measures
apiece.* What are the two measures—what is the
third? Surely the twofold fear is common and well
known to everyone, but the third kind is less common and less well known. The first fear is that we

*RB 5.12

*Dt 24:1

Jn 2:7

*Gen 29:16-30

*Si 15:3

*Ps 36:9 [35:10];
Pr 13:14
°Ps 111 [110]:10;
Si 1:16
†Is 11:3
*1 Jn 4:18

Is 26:18 VL

Jn 2:6

may be tortured in hell. The second, that we may be excluded from the vision of God and deprived of so inestimable a glory. The third fills the timid soul with great anxiety that it may by some chance be abandoned by grace.

9. All fear of the Lord quenches sinful desire, just as water quenches fire.* This is especially true of the [third], when it counters every temptation in order to prevent the loss of grace. Persons left to themselves sink daily from bad to worse, from little risks to serious faults. We see many who are like this: already filthy, they are filthy still.* In the face of this [third kind of] fear the soul cannot delude itself either about the slight importance of the sin or about future amendment. The first two kinds of fear are to some extent blocked by such delusions.

The Lord instructs us therefore to fill the jars with this water. Sometimes they are empty and full of air—if anyone by his eagerness for vanity is harebrained enough to empty those observances I described earlier of their everlasting reward—as was the case with the foolish virgins whose vessels contained no oil.* Sometimes—and this is worse—[the jars] are indeed full, but full of poison—envy, murmuring, rancor, and slander. For this reason, to keep all these from getting in when wine is lacking, we are commanded to fill the jars with water, so that the Lord's commandments may be kept in fear, which is then changed into wine when fear is cast out by love,* and everything is filled with spiritual fervor and joyous devotion.

*Si 3:30, 33

*Rv 22:11

*Mt 25:3

*1 Jn 4:18

ON THE FEAST OF THE CONVERSION
OF SAINT PAUL

How We Ought to Be
Converted to His Example

1. **W**ITH GOOD REASON, dearly beloved, is the conversion of the Teacher
of the Nations* being celebrated
today by all the nations with joyful festivities. We
see the many branches that have come forth from
this root. Paul, once converted, became a minister
of conversion to the whole world.* Long ago, while
still in the flesh but no longer walking according to
the flesh,* he converted many to God through his
task of preaching. Now as well, while living more
happily in and with [God], he still has not stopped
converting people. I mean by his example, by his
prayer, and by his teaching.

    The commemoration of his conversion* we cele-
brate because it too is found to be of use to those
who remember it. In this commemoration sinners
conceive a hope of pardon—so as to be aroused
to repentance—and those who already repent receive a pattern of perfect conversion. Who can altogether despair over the enormity of any crime
whatever when they hear that Saul, still breathing
threats and murder against the Lord's disciples,*
suddenly becomes a vessel of election?* Who, when
oppressed by the weight of evil, can say, 'I am not

1 Tm 2:7

Rm 1:8

Rm 8:8, 4

Ac 9

Ac 9:1

Ac 9:15

194

strong enough to rise to better things right now',
when on the very journey on which he was thirsting for christian blood and whole-heartedly puffing
out deadly venom, this cruelest of persecutors was
instantaneously changed into the most faithful of
preachers? Indeed, this one conversion marvellously
puts before us both the great extent of mercy and
the effectiveness of grace.

2. *Suddenly*, writes Luke, *a light from heaven flashed
around him*. O the unimaginable condescension of
divine loving-kindness! With a lightning flash from
heaven and from outside it enlightens someone as
yet incapable of receiving light within. *And a voice
came*: the testimonies of light and voice have become
very credible.* We cannot doubt a truth that enters
through both windows—that is, both eyes and ears.
So too at the Jordan did a dove appear above the
Lord's head and a voice sounded;* yes, and on the
mountain when he was transfigured before his disciples, a radiance was seen and the Father's voice
was heard.*

Saul, Saul, why are you persecuting me? Paul was really
caught. He had no place for pretense, no capacity
for denial. In his hands are the letters of his entirely
cruel commission, of his detestable authority, of his
iniquitous power. *Why are you persecuting me?* [Jesus]
asks. Wasn't the person who was butchering Christ's
members* on earth persecuting Christ? Were those
who nailed that most sacred body to the gibbet of
the cross* persecuting Christ while this man raging
with violent hatred* against his body—which is the
Church, for that is his very body*—was not persecuting him? If [Christ] gave his own blood* as the
price of our souls' redemption,* does he not seem to
you to be enduring an even worse persecution from
the man who used evil suggestion, bad example,
and opportune scandal to turn away from [Christ]

Ac 9:3; Mk 1:11

Ac 9:4
*Ps 93 [92]:5

*Mt 3:13-17

*Mt 17:1-5
Ac 9:4

*1 Cor 6:15

*Col 2:14
*Ps 25 [24]:19
*Col 1:24
*Heb 9:12
*Ps 49:8 [48:9]

the souls he had redeemed? Is this persecution not worse than that of the Jews who shed his blood?

3. Recognize, dearly beloved, and fear the comradeship of those who hinder the salvation of souls. This is a thoroughly dreadful sacrilege, one that seems even worse than the crime of those who laid sacrilegious hands on the Lord of majesty.

It seemed as if the time of persecution had already ceased, but—as became clear—Christians never lack persecution, and nor does Christ. What is even more serious, those who are called Christians after him persecute Christ. Your friends, God, and your companions have drawn near and stood against you! The whole christian people, from the least on up to the greatest,* seem to have banded together against you.* From the sole of the foot even to the head there is no soundness. Wickedness has come forth from elder statesmen*—your own vicars—who were supposed to govern your people.

We can no longer say, *Like people, like priest* because the people are not like the priest. Woe, woe, Lord God,* because those who are eminent in persecuting you are those who seem to love the preeminent places in your Church and to hold the highest offices.* They have gained possession of the citadel of Zion,* they have seized its rampart, and they are boldly and authoritatively turning the entire city over to the flames.* Their wretched undertaking is the overthrow* of your wretched people.

If only their harm was confined to this! Then perhaps someone forewarned and forearmed by the Lord's teaching would take care, not to imitate their example, but to observe their precepts.* Now, however, holy offices are given out as a source of sordid profit, and people suppose that gain is godliness. They are found brimming over with godliness* in undertaking—or rather in accepting—the care of souls, but

*Gen 19:11

*[Ps 37:12]

*Susannah 5 [Dan 13:5]

Is 24:2

*Jer 4:10

*3 Jn 9, Mt 23:6

*2 Sm [K] 5:7

*Jgs 1:8

*conversio . . . subversio

*Mt 23:3

*1 Tm 6:5

with them this is a minor concern, and the very last thing they think about is the salvation of souls.* *1 Pt 1:9*

Could any persecution be worse for the Saviour of souls? Others too act wickedly against Christ, and there are many antichrists in our day. With good reason does [Christ] consider more cruel this persecution from his own ministers for benefits received and feel it more grievously because of the powerfulness he tolerates from his own ministers—even though many others seem to be acting against their neighbor's welfare at various times and in various ways,* and at various opportunities. *Heb 1:1*

All this Christ sees, and is silent. This the Saviour suffers and takes no notice. Therefore we too must take no notice and be silent for the present—especially with regard to our prelates, the leaders of the churches. This, of course, suits them, too, as they now escape human judgement. A severe judgement, however, is going to come upon those in leadership positions and the mighty will suffer mighty torments.* *Ws 6:7*

4. I fear, dearly beloved, that even among us may be a Lord's persecutor, for reason has plainly taught that to impede salvation is to persecute the Saviour. What thanks can I give for my soul's salvation to the brother who gives me the poison of brotherly slander to drink? Slanderers are justly described as hateful to God because they persecute him. And what about someone whose example encourages others to act rather remissly, or who disturbs them by his antics, or upsets them by his curiosity, or annoys them with his impatience and complaining, or in any other way grieves the Spirit of God who is in them,* putting a stumbling block before one *Eph 4:30* of these little ones who believe in him?* Is this not *Mt 18:6* openly to persecute Christ?

In order, then, to keep both the name and the sin of 'persecutor' far from us always, I appeal to you, dearly beloved, always to be kind and gentle, bearing with one another in all patience and urging one another on to what is better and more perfect. What servant supposes it enough not to persecute his master, but not to obey him either? What grace will someone have who, if he does not resist, does not assist either? If someone is so faint-hearted as to think it enough to be neither God's persecutor nor his coadjutor,* let them listen to what He himself says: *Who is not with me is against me, and whoever does not gather with me scatters.*

5. *Saul, Saul, why are you persecuting me?* And he [answered]: *Who are you, Lord?* We are clearly meant to understand by this that the brightness was around him but not within him. Paul heard the Lord's voice, but he did not see the Lord's face; he was being educated for faith and, as he himself later taught, *faith comes from what is heard.*

Who are you? he asked. He was persecuting someone he did not know, and this was why he received mercy, because he acted ignorantly in unbelief.* Learn from this, brothers, that God, the righteous judge,* considers not only what you do, but the attitude with which you do it. Be wary from now about thinking it slight whenever you knowingly slack off, however slightly. No one should not say at heart, 'These things are trivial. I won't bother to correct them. It's no great matter if I continue in these pardonable and insignificant sins'. This, dearly beloved, is impenitence. This is blasphemy against the Holy Spirit, unforgivable blasphemy.* Paul was indeed a blasphemer, but not against the Holy Spirit because he acted ignorantly in unbelief. He did not speak blasphemy against the Holy Spirit, and as a result he received mercy.

6. *Who are you, Lord?* And the Lord answered him, *I am Jesus the Nazarene, whom you are persecuting.* 'I

*1 Cor 3:9

Lk 11:23

Ac 9:5

Rm 10:17

*1 Tm 1:13

*2 Tm 4:8

*Mk 3:29

Ac 9:5; 22:8

am the Saviour, and in persecuting me you are de-
stroying yourself. I am the One whom you read in
your Law had been foretold, but you do not know
has been fulfilled: *He will be called a Nazarene'.*[aq] And   *Mt 2:23*
he said: *Lord, what do you want me to do?* Here plainly,
my brothers, is the pattern of perfect conversion.
My heart is ready, O God, he says, *my heart is ready.*   *Ps 57:7 [56:8]*
I am ready and am not troubled, that I may keep your
commandments.   *[Ps 118:60]*

   Lord, what do you want me to do? O brief but bursting word, but full, living and active, worthy of full
acceptance!* How few are found in this pattern of   **Heb 4:12;*
perfect obedience who have so renounced their   *1 Tm 1:15*
own wills that they do not even have hearts of their
own! At every hour they are seeking not what they
themselves want, but what the Lord wants, as they
say without interruption, 'Lord, what do you want
me to do?' and also the words of Samuel, *Speak,*
Lord, for your servant is listening.   *1 Sm [K] 3:10*

   Alas, we have more imitators of the blind man in
the Gospel than we do of the new Apostle. *What*
do you want me to do for you? says the Lord to the
blind man.* How great is your mercy, Lord, how   **Mk 10:51*
great your condescension! Is it possible the Lord is
seeking to do his servant's will? That man truly was
blind because he did not consider, he did not tremble, he did not cry out, 'Don't let this happen, Lord!
Instead, tell me what *you* want *me* to do! For you to
ask and do my will is not fitting, it is not right at all.
I should instead ask and do your will'.

   You see, brothers, that conversation was truly necessary in this case. Indeed, to this very day the faint-
heartedness and perversity of people demands that
they be asked, 'What do you want me to do for you?'
instead of them asking, 'Lord, what will you have
me do?' A servant and representative of Christ must
consider what people are willing to be commanded

to do; these people do not consider what may be the will of the One who gives the commands. Their obedience is not complete, they are not ready to obey in all things, they have not made up their minds to follow in everything the One who came to do not *Jn 6:38 his own will but the Father's.* They distinguish and discriminate, choosing in what things they will obey the One giving order—or in fact, in what things the One who commands them must obey their wills.

Even though people like this may see themselves tolerated and humored, and have their weakness indulged, I appeal to them to move on, to be ashamed always to be found little children, lest someday they hear, *What ought I to have done for you that I did not* Is 5:4 *do?* May the great number of mercies they have been shown not become a full measure of well-deserved condemnation for those who have abused the patience and kindness of their superior!

7. *Lord, what will you have me do? And the Lord said to him, 'Get up and go into the city, and there you will be* Ac 9:6-7 *told what you are to do'.* O Wisdom, sweetly indeed *Ws 8:1 ordering all things!* You send the one to whom you are speaking to someone else to be instructed about your will! In this way you are commending the advantage of community life. Once he has been taught by a human being, he will himself learn how to bring help to other people according to the grace *Rm 12:6;\n1 Cor 3:10 given to him.*

*Ps 48:8 [47:9] *Go into the city.* You see, my brothers, that your entering the city of the Lord of hosts,* wanting to learn the divine will, was not done without divine counsel. Plainly the One who filled you with wholesome awe and directed your heart to desire his will, himself said to you: *Get up and go into the city.*

But now, listen to how clearly he commends, in what follows, voluntary simplicity and christian meekness. Once the man's eyes had opened he saw

nothing; he was led by the hand by his companions.
Happy blindness, by which the eyes once brightened
by maliciousness are at length wholesomely blinded
by conversion! That Paul remains for three days
without food, persisting in prayer,* is clearly relevant   *Ac 9:9
to those who have newly renounced the world but
are not as yet refreshed by heavenly consolation. They
too must wait for the Lord with utmost patience.*   *Ps 27[25]:14;
They must pray without ceasing,° asking, searching,   2 Tm 4:2
°1 Thes 5:17
and knocking,† because in due season* the heavenly   †Mt 7:7-8
Father will hear them. He will not forget them for   *Ps 145 [144]:14
ever;° *he will come, he will not delay.* If you wait three   °Ps 13 [12]:1
Hab 2:3; Heb
10:37
days for him, having nothing to eat, be assured that
the gracious and merciful Lord* will not send you   *Ps 111 [110]:4
away fasting.°   °Mk 8:2-3

8. After that Ananias is given instructions to lay
hands on Saul; as a well informed person, however,
he does not immediately agree.* (Notice that Paul   *Ac 9:13-14
himself subsequently passes this teaching on to his
disciple when he says, *Do not lay hands hastily on anyone.*) *He has seen a man laying his hands on him that he*   1 Tm 5:22
may regain his sight, the Lord tells [Ananias].

Brothers, although Paul had seen this, he was not
immediately enlightened [from blindness]. Did he
not have to wait for Ananias' hand because he fore-
saw—perhaps in a dream—that he was going to
come to him?

I say this, dearly beloved, because I am afraid that
some among you, who imagine—only by a dream—
that they have been enlightened, may perhaps no
longer uncomplainingly allow themselves to be led
by the hand, but will profess to be guides for others.
Why should those who have not yet been charged
with the responsibility of administration, who have
not yet been entrusted with a commission,* who   *1 Cor 9:17
have not yet been ordered to receive their sight and
to look out for those who, having their eyes open,

still see nothing—why should they attempt to take these things upon themselves, is not because they are plotting vain things and pursuing empty dreams?* Let us beware of this vice, brothers. Always, as far as we can, let us choose to be abject* and to be led by the hand as we learn meekness* and humility from Christ the Lord:

to whom be honor and glory forever and ever. Amen.*

*Ps 2:1

*[Ps 83:11]
*2 Cor 10:1

*1 Tm 1:17

A cumulative index to the four volumes of liturgical sermons
of Saint Bernard will appear in
Bernard of Clairvaux: Sermons for Autumn and the Harvest Season
Cistercian Father Series 54.

TEXTS IN ENGLISH TRANSLATION

THE CISTERCIAN MONASTIC TRADITION

Aelred of Rievaulx

- Dialogue on the Soul
- The Historical Works
- Liturgical Sermons, I
- The Lives of the Northern Saints
- Spiritual Friendship
- Treatises I: Jesus at the Age of Twelve; Rule for a Recluse; Pastoral Prayer
- Walter Daniel: The Life of Aelred of Rievaulx

Bernard of Clairvaux

- Apologia to Abbot William (Cistercians and Cluniacs)
- Five Books on Consideration: Advice to a Pope
- Homilies in Praise of the Blessed Virgin Mary
- In Praise of the New Knighthood
- Letters
- Life and Death of Saint Malachy the Irishman
- On Baptism and the Office of Bishops
- On Grace and Free Choice
- On Loving God
- Parables and Sentences
- Sermons for the Summer Season
- Sermons on Conversion
- Sermons on the Song of Songs, I-IV
- The Steps of Humility and Pride

Gertude the Great of Helfta

- Spiritual Exercises
- The Herald of God's Loving-Kindness, Books 1 and 2
- The Herald of God's Loving-Kindness, Book 3

William of Saint Thierry

- The Enigma of Faith
- Exposition on the Epistle to the Romans
- Exposition on the Song of Songs
- The Golden Epistle
- The Mirror of Faith
- The Nature and Dignity of Love
- On Contemplating God, Prayer, Meditations

Gilbert of Hoyland

- Sermons on the Song of Songs, I-III
- Treatises, Sermons, and Epistles

John of Ford

- Sermons on the Final Verses of the Song of Songs, I-VII

Other Cistercian Writers

- Adam of Perseigne, Letters, I
- Alan of Lille: The Art of Preaching
- Amadeus of Lausanne: Homilies in Praise of Blessed Mary
- Baldwin of Ford: Commendation of Faith
- Geoffrey of Auxerre: On the Apocalypse
- Guerric of Igny: Liturgical Sermones, I-II
- Helinand of Froidmont: Verses on Death
- Idung of Prüfening: Cistercians and Cluniacs. The Case of Cîteaux
- In The School of Love. An Anthology of Early Cistercian Texts
- Isaac of Stella: Sermons on the Christian Year, I-[II]
- The Letters of Armand-Jean de Rancé, Abbot of la Trappe
- The Life of Beatrice of Nazareth
- Mary Most Holy: Meditating with the Early Cistercians
- Ogier of Locedio: Homilies [on Mary and the Last Supper]
- Serlo of Wilton & Serlo of Savigny: Seven Unpublished Works (Latin-English)
- Sky-blue the Sapphire, Crimson the Rose: The Spirituality of John of Ford
- Stephen of Lexington: Letters from Ireland
- Stephen of Sawley: Treatises
- Three Treatises on Man: A Cistercian Anthropology / Bernard McGinn

EARLY AND EASTERN MONASTICISM

- Besa: The Life of Shenoute of Atripe
- Cyril of Scythopolis: The Lives of the Monks of Palestine
- Dorotheos of Gaza: Discourses and Sayings
- Evagrius Ponticus: Praktikos and Chapters on Prayer
- Handmaids of the Lord: Lives of Holy Women in Late Antiquity and the Early Middle Ages / Joan Petersen
- Harlots of the Desert. A Study of Repentance / Benedicta Ward
- Isaiah of Scete: Ascetic Discourses

- John Moschos: The Spiritual Meadow
- The Life of Antony (translated from Coptic and Greek)
- The Lives of the Desert Fathers. The *Historia monachorum in Aegypto*
- The Spiritually Beneficial Tales of Paul, Bishop of Monembasia
- Symeon the New Theologian: The Practical and Theological Chapters, and The Three Theological Discourses
- Theodoret of Cyrrhus: A History of the Monks of Syria
- Stewards of the Poor. [Three biographies from fifth-century Edessa]
- The Syriac Book of Steps *[Liber graduum]*
- The Syriac Fathers on Prayer and the Spiritual Life / Sebastian Brock

LATIN MONASTICISM

- Achard of Saint Victor: Works
- Anselm of Canterbury: Letters, I–III
- Bede the Venerable: Commentary on the Acts of the Apostles
- Bede the Venerable: Commentary on the Seven Catholic Epistles
- Bede the Venerable: Homilies on the Gospels, I–II
- Bede the Venerable: Excerpts from the Works of Saint Augustine on the Letters of the Blessed Apostle Paul
- The Celtic Monk [An Anthology]
- Gregory the Great: Forty Gospel Homilies
- Guigo II: The Ladder of Monks and Twelve Meditations / Colledge, Walsh edd.
- Halfway to Heaven
- The Life of the Jura Fathers
- The Maxims of Stephen of Muret
- Peter of Celle: Selected Works
- The Letters of Armand-Jean de Rancé, I–II
- The Rule of the Master
- The Rule of Saint Augustine
- Saint Mary of Egypt. Three Medieval Lives in Verse

STUDIES IN MONASTICISM / CISTERCIAN STUDIES

Cistercian Studies and Reflections

- Aelred of Rievaulx. A Study / Aelred Squire
- Athirst for God. Spiritual Desire in Bernard of Clairvaux's Sermons on the Song of Songs / Michael Casey
- Beatrice of Nazareth in her Context, I–II: Towards Unification with God / Roger DeGanck
- Bernard of Clairvaux. Man. Monk. Mystic / Michael Casey
- The Cistercian Way / André Louf
- Dom Gabriel Sortais. An Amazing Abbot in Turbulent Times / Guy Oury
- The Finances of the Cistercian Order in the Fourteenth Century / Peter King
- Fountains Abbey and Its Benefactors / Joan Wardrop
- A Gathering of Friends. Learning and Spirituality in John of Ford
- Hidden Springs: Cistercian Monastic Women, 2 volumes
- Image of Likeness. The Augustinian Spirituality of William of St Thierry / D. N. Bell
- Index of Authors and Works in Cistercian Libraries in Great Britain / D. N. Bell
- Index of Cistercian Authors and Works in Medieval Library catalogues in Great Britain / D. N. Bell
- The Mystical Theology of Saint Bernard / Etienne Gilson
- The New Monastery. Texts and Studies on the Earliest Cistercians
- Monastic Odyssey [Cistercian Nuns & the French Revolution]
- Nicolas Cotheret's Annals of Cîteaux / Louis J. Lekai
- Pater Bernhardus. Martin Luther and Bernard of Clairvaux / Franz Posset
- Rancé and the Trappist Legacy / A. J. Krailsheimer
- A Second Look at Saint Bernard / Jean Leclercq
- The Spiritual Teachings of St Bernard of Clairvaux / John R. Sommerfeldt
- Studies in Medieval Cistercian History
- Three Founders of Citeaux / Jean-Baptiste Van Damme
- Understanding Rancé. Spirituality of the Abbot of La Trappe in Context / D. N. Bell
- William, Abbot of Saint Thierry
- Women and Saint Bernard of Clairvaux / Jean Leclercq

Cistercian Art, Architecture, and Music

- Cistercian Abbeys of Britain [illustrated]
- Cistercian Europe / Terryl N. Kinder
- Cistercians in Medieval Art / James France
- SS. Vincenzo e Anastasio at Tre Fontane Near Rome / J. Barclay Lloyd
- Studies in Medieval Art and Architecture, II–VI / Meredith P. Lillich, ed.
- Treasures Old and New. Nine Centuries on Cistercian Music [CD, cassette]
- Cistercian Chants for the Feast of the Visitation [CD]

Monastic Heritage

- Community and Abbot in the Rule of St Benedict, I–II / Adalbert de Vogüé
- Distant Echoes: Medieval Religious Women, I / Shank, Nichols, edd.
- The Freedom of Obedience / A Carthusian
- Halfway to Heaven [The Carthusian Tradition] / Robin Lockhart
- The Hermit Monks of Grandmont / Carole A. Hutchison
- A Life Pleasing to God: Saint Basil's Monastic Rules / Augustine Holmes
- Manjava Skete [Ruthenian tradition] / Sophia Seynk
- Monastic Practices / Charles Cummings
- Peace Weavers. Medieval Religious Women, II / Shank, Nichols, edd.
- Reading Saint Benedict / Adalbert de Vogüé
- The Rule of St Benedict. A Doctrinal and Spiritual Commentary / Adalbert de Vogüé
- Stones Laid Before the Lord [Monastic Architecture] / Anselme Dimier
- What Nuns Read [Libraries of Medieval English Nunneries] / D. N. Bell

Monastic Liturgy

- From Advent to Pentecost / A Carthusian
- The Hymn Collection from the Abbey of the Paraclete, 2 volumes
- The Molesme Summer Season Breviary, 4 volumes
- The Old French Ordinary and Breviary of the Abbey of the Paraclete, 5 volumes
- The Paraclete Statutes: *Institutiones nostrae*
- The Twelfth Century Cistercian Hymnal, 2 volumes
- The Twelfth Century Cistercian Psalter [NYP]
- Two Early Cistercian *Libelli Missarum*

MODERN MONASTICISM

Thomas Merton

- Cassian and the Fathers: Initiation into the Monastic Tradition
- The Climate of Monastic Prayer
- The Legacy of Thomas Merton
- The Message of Thomas Merton
- The Monastic Journey of Thomas Merton
- Thomas Merton Monk
- Thomas Merton on Saint Bernard
- Thomas Merton: Prophet of Renewal / John Eudes Bamberger
- Toward An Integrated Humanity [Essays on Thomas Merton]

Contemporary Monastics

- Centered on Christ. A Guide to Monastic Profession / Augustine Roberts
- Inside the Psalms. Reflections for Novices / Maureen McCabe
- Passing from Self to God. A Cistercian Retreat / Robert Thomas
- Pathway of Peace. Cistercian Wisdom according to Saint Bernard / Charles Dumont
- Poor Therefore Rich / A Carthusian
- The Way of Silent Love / A Carthusian

CHRISTIAN SPIRITUALITY PAST AND PRESENT

Past

- A Cloud of Witnesses. The Development of Christian Doctrine [to 500] / D. N. Bell
- Eros and Allegory: Medieval Exegesis of the Song of Songs / Denys Turner
- High King of Heaven. Aspects of Early English Spirituality / Benedicta Ward
- In the Unity of the Holy Spirit. Conference on the Rule of Benedict

- The Life of St Mary Magdalene and of Her Sister St Martha [Magdalene legend]
- The Luminous Eye. The Spiritual World Vision of St Ephrem / Sebastian Brock
- Many Mansions. Medieval Theological Development East and West / D. N. Bell
- The Name of Jesus / Irénée Hausherr
- Penthos. The Doctrine of Compunction in the Christian East / Irénée Hausherr

CISTERCIAN PUBLICATIONS Titles Listing

- Prayer. The Spirituality of the Christian East II / Tomás Spidlík
- Russian Mystics / Serge Bolshakoff, Introduction by Thomas Merton
- Silent Herald of Unity. The Life of Maria Gabrielle Sagheddu [Patron of Ecumenism] / Martha Driscoll
- The Spirituality of the Christian East / Tomás Spidlík
- The Spirituality of the Medieval Latin West / André Vauchez
- The Spiritual World of Isaac the Syrian / Hilarion Alfeyev
- The Venerable Bede / Benedicta Ward

Present

- Bearers of the Spirit: Spiritual Fatherhood in the Romanian Orthodox Tradition
- The Call of Wild Geese / Matthew Kelty
- The Contemplative Path. Rediscovering a Lost Tradition
- Drinking from the Hidden Fountain / Tomás Spidlík

- Entirely for God. The Life of Michael Iwene Tansi / Elizabeth Isichei
- Grace Can Do More. Spiritual Accompaniment / André Louf
- Interior Prayer / A Carthusian
- A Hand On My Shoulder. Memoirs of John Willem Gran, I–II
- The Hermitage Within / A Monk
- How Far to Follow. The Martyrs of Atlas / Bernardo Olivera
- Memoirs. From Grace to Grace / Jean Leclercq
- Mercy in Weakness / André Louf
- No Moment Too Small / Norvene Vest
- The Prayer of Love and Silence / A Carthusian
- Praying the Word / Enzo Bianchi
- Praying with Benedict / Korneel Vermeiren
- Sermons in a Monastery / Matthew Kelty
- Tuning In To Grace / André Louf
- Words To Live By. Journeys in Ancient and Modern Egyptian Monasticism / Tim Vivian

---

EDITORIAL OFFICES

Cistercian Publications • WMU Station
1903 West Michigan Avenue
Kalamazoo, MI 49008-5415   USA
tel 269 387 8920   fax 269 387 8390
e-mail cistpub@wmich.edu

CUSTOMER SERVICE—NORTH AMERICA: USA AND CANADA

Cistercian Publications at Liturgical Press
Saint John's Abbey
Collegeville, MN 56321-7500 USA
tel 800 436 8431   fax 320 363 3299
e-mail sales@litpress.org

CUSTOMER SERVICE—EUROPE: UK, IRELAND, AND EUROPE

Cistercian Publications at Columba Book Service
55A Spruce Avenue
Stillorgan Industrial Park
Blackrock, Co. Dublin, Ireland
tel 353 1 294 2560   fax 353 1 294 2564
e-mail sales@columba.ie

WEBSITE
www.cistercianpublications.org

Cistercian Publications is a non-profit corporation.